The Path to Mindfulness and Spiritual Awakening

# *Mindful*
# DREAMING

## A Practical Guide for Emotional Healing
## Through Transformative Mythic Journeys

### DAVID GORDON, Ph.D.

Foreword by Jeremy Taylor, author of **Dream Work**

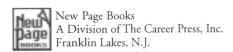
New Page Books
A Division of The Career Press, Inc.
Franklin Lakes, N.J.

MINDFUL DREAMING
EDITED BY JODI BRANDON
TYPESET BY GINA TALUCCI
Cover design by Conker Tree Design
Printed in the U.S.A.

All the names in this book have been changed to protect the privacy of those indivuduals portrayed in the examples throughout the text.

For the poem Lost: Traveling Light: Collected and New Poems. Copyright 1999 by David Wagoner. Used with permission of the poet and the University of Illinois Press.

Printed with permission from Many Rivers Press, Langley Washington. *www.davidwhyte.com*

To order this title, please call toll-free 1-800-CAREER-1 (NJ and Canada: 201-848-0310) to order using VISA or MasterCard, or for further information on books from Career Press.

The Career Press, Inc., 3 Tice Road, PO Box 687,
Franklin Lakes, NJ 07417
**www.careerpress.com**
**www.newpagebooks.com**

**Library of Congress Cataloging-in-Publication Data**

Gordon, David, 1947, Feb. 2-
  Mindful dreaming : a practical guide for emotional healing through transformative mythic journeys / by David Gordon.
    p. cm.
  ISBN-13: 978-1-56414-922-0
  ISBN-10: 1-56414-922-6
    1. Dreams. 2. Self-realization. 3. Myth--Psychological aspects. I. Title.

BF1099.S36G67 2007
154.6 ' 3--dc22

2006025948

# Dedication and Acknowledgments

This book is dedicated to my dad, who through the example of his life has been the North Star on my Journey. For his compassion, love of life, and fearless heart I am eternally grateful.

## *Acknowledgments*

An ancient adage reminds us that the teacher and the student create the teaching. So it has been with *Mindful Dreaming*, a book that would not have been born without the devotion, creative contributions, and profound dreams of my many (anonymous) clients, friends, and family, as well as dream group members. Thanks in particular to those in our present group: Dianne, Gary, Carol, Barbara, Ray, Karima, Amy, and Sheri. A special thanks as well to my "extended family" of incredible dreamers and friends in the International Association for the Study of Dreams (IASD) for their seminal contributions to the field of dreamwork.

I especially want to thank my friend Rev. Jeremy Taylor, whose contributions to the field of dream study and extraordinary talents as a dreamworker have been an ever-present inspiration on my own Journey. And for the guidance and unfailing encouragement of my friend, colleague, and "coach" Kathleen Brehony, I offer my great appreciation. Thanks as well to Jon and Robin Robertson and Lisa Ross for their astute editorial contributions. Special kudos to my editor Jodi Brandon, whose patience and equanimity carried me through the final days of this project.

So many people and so little space, but my heartfelt thanks (and smiles) go to Jessica C. and Robyn for your belief in me—never forgotten. To everyone at the White Doe who made my creative retreats a warm and wonderful experience, many thanks to Beth, Bebe and Bob, Aisha—and especially Myra.

To Jessica and Jonathan, please know my heartfelt gratitude for your unwavering belief in my dream over all these years. Many thanks as well to Hayden and Schyler for your neverending patience and understanding—and for not confusing me with my computer. Thanks to Jackie, whose constant support and encouraging dreams kept me on track when no end was yet in sight.

And to my beautiful wife Dani, who has been my muse, spiritual inspiration, and tender mid-wife throughout the joyful highs and grinding lows of this project: No words can express my gratitude. Whatever may be worthy in this book bears her spark and genius.

# Contents

Foreword                                                                                    7

Introduction                                                                                9

Section I: Preparing for the Journey:
   10 Steps to Mindfulness We Learn From the Mythic
   Journey and the Compass of Dreamwork                        14

   Chapter 1: *The Journey to Mindfulness in
      Our Everyday Lives and Dreams*                                 27

   Chapter 2: *Receiving the Gift of Direct Experience
      From Your Dream Mentors*                                          44

   Chapter 3: *The Grammar of Co-Creation in Our Dreams*    56

   Chapter 4: *The Integrative Practice of Mindful Dreaming*   68

Section II: The Time of Your Calling: Embracing 4 Lessons in
   Mindfulness  Our Nightmares Teach Us                            77

Chapter 5: *Dreams of Distraction:*
   *Nightmares That Teach Us Mindfulness of Solitude*            97

Chapter 6: *Dreams of Control:*
   *Nightmares That Teach Us Mindfulness of Humility*           109

Chapter 7: *Dreams of Judgment: Nightmares That*
   *Teach Us Mindfulness of Compassion*                         130

Chapter 8: *Dreams of Attachment: Nightmares That Teach Us*
   *Mindfulness of Grief and Letting Go*                        142

Chapter 9: *Inspirational Dreams in the*
   *Time of Our Calling*                                        163

Section III: The Time of Your Quest:
   Practicing Mindfulness of Impatience and the Art of
   Waiting in the Present Moment                                169

Chapter 10: *Dreams of the Quest*                               190

Section IV: The Time of Your Illumination:
   Finding the Divine Mirror                                    **200**

Chapter 11: *Dreams of Apprenticeship*                          210

Chapter 12: *Dreams of Embrace and Mastery*                     223

Chapter 13: *Dreams of Embodiment*                              229

Chapter 14: *Dreams of Being (Witnessing Consciousness)*        238

Section V: The Time of Your Return:
   Becoming Your Own Mentor                                     247

Chapter 15: *Dreams of Resolve and Dreams of Charity*           251

Appendix                                                        265

Notes                                                           266

Bibliography                                                    274

Index                                                           283

About the Author                                                288

# Foreword

I have known David Gordon for many years, and have come to rely on his good judgment, advice, and dream wisdom. He is both a valued colleague and a friend, and now he has written this extraordinary book. It is my privilege to invite you to read it, and to offer a few of my thoughts about its particular merits.

David organizes his insights into a pattern of archetypal psycho-spiritual categories derived from both Western and Eastern wisdom traditions. By writing in this way, he joins the ranks of post-modern dream explorers and ancient wisdom keepers who have discovered through their own dreams and the dreams of others that there are as many different legitimate ways to understand and make use of our dreams as there are dreamers who remember them—all valid, all interesting, all worth noting and acknowledging.

The dream world is many worlds, all blending and melding into one, rather like individual people and nations of the Earth, often at odds with one another, yet still and always members of a single human family, striving toward the same human goals and aspirations. Each dream we recall from sleep is a revelation of the deeper truth of our own individual lives, and at the same time, it is part of a stream of dreams that feeds into a collective sea that bathes and nurtures and nourishes all living things. David knows this. He also knows that the many simultaneous meanings of our individual dreams cluster around and always point in the direction of the deepest truths we humans are capable of comprehending.

What is a dreamer to make of this ambiguous soup of multiple meanings and possibilities? David not only offers wise and gentle guidance to help us sort the levels of our dreams, but he also offers us a set of clear, concrete exercises to help us connect with the healing and transformative energies of our dreams in each particular instance.

This clarity and gentle, practical wisdom alone would make this book worth reading, rereading, and passing on to friends.

David also brings us other gifts, literary and emotionally expressive gifts gleaned from and reflecting his lifetime of reading and movie-going, living and working, playing and loving. thinking and feeling. He shares moving and compassionate exemplary stories from his own life and practice, and from wisdom traditions from all over the world. Like the dreams themselves, David's insights are not limited to or bound by fashion or convention. (It seems to me that he also makes it quite clear that he could tell us, and show us, even more, if we would only loosen our white-knuckled grip on our limited waking opinions about the passage of time, and our culturally determined insistence on linear cause and effect.)

This is a book full of poetry and possibility. David's wide reading and omnivorous interests give us back the whole world to play in and to learn from. All of David's wisdom is carefully presented in such a way as to invite us back to our own inner source, the unique wisdom and healing energy of our own dreams.

—Jeremy Taylor
Fairfield, California
September 2006

# Introduction

*Dreams are the workshop of evolution.*

—Sandor Ferenczi

I've often wondered how many of us would willingly make a journey that we knew at the outset would be frightening. Would Frodo have gone to return the Ring of Power if he truly understood the terrible adventure in store for him? Some degree of fear is ever present as we grow, because we humans are caught in a paradox: Growth requires that we change, yet as a species we are born to fear change as we fear the night—the dark womb of the Unknown.

Yet the dark night holds tremendous healing power. If we learn how to use them, our nightly dreams can serve as both a compass and a guide in life's journey. This is a perennial truth that underlies virtually every spiritual tradition on our Earth. Buddha told of five dreams that caused his spiritual awakening.[1] Mohammed received his own spiritual calling from a dream that inspired the sacred Muslim holy book—the Qur'an.[2] The Old Testament emphasized the importance of dreams when God spoke to Moses, saying, "If there be a prophet among you I will…speak to him in a dream."[3] Jacob of course, dreamed of a ladder to heaven on top of which God stood and promised that Jacob's offspring would spread throughout the world.[4] In the Christian tradition Joseph is told of the source of Mary's pregnancy in a dream and instructed to name the child Jesus.[5] In Native American and many other indigenous cultures dreams have always been an integral part of the spiritual life of the community, used to teach, guide, heal, and prophesy.

Dreams push us to find a new way—and in so doing, prompt us to confront spiritual questions we may never have considered. Toward what end, what purpose are your dreams urging you in this lifetime? Where are they leading you—and why?

> Our dreams unfold with an undeniable sequence and purpose—urging us to rid ourselves of values learned from our families and collective culture that now sustain only our unhappiness, and prevent our necessary growth.

The desire to open to new experience and unleash life energy, versus the desire for the familiar and permanent, is a prime example of what analyst Carl Jung called our struggle with the "tension of opposites."[6] We suffer in this struggle for lack of a compassionate, objective mentor—a source from which to receive guidance about our nature, attitudes, and actions—and deliverance from the places in which we find ourselves consistently stuck. We turn again and again to family, friends, lovers, therapists, or clergy for help in discovering the truth about ourselves. Sadly, we are often disappointed. This is because we are all wounded by life, and those we depend on are limited in their ability to serve as reliable guides.

When we persist in seeking others' advice, their very human perspective and judgment becomes the flawed mirror and measure of our self-esteem. Trying to base our self-image on the shifting and biased judgments of others can be thought of as looking for a true reflection in a circus house of distorted mirrors.

The answer to our human dilemma lies in finding a compassionate mirror for our suffering. Although meditation and prayer are powerful sources of help, in the Zohar, an ancient Hebrew text, it is said that our dreams are our "closed-eye"[7] wisdom, the wisdom of our inner knowing—and the most direct source of consistent guidance and healing available to us.

For the last 30 years of my life as a therapist, and the last 20 as a dreamworker, I've helped clients transcend their fears and find the courage to change. In serving as their guide, and in my own experience, I've developed a deep and abiding reverence for the healing power of dreams. But I also slowly awakened to the broader reality of their spiritual meaning and value. Yes, dreams do point to where we are stuck and in conflict, but they always offer a new, wiser perspective as well—one that we could never have conceived of consciously. A powerful sequence of dreams that I had (which I will share with you later in this book) changed my life and coalesced what I knew, professionally and personally, about dreams.

Over time what I was learning from these dreams drew me to deepen my understanding of two great pioneers in the field of consciousness studies: Carl Jung and Joseph Campbell. Swiss analyst Carl Jung spoke about how our dreams and our psyche draw their wisdom from a deeper well of knowledge that Jung called our "Collective Unconscious."[8] Joseph Campbell spent his life distilling the essential lessons that myth, fairytales, and fables teach us about life. He concluded that every one of these stories share in common a four-stage pattern or sequence he called the Heroic or Mythic Journey.[9] The four phases of the Journey may be described in brief as: The Calling, Quest, Illumination, and Return. Campbell showed us how these stages chart our perennial search for meaning and heart in life—the reason he said we must "follow our bliss."[10]

> As you learn the simple language with which dreams speak to you each night, you'll find a compassionate mentor. Our dreams are both the gateway and mirror we seek.

I've also been a lifelong student of Buddhist and Asian philosophy. As I studied dreams over the years, I found that my dreams and those of the many thousands of others I've worked with reflect the view of reality embodied in Buddhist as well as Asian thought generally. Much as certain schools of Buddhism assert that dreams are powerful sources of assistance and can serve as a path to awakened consciousness, my spiritual practice evolved based on the guidance provided by my own dreams.

I found that the recurring nature of specific dream motifs and imagery serve as lessons in mindfulness about the attitudes necessary to achieve expanded or awakened consciousness. Interestingly, when these very Buddhist-like lessons are practiced in waking life, our dreams affirm the progress we have made and provide us with new experiences of expanded consciousness from which to learn.

Inspired by these perennial ideas, *Mindful Dreaming*'s simple model reminds us that every dream has a place, meaning, and purpose— a lesson in mindfulness— corresponding to the stage of the Mythic Journey in which we find ourselves.

You may have read that there are many types of dreams, such as problem-solving dreams, healing dreams, spiritual or archetypal dreams, turning-point dreams, and so on. However, I have found that the type of dream we have is less important than the purpose our dream serves in helping us to identify the stage or time of our Journey and the lessons in mindfulness we must learn to progress along our path.

This discovery is at the heart of *Mindful Dreaming*. Our dreams do not simply reflect conflicts in our lives, or try to make us healthier on some popular psychological scale of self-esteem. Rather, they prompt and lead us, actually suggesting a direction we need to take in life and a way to achieve the mindfulness required to get there. Whether in regard to relationships, career problems, or creative blocks, dreams can offer perspective and guidance well beyond our immediate conflicts.

*Mindful Dreaming* is a guidebook that offers you an entirely new perspective on the nature of dreaming—one that will help you discern the relevance of your nightly dreams to your daily experiences and, more importantly, to the stages of mindfulness and growth on your own life Journey.

Distilled from thousands of dreams shared by clients, friends, and myself, what follows is a much-needed map and manual that will serve as a foundation for a lifelong, fulfilling spiritual practice—a field guide for your own daily Journey through life.

*Mindful Dreaming* is a highly practical book. As you read about each phase of your Journey you'll find many exercises to help you embody the healing energy of each night's dreams. With your new understanding of dreams, and the Mythic Journey stages to which they correspond, you'll have the keys to mindfulness on your spiritual path. Most importantly, you'll come to view even your most painful times in life as a necessary step in the natural cycle of growth to which the Journey is always calling us.

You'll also learn that every dream contains a Dream Mentor who will teach you one of 10 lessons in mindfulness needed to transcend the fear that suffocates your full potential, release chronic conflict in relationships, and discover your own path to the quality of love you want to receive and give.

As your dreams help you release the old wounds and collective values with which you were raised, you will open to an expanded consciousness of life-sustaining values. You will also unearth the passionate energy trapped beneath the self-defeating attitudes that have kept you stuck, frustrated, and unfulfilled in your life.

In fact, because every dream image is a hologram of living, healing energy on which you can draw, you'll discover that dreamwork releases energy that you will actually feel in your body. Work with your dreams will literally open you to a fresher, fuller, more immediate experience of life.

In the coming chapters you'll discover more about dreamwork as a spiritual practice. You'll learn how your dreams and Dream Mentors teach the values of mindfulness you need to make progress through the four recurring phases of your own personal life journey—the Calling, Quest, Illumination, and Return. In this process, your understanding of the perennial spiritual values you've heard about all your life will be enriched and renewed. You'll find that your Dream Mentors address the same 10 core lessons in mindfulness taught by our spiritual traditions throughout the millennia.

Above all, *Mindful Dreaming* provides the knowledge of a profound spiritual map—the Mythic Journey—10 sacred principles in mindfulness by which to live and the gift of dreamwork to guide you in daily life and relationships. Embrace each phase of your Journey and awaken to the energy of the Divine in your everyday life.

If you're stagnating in a job or career that's not your heart's path, or you seem to have everything but feel empty inside, this book will help you find in your nightly dreams the mentor and muse for which you've been longing—and the mindfulness to embrace what you have learned.

# Section I

## Preparing for the Journey:
## 10 Steps to Mindfulness We Learn From the Mythic Journey and the Compass of Dreamwork

*During the dream state there clearly is a form of consciousness in which one may engage in certain types of spiritual practice. For example...one might cultivate compassion or insight.*

—The Dalai Lama

We are born into a culture whose prevailing beliefs suggest an inherent flaw in our character as human beings. This is the moral of our creation myth in which we suffer the burden of Original Sin—and the subject of continuing sermons in many of our mainstream churches. It's also the underlying psychology of Freud that we are all at bottom seething cauldrons of infantile and selfish impulses demanding to be expressed. Remarkably, it's just in the last couple of years that a revolutionary, though fledgling, field of Positive Psychology has emerged, asserting there is more to human nature! The founders of this movement state that they "have discovered... a set of human strengths to buffer mental illness: courage, optimism, interpersonal skill, work ethic, hope, honesty and perseverance."[1] Sadly, Positive Psychology and its "discovery" that people have innately adaptive traits stands out as a refreshing perspective in the "modern" study of human behavior.

In Western culture we carry many unspoken beliefs about our inherent lack of worth, integrity, and order within—beliefs that yield in us a deep and abiding mistrust of who and what we are and the limits of what we can become. As if in a struggle against deep inner flaws, we battle with constant self-criticism and strategies for "improving." This is why the Dalai Lama, when he first visited the West, was shocked and bewildered to hear that so many of us feel self-hatred. "What's that? What is self-hatred?" he asked.[2,3] Subsequently he began to emphasize that we cannot have compassion for others until we have learned self-compassion—a given in his own culture.[4]

Adding to our emotional and spiritual alienation is the fact that, although our religions offer us hope, inspiration, and bits of guidance, we are asked to follow rules without the validation of our own experience—and so faith must take the place of direct knowing. Buddhist scholar Robert Thurman tells the story of a child in church who is asked to explain what faith means: "Sure," says the boy, "that's just believing in what you know ain't true."[5]

A close friend of mine and therapist recently shared with me a powerful dream as she struggled to find her own path free of the distortions, hierarchical rules, and dogma that dictate our spiritual experience. This is her dream:

I see a group of people who appear rough and primitive. They possess little language and are clothed primarily in rags and fur. These people had been aware of an unnamed spiritual dimension of consciousness throughout the history of their culture. However, they had not found a way until now to commune with or experience it directly. In so doing they found such bliss and joy that they were transformed. Their newfound consciousness had liberated them from their many fears and made them aware of a new reality that gave their lives meaning and purpose.

A group of priests, politicians, and shamans hear about their experience and feel very angry and threatened in their roles as intermediaries to the Divine. So they conspire to end the threat to their power by devising a special form of torture. What makes this torture especially painful is that it forces each person to forget all that they had learned. That's the point at which I woke up and that's when I realized my work was to help us to remember.

This dream points to the way in which we have become afraid and, indeed, forgotten how to trust the wisdom of our hearts—to look within our own selves for guidance.

As a result of this same "forgetting," most of us harbor some degree of fear that without the constant manipulation and strategizing of our egos we would have no other ground of consciousness on which to stand. Our culture teaches us to rely instead on the proud worship of our own ego. Buddhism reminds us that to end suffering it's the desires of our ego that must be released, but it's helpful to understand that there are actually five strategies for obtaining what our egos desire that cause us distress: distraction, control, judgment, attachment, and impatience.

Each of these five ego strategies contains within it both a desire and a fear: What we desire is always the same at bottom—to feel the lasting peace and fulfillment of unconditional acceptance—to feel fully okay as we are without reservations and doubt. "In the final analysis," says the Dalai Lama, "the hope of every person is simply peace of mind."[6]

> What feels as if an ever-present potential for disorder or chaos within comes from our intuitive sense that we are alienated from our authentic selves.

But the fearful premise underlying our five ego strategies is that we are not okay as we are, that we must strive constantly to find the love that is missing, not within us but in our external relationships: In our fear of never finding the source of love and security we desire we allow ourselves to engage in neverending distractions, restlessly searching, continually wanting "something" that will make us happy; in our fear of never obtaining what we desire, we make plans to take control and have what we want; in our fear of never being desired by others, we judge ourselves as unworthy and others as bad for failing to mirror our worth; in our attachment to all that is impermanent and changing, we live in constant insecurity, ever-fearful of loss, believing that "we are what we have" and what we identify with; and in the groundless, always-shifting sands of our insubstantial and saccharine culture, we fear that we won't find what we desire—or be what we want—soon enough, and so stand ever impatient for the next fix to fill the gnawing emptiness of our lives.

Out of these five strategies arise the ills of our modern life. "What are the roots that clutch," asked T.S. Elliot in The Waste Land, "what branches grow out of this stony rubbish? Son of man you cannot say, or guess, for you know only a heap of broken images..."[7]

Where then are we to find the images of wholeness that will guide us on our Journey—images that will inspire us to live life more fully and joyously in the present moment? The answer lies in our nightly dreams. In contrast to our ego values, our dreams serve the living consciousness of the Source that announces our Calling in life to grow and to open the gates of a new awareness about ourselves and the world in which we live.

When we say we are feeling "Called" to change our life, we mean that we are called to change and move on from what we have been—to release the old roles and social persona built upon our ego's five strategies that have limited the depth and breadth of our conscious awareness. The presence of these limitations explains why our Calling is always preceded by feelings of emptiness and why in the metaphor of myth, fable, and film the land has become barren and the king sick and ineffective.

For this reason too, in the time of our Calling, our dreams are nightmares that reflect the way in which our traditional values and beliefs are embattled and no longer serving us. In our waking lives, we may find that our once-cherished marriage is failing, a fulfilling career no longer satisfies, or our physical health is waning.

Yet when we respond to the Call for healing and change—our ego always views this moving-on process as dark and threatening. We may never before have attended to any task other than maintaining and building the walls of our ego, which we call our identity and which we have thought necessary for our social acceptance and survival. "Let go and trust what?!" we ask. "What other ground is there on which to stand?"

My client Lenny dreamed about a friend, William, who was in waking life training as a spiritual healer. In the dream, Lenny is led by William through a twisted, viny forest, and Lenny follows him, complaining loudly and worrying that they are lost:

> Finally, after wandering for what seemed hours, we come to a clearing and see a sharp precipice in front of us rising up hundreds of feet over a blue lake far below. Suddenly a moose appears from behind some trees and charges us. William quickly strips down naked and, gesturing that I should follow him, leaps over the edge. Very reluctantly and with only moments to spare, I step out into midair, arms and legs flailing in wild panic.

Now, I've fallen into a river and I'm thrashing in the water, choking, coughing, and gasping for air as I go under for what may be the last time. In my panic, I hear William's far-off voice, but it's getting louder and louder: "Lenny! Lenny! Stand up! Lenny! Stand up!"

So goes the universal Journey for us all. It's hard for us to believe there is any other ground of reality or consciousness than the one conditioned by our family and society—and so we cling tenaciously to outworn, painful, and damaging paths, rather than taking the leap or at least giving the benefit of the doubt to a consciousness that is wiser than our ego.

In fact, our attachments stand between us and our awareness of the Divine. This is why when asked to define God, Jung said, "God is the name by which I designate all things which cross my path violently and recklessly, all things which alter my plans and intentions, and change the course of my life...."[8] In other words, all things that alter the plans and intentions of our ego emanate from God and are part of the Divine.

The stages of what the great mythologist Joseph Campbell called the Mythic Journey—the Calling, Quest, Illumination, and Return—and its 10 steps to mindfulness help us find this "other" ground and recognize that the values to which our ego is attached are not the ground of our true self.

For this reason, the five lessons in mindfulness we learn in the first half of our Journey—the Calling and Quest—cannot be the lessons of Spring that our culture, mainstream religions, or new age philosophies emphasize. These first lessons are not about rebirth, growth, oneness, and union. Rather, they are about the need to release distraction, control, judgment, attachment, and im-patience—lessons we learn from the Autumn and Winter of our life. The dark seasons of Autumn and Winter are about the dissolution of old forms—a time when vegetation undergoes a process of deepening its roots and its con-nection with the earth even though its leaves and blossoms, its outward beauty, fall away.

To accept our Call we must honor and practice mindfulness of our dark Winter soul. Our Winter soul dreams of being lost, confused, or despairing. "It is nighttime in my dream and there are lots of homeless people...I'm one of them...." "There's a war and I have to kill someone." "I'm crying over the death of an old and dear friend."

Though we may struggle to hold on, our Winter soul knows the spiritual importance of letting go. So in the time of our Calling and Quest we learn the first five of the 10 steps needed to release our habitual modes of reacting—ego strategies—and make room for new ways of experiencing and perceiving ourselves in the world.

To invoke help from the Source we practice mindfulness of distraction, control, judgment, attachment, and impatience, setting the intention to release our ego's core values—values that make us feel more fragmented and separate.

Sacrifice literally means, from the Latin, "to make sacred," and it's through the willing sacrifice of these favorite ego strategies—the letting go—that we clear a space for the sacred in our life—and discover our deep interconnectedness. "If you could get rid of yourself just once," wrote Rumi, "the secret of secrets would open to you."[9]

Now in the second half of our Journey our Dream Mentors help us become conscious and mindful of the life-enhancing values we must nurture to reclaim this vital life energy and prepare us to embody the new perspectives we have learned.

Until now we have held back. We have explored the reasonableness of the lessons we have been learning through the first half of the Journey, even practiced them when time allowed. But we were not ready to embrace them wholeheartedly. As author and adventurer W. H. Murray said:

> *Until one is committed there is always hesitancy,*
> *the chance to draw back, always ineffectiveness.*
> *Concerning all acts of initiative and creation,*
> *there is one elementary truth, ...*
> *the moment one definitely commits oneself, then providence moves too.*[10]

In the clearing of this sacred space then flows a new energy that is more joyful, life-sustaining, and promoting of compassion for ourselves—and it is here too as we practice mindfulness of these ego strategies that we become aware of a more ancient pulse within us—one driven by a wellspring of intelligence, inherent order, and rhythm.

Now, having learned to "step out of the way" of the natural healing energy within us, we are ready to commit. In the time of the Illumination and Return on our Journey, the final five steps to mindfulness introduce us to a profoundly new experience of ourselves in the world. Now we approach life with an open-hearted embrace, the resolve to hold firm to our new-found reality and model for others what we have learned: Having become mindful of our distractedness, we fully embrace the value of solitude. Having relaxed our grip on control, we open to humility and to receiving guidance from the Source. Mindful of our destructive rush to judgment, we embrace compassion for our own suffering—not just that of others. Seeing through the illusion of permanence, we let go of our attachments and outworn identities, grieving for the limitations and losses that life imposes. Finally, having become more mindful of our impatience we learn the benefits of correct waiting and open to a new expanded consciousness that arises from our unresisting embrace of the present moment.

In this way we achieve release from our suffering—find redemption—and embrace the time of our Illumination. From the fruits of our Illumination and with continued mindfulness we discover the resolve of self-impowerment, sharing with others in the time of our Return the wisdom with which we have been gifted along our way.

When speaking about the creation of his statue of David, Michelangelo explained "David was already there, perfectly formed in the marble. All I had to do was chip away everything that was not David.[11] The goal of mindfulness is awakened consciousness—after chipping away and releasing the chaotic, confusing thoughts and plans of our everyday ego—we discover the innate experience of well-being, peace, and unity with the world, "Mindfulness…is the miracle," says Thich Nhat Hanh, "which can call back our dispersed mind and restore it to wholeness so that we can live each minute of life."[12]

Our own science of Chaos Theory demonstrates that out of every apparently chaotic condition arises not more chaos but order. As Nietzsche reminds us, "To give birth to a dancing star, one must first have chaos within."[13]

Mindful Dreamwork views every person, animal, and angelic or demonic being as our Dream Mentors, prompting us to give the benefit of the doubt that within us is not a black abyss. Rather Mentors point the way in our every dream to the eternal ground of intelligence, wisdom, order, and compassion—always present in this moment and beyond the grasp of our waking life egos.

In contrast to our Western perspective, indigenous cultures and the spiritual philosophy of the East take this ordered world for granted. These cultures view human nature as in its essence trustworthy and good. The Perennial view teaches us that the dark abyss we fear is an illusion created by our habitual modes of thinking and of perceiving ourselves. As a result, we remain blind to the underlying order and harmony in the universe and our oneness with it.

> What we in our culture view as routine and mundane events are, for indigenous people, mirrors of a greater Truth embedded in a universe that is innately ordered, harmonious, and life-supporting.

Ironically, it was our foremost physicist Albert Einstein who felt compelled to warn us of this blindness: "The intuitive mind is a sacred gift," he said, "and the rational mind its faithful servant. We have created a society that honors the servant and has forgotten the gift."[14]

Whether through dreamwork, meditation, prayer, or other spiritual practice, many of us long for that gift of guidance and truth that the intuitive dimension of life offers. In contrast to our own society, earth-based cultures are at their core immersed in an intuitive worldview in which the daily affairs and decisions of life are experienced as a seamless part of the sacred natural world. All of the problems, accidents, injuries, illnesses, dreams, and joys of life are received simply as feedback from the Source.

In these cultures, everyday experiences inform them of the degree to which they and their community are aligned correctly with Divine purpose and energy.

In his book, *Secrets of the Talking Jaguar*, Mayan shaman Martin Prechtel wrote:

> *[We] shamans were taught to read messages from the spirits in how candles burn down, how birds sing, in animal tracks, in weather formations,*

*in the twitching of our muscles, in goose bumps, in the sounds of crack-*
*ling fires, in the forms of hot embers, in the daylight reflections of a*
*bowl of water, the positions of tossed knuckle bones, the actions of dogs,*
*the flight of meteorites, our own premonitions and gut feelings. But*
*above all and beyond all of these, we learned to listen, and read our*
*dreams.* [15]

In perennial cultures, feelings of confusion, conflict, anxiety, and unhappi-
ness are viewed as the result of one's community and oneself living out of
alignment with the natural rhythms and sacred energies of nature. Campbell
often spoke about the gods of myth and the images of our dreams as embodiments of these energies—as "personifications of the energies that inform life—
the very energies that are building the trees and moving the animals and
whipping up the waves on the ocean. The very energies that are in your body....
They're alive and well in everybody's life."[16]

This perennial perspective leads us to understand that healing and spiritual growth result from any method that helps us realign with the creative
energies of nature. As first-century Roman poet Juvenal said, "Nature never
says one thing, Wisdom another."[17]

We honor the Call of our psyche or the Source by aligning ourselves with
the flow and pattern of nature's energy in which we all participate—the blueprint which guides our nature and that of the world around us.

Depending on our spiritual practice, we accomplish this realignment by
learning from our healer, guru, or Dream Mentors how to identify and stay
mindful of the thoughts that stand in the way of our own natural process of
healing and growth—thoughts that limit our experience of what and who we
are. Our teachers and Mentors help us become more conscious of these habits
of thought and the suffering they cause in us.

Sadly, in our culture we have separated our waking consciousness from the
natural cycle and have difficulty appreciating those spiritual traditions based
in observations of nature. Zen scholar D. T. Suzuki said it so well: "God against
man. Man against God. Man against nature. Nature against man. Nature against
God. God against nature—very funny religion!"[18]

# What Is Mindful Dreaming? A Brief Review

Those of us who search for a greater spiritual grounding in life seek a guide to help us remove the veil between knowledge and experience and learn how to commune directly with the Source without the threats of recrimination and judgment found in many of our mainstream religious traditions. I have written *Mindful Dreaming* as just such a guide—one that speaks directly to our unique daily experiences so that we may feel the relevance of what we are being taught. This book is intended to help you experience what you seek, rather than to imitate those who have walked before you. This is why the Buddha was said to have told his followers: "If you see the Buddha along the road, kill him." We are meant to experience the fullness of life, not to act as those who do.

Regardless of who we are, when we live, or the nature of the Grail we seek, the four stages of the Mythic Journey—the Calling, Quest, Illumination, and Return—and its 10 lessons in mindfulness assist us in aligning with the wiser source of guidance and healing within.

The practice of Mindful Dreaming is grounded in the premise that all dream figures are our Mentors, and that these Mentors provide us with 10 lessons in mindfulness that guide us toward an expanded or Awakened consciousness and release from our suffering.

In this perspective, every dream is a lesson in mindfulness—a tangible answer to our prayers—about the stage of our spiritual journey, the thoughts that keep us stuck, and the intentions we must embrace and embody to grow. *Mindful Dreaming* teaches that dreams mirror our ego's attitude toward the guiding wisdom of the Self or Source—for better or worse.

During the first half of our Journey—the Calling and Quest—Mentors assist us in mindfulness of our five core ego values: distraction, control, judgment, attachment, and impatience. In waking life and dreams we experience suffering to the degree that we cling to these favorite ego strategies.

In the second half of our Journey—the Illumination and Return—we are guided to become our own Mentor, increasingly grounded in a wholly new, expanded consciousness. In waking life and dreams we experience redemption from our suffering and joy to the degree that we mindfully replace our ego strategies with the five core values of the Self or Source taught by our Mentors. Releasing distraction, we embrace solitude; spurning control, we embrace humility and follow guidance; refusing to judge, we embrace compassion for our own suffering; accepting the futility of attachment, we embrace grief and let go; releasing impatience, we embrace the present moment in which resides the Witnessing Consciousness—the Grail on our Journey.

In the following chapters of this section you will learn more about the stages of the Mythic Journey throughout your life and how your dreams reflect the phases of your own personal Journey. You'll also learn about Dream Mentors—the language with which they speak and the great gifts of healing and spiritual guidance they offer us each night.

# Practices for the Start of your Journey

## The Practice of Recording Your Dreams

When we set the intention to work with our dreams, each step along the way becomes an important aspect of practice and should be approached with reverence and clear intention. In this manner we honor our commitment to inner work and our deep and sincere desire to open to the guidance of the Source.

- Place a journal or spiral notebook to keep by your bedside. Remember that this journal will be your companion on your Journey and in many respects will contain your personal sacred text, so find or make a journal that is sturdy, aesthetic, and dedicated only for the recording of your dreams and inner work.

- Each night before bed, place the date on the top of the page and invite a dream that will provide you with whatever lesson is most important for you to receive. Set the intention to recall this dream upon waking. Practice setting this intention with reverence and focus.

- If you are desiring special guidance from your dreams, you can request a dream to provide this guidance. (This is called Dream Incubation. Read more about incubation in Chapter 3.)

- When you awaken in the morning or in the middle of the night, immediately write the dream down. This takes discipline and commitment, as we will often tell ourselves that we can wait until later, and later the dream is usually forgotten. (To record middle-of-the-night dreams, it may be helpful to have a pen with a light or a small flashlight so that you do not awaken anyone else that may be sharing the room.)

## Practices That Help Us Remember Dreams

Everyone dreams, and although some of us may find it easier to recall our dreams than others, there are simple techniques that can be used to enhance recall. You will also find that once you set the intention to work with your dreams and open to the healing energy they provide, that dream recall will improve considerably.

- ≈ Remembering our dreams depends upon kinesthetic memory. This means that dreams are most easily recalled while in the physical position in which they occurred. As you awaken, do not move or shift position.

- ≈ Before moving, "rehearse" your dream. Repeat your dream as if you were telling yourself a story, emphasizing its beginning, middle, and end.

- ≈ If you recall only a tiny fragment of your dream—even just an image—write it down. Remember that a picture is worth a thousand words. All dreams are important. Often the simplest and shortest dreams are the easiest to work with, and very powerful sources of insight.

- ≈ After rehearsing your dream, immediately turn over and write down everything you remember. Don't wait. You will forget more detail with each passing moment.

- ≈ After writing down your dream, include a few words about your mood on awakening. Later in the day, reread your dream and give it a short title in your journal—a single word or phrase. Titling always helps get to the heart of our dream's meaning.

- ≈ Whenever possible, note the Journey stage of your dream in your journal as well as the lesson in mindfulness that it teaches. (You'll learn more about the stages and lessons and how to identify them shortly.) This will help you build cumulative insights about your dream Journeys, and their relevance to your Journey through life.

## Journal Practice: The Roots of Judgment

You read in this section about the ways in which our cultural conditioning influences our perception of ourselves and the world in which we live. Consider these questions:

- ≈ Do you believe you are an innately "good" and lovable person? Do your parents think so? If yes, could you tell by their behavior toward you or did you have to infer their unconditional love?
- ≈ What did you learn about "good and evil" growing up in your church, synagogue, or mosque?
- ≈ Do your parents view good and evil the way you do?
- ≈ How much have your parents' attitudes about good and evil affected you?
- ≈ What do you feel is at the core of your being or true nature— something that feels positive, or negative? What do your parents feel is at the core of your true nature?
- ≈ Do you feel the universe, as we know it, is innately ordered or largely the result of chance occurrence? A little of both?

## Journal Practice: Exploring Your Favorite Ego Strategies

In this section you were introduced to our ego's five preferred strategies: distraction, control, judgment, attachment, and impatience. Because we engage in all of these at various times in our lives, take a moment to journal and reflect on each of them. Typically there is some protective impulse in the development of an Ego strategy. Perhaps it would be helpful to honor this as well. You might say:

> *I often stay busy and preoccupied, taking on many projects I don't really care about. I am using distraction to protect myself from feeling lonely and sad. I would rather feel my sadness and heal my life so that I can access more life energy for things I really care about.*

It may also be helpful to explore which of the strategies is your favorite and to consider feedback you've received from family and friends. Usually such feedback is couched in good-natured teasing about our foibles or in more painful arguments in which we are accused or admonished. You might say:

> *I don't feel like I am controlling, but I am often frustrated and stuck in my dreams. In waking life my friends seem a little upset with me and often will say that I need to relax and trust that things will be okay. I feel like that is irresponsible but I do think I would be happier if I could relax a bit more.*

# Chapter 1

# The Journey to Mindfulness in Our Everyday Lives and Dreams

*There are only two or three human stories, and they go on repeating themselves as fiercely as if they had never happened before.*

—Willa Cather

*The universe is made of stories, not of atoms.*

—Muriel Rukeyser

Dorothy struggling to find "home." Luke Skywalker determined to master "The Force." Frodo and his Hobbit companions risking their lives to destroy the Ring of Power. We might think that these are unrelated adventures about rings, invisible power, and a long trek home to a farm in Kansas. But in truth, they are the same story. Dorothy, Luke, and Frodo are all traveling the same path—a universal Journey of change and transformation.

When you think about it, within every compelling novel, film, fable, or spiritual story, the main characters have one central goal, though initially they are often unaware of it. That goal is to transcend the grip of limited perspectives created by family or society, lovers or friends who have blinded them to their full human potential.

We never weary of this one grand tale. We tell it, read it, and see it again and again, marveling at the new variations of character, setting, and adventure. But the heart of the story remains the same. And because it is the elemental human story, it speaks to us directly. There is always the Unknown, and the fearful moment when we realize that our old defenses and lifelong values will not serve us in this new land. There is a point of discovery, a realization that the only way we can transcend our fear of the Unknown is by living with a new fierceness of heart. And inevitably, as we search for the courage to trust our own inner authority, there is suffering to endure. The pivotal point of transformation is when we release our belief that only others have the power to define reality—and instead empower ourselves to live by our own heart's wisdom. Only then can we find our way "home," back to our true selves, which are at once familiar and newly transformed.

# Resisting the Call

The only variation in the classic heroic journey motif—though the lesson remains the same—is the tragedy that occurs when protagonists refuse or fail to follow their calling.

We don't often see movies or books that illustrate this variation, because, by definition, it is an unfinished story. The result of refusing one's Calling is continued frustration, or misery. Remember, for example, in Tennessee Williams's *The Glass Menagerie* when Tom finally breaks away from his oppressive relationship with his mother, but remains emotionally ensnared in a web of guilt about leaving behind his disabled sister, Laura. One can imagine that Tom would increasingly close down as a person, or try to drown out his inner voice with alcohol or drugs.

In every hero's tale—whether played out on the screen, in books, or in daily life—the hero or heroine has little interest in change initially. Once it is clear, metaphorically, that "we are not in Kansas anymore," the fear of change and growth sticks deep in all of us. As Goethe once remarked, "Everybody wants to be someone; nobody wants to grow."[1] Though each tale ends with a compassionate gift, we usually resist with all our might that inner Call to change. Given the choice, at least initially, we would like to hold on to those painful, deadening (though familiar) strategies that no longer work, and skip the transformation. As they prepare to confront the Wicked Witch in *The Wizard of Oz*, the Lion implores the Scarecrow and Tin Man, "There's only one thing more I'd like you fellows to do." "What's that?" they ask. "Talk me out of it."

Despite this fear, the impulse to grow, to "become someone," seems a divine mandate hardwired within us. An ancient Roman adage reminds us that "the fates lead those who will—and drag those who won't." And though we may have allies and Mentors along the way, the decisions to accept the risks of the Journey are ours alone to make. When we seek redemption for our suffering, we must always find our own rocky path toward that end.

If our life were a movie, we'd recognize our Calling. As the movie score surged to dramatic heights, we would identify the moment of truth, and (with our face to the camera), garner the fierceness of heart that our own grand mission requires.

In real life, the markers are obvious. What is our Calling? What is the core spiritual impulse that prompts us toward fulfillment of our personal destiny, that urges us toward discovery of our entire potential, and that drags us, albeit kicking and screaming, toward a deeper understanding of life? Is there a purpose and direction our psyche has in mind for us when we dream, a unique journey our dreams are calling us to take?

# The Journey in Our Everyday Life

My work with dreams during the past 20 years has been to solve these riddles: I've discovered that indeed dreams teach us the steps to mindfulness that, when practiced, help move us through the everyday problems in which we find ourselves stuck, expand our consciousness, and return us to an awareness of our true spiritual nature.

Initially, the stimulus of my own dreams brought a new depth of understanding to my reading of Swiss analyst Carl Jung and opened me to the work of Joseph Campbell, the late, great mythologist. Jung spoke about how our dreams, and indeed our psyche, from which our dreams spring, participate in and draw their wisdom from a deeper ground of nature—a "quantum field of information" as physicists might say—that Jung called our "Collective Unconscious." Joseph Campbell, for his part, spent his life peering into this well of shared knowledge and wisdom, and distilling a universal pattern embedded in our world myths, fairytales, fables, spiritual literature, and popular books and films.

Campbell dubbed this pattern the heroic or Mythic Journey, but it is most popularly known in our culture as the search for the Holy Grail. The Grail is derived from Christian imagery, in one version a mythical chalice from which Jesus drank at the Last Supper, which was said to have captured his blood as he died on the cross. It came to be seen in medieval literature as a source of redemption and eternal life for King Arthur's knights, or anyone who might find and drink from it.

Campbell helped us see that we are all on a journey for the Holy Grail, something that will bring meaning and redemption to our lives. The search may take many forms— for example, we may focus on finding the financial security and quality of life that will liberate us from worry; the person who will finally love us as we always wished to be loved; the invention or work of art that demands expression, or the spiritual awakening and enlightenment that will make sense of our life once and for all. In fact, our personal Grail will change and deepen over time as we mature and our consciousness evolves.

> Joseph Campbell identified the four recurring stages, or sequence, of the Mythic Journey: the Calling, the Quest, the Illumination, and the Return. These distinct stages chronicle the unending search for meaning and heart in our lives, the search for our Grail— or, as Campbell called it, our "search for bliss."

Regardless of who we are, when we live, or the nature of the Grail we seek, the stages of the search and the lessons that it teaches are universal.

*The Wizard of Oz* is a classic hero's tale, one long Journey dream with each of the four stages represented. Dorothy's Calling—her search for heart and meaning—leads her on a remarkable *Quest*, full of danger, confusion, and insight, before she finally returns "home," transformed.

When we meet her, Dorothy is an orphan who feels out of place and alone on her farm in Kansas. This sense of disconnection from the love and understanding of those around us is a common element of a *Calling*. When Dorothy awakens to find that she's "not in Kansas anymore," she has responded to her Call. She has taken herself "over the rainbow," and crossed the threshold into another world of experience. Her *Quest* begins.

Immediately, Dorothy encounters the good witch Glinda, who, as do all good Mentors, gifts her with the tools that she will most need on her Journey—the path of the Yellow Brick Road, the direction she must follow, and ruby slippers, her power to return home. Ironically, at the start of our Journey we never appreciate the nature of the gifts we have been given, or the powers of self we already possess. Instead, we feel incomplete, without the heart, brains, or courage to complete our Journey. During the *Quest* stage, in life or dreams, we are continually tested and prompted to discover, trust, and become mindful of our own inner authority and resources. Dorothy is no exception to this rule. She encounters numerous challenges, threats and obstacles—"Lions, and tigers, and bears, oh my!"—that teach her essential lessons about her many strengths.

In the language of dreams, the Wicked Witch is as powerful a Mentor for Dorothy as Glinda, the good witch. Dream Mentors can be frightening and foreboding—"Surrender, Dorothy!"—taunting and pushing us to look beyond our defenses and release attachment to our limited self-image.

With all of her allies and mentors—including the Tin Man, Scarecrow, and Lion—who embody her different perspectives on life, Dorothy perseveres through the ordeals of the *Quest* and enters the time of *Illumination*. She realizes—as we do in every successful Journey—that she has had within her all that she needed from the start. Dorothy has learned to trust her courage, intelligence, and heart, and "to look for her heart's desire" within herself—in her "own backyard." One of her final epiphanies is the importance of trusting her own intuition—when Toto pulls away the veil that hides the very human man beneath the grandiose authority of the wizard. We, too must learn that no authority is so great that we can not challenge it. In doing so, we learn to trust our perspective and the power of our own heart's wisdom.

Yet insight is of no use if we fail to honor and remain mindful of the new values we have discovered on our Journey. We must resolve to live what we have learned. So in the last stage of our Journey, we are challenged to hold firm to our new insights, and to integrate these into our daily life. In the time of our own *Return*, as Dorothy does, we must practice mindfulness that "there's no place like home." Of course, Dorothy's home is not literally where Aunt Em lives. Dorothy's home is her newfound sense of herself as an emotionally integrated person, grounded in an awareness of her own transformed capacity for trust and love. Finally, Glinda reminds Dorothy that she has had the power within her all along to return home—but "Dorothy wouldn't have believed me. She had to learn it for herself"—and so must we.

In this and every story there are two parallel tales: an outer and inner journey. Outwardly, Dorothy is called to find her way home, while helping her friends find what they feel they need to complete themselves. However, by accomplishing this outer Calling, she affirms a more profound inner Calling. Dorothy is helped by her mentors to find the resolve to act compassionately on behalf of her own needs, and to nurture within herself the same compassion for others. Whether it is Elliott in *E.T.*, Rick and Ilsa in *Casablanca*, Neo and Morpheus in *The Matrix*, Frodo and Sam in *Lord of the Rings*, or Dorothy and her friends, the Journey always has the same goal: to practice mindfulness of the lessons our mentors teach us—and in so doing transcend our fears, and find the courage and inner authority to listen to our heart.

# The Journey in Our Dreams

It is no surprise then that the Journey motif is present even in our dreams, because it is the story of life's greatest heroic changes. We feel overwhelmed and terrified when we resist the pressures and sanctions of family and society to conform. Outwardly, we fear the punishment of being rejected and abandoned, while inwardly we fear discovering that we have been selfish and even "bad" for following our heart's desire. Dorothy is horrified when she inadvertently melts the Wicked Witch. Fortunately however, just as in the films and stories we love to watch, we are provided by our psyche with Dream Mentors—frightening as they may be—to help us learn the courage we need to live life as we desire, and to become the heroes or heroines of our own life stories.

At the start of our own Journey when we sense that we are being called to change and grow, just as Dorothy and the Wicked Witch, we too are frightened and our Calling dreams tend to be nightmares in which we feel mortally cheated.

This is because we fear the consequences of questioning, let alone opposing the collective wisdom of our family and society. Consequently, in our nightmares we deeply mistrust and run from our Dream Mentors, though ironically (as you'll learn in Section II) they come only to guide and liberate us from our suffering.

In the meantime, we dream of being hunted down by serial murderers, we endure tornadoes, hurricanes, and earthquakes, and experience the loss of what we have most prized in life: "I was walking along the beach. It was one of those perfect days. I could feel the fine grains of sand beneath my feet and the cool waves lapped at my toes. Then out of nowhere the ground began to tremble. I saw a huge bubble of churning water rise right out of the center of the ocean and become a gargantuan Tsunami wave, like the one in that movie *Deep Impact*. The wave towered over my head, paused for a moment and then crashed down on my home behind me, leveling it entirely as I watched It was horrible." We are not yet aware that the old identity and values to which we are most attached are what most need to be released if we are to end our suffering.

As we move though the lessons of the Calling we slowly release the fears that bind us, and now in the Quest our dreams do not feel mortally threatening. As we no longer fully identify with the rules of the Collective Unconscious, we no longer feel that we will die—that we will be unlovable and abandoned—if we change. Our fear remains, but is more "manageable." We dream of feeling anxious, confused, lost, and hopeless—still attached to what is not in our best interest: "I'm a nurse in a war that we are losing and I'm trying to save everyone who is wounded. It seems impossible but I keep trying. I wake up overwhelmed just like I feel everyday of my life."

Just as Dorothy experienced numerous challenges to grow on her path, our Quest dreams continually test and prompt us to become mindful of our own inner resources and capacity for living in the Present Moment—and as you will learn in subsequent chapters, to release the ego strategies, the pattern of destructive thoughts that keep us stuck in our very limiting self-image and perspective about reality.

Eventually, we master the challenges of our Quest and more fully embrace new values we have learned from our Mentors in waking life and dreams.

Now in the time of our Illumination our perspective has transformed and the enemies we perceived in our Calling and Quest dreams have become great teachers with words of wisdom that inspire us to remain on our path and to direct experiences of expanded consciousness to demonstrate that redemption is possible.

We have transcended our fear of change and of opposing the collective wisdom with which we have been raised. As Dorothy did, we have torn the veil from the face of the Wizard and found him powerless and ineffectual. Gardens in our dreams grow beautiful and lush, and we meet loving Mentors who guide and lead us to profound breakthroughs, insight, clarity, and epiphany. We experience redemption from our suffering and now know it was worth the struggle to endure. A friend of mine dreamed:

> I've completed a sad and painful divorce, just as I had in waking life. In the dream I wonder about the decision I've made and how I ever gave up the childhood values I cherished. I feel like it's taken everything out of me. Then I hear the bells of a church tolling in the distance and as the chimes get louder an ecstasy builds in my chest until I'm going to explode with joy. I realize right in my dream that this is the joy of liberation—I've liberated my soul not from my marriage as I once thought, but from the prison of deadening rules I had made for myself all my life. I feel no more of that agonizing doubt and now know in my heart that I have done the right thing.

Finally, in the time of our Return we arrive back home to a newfound experience of ourselves and, as Dorothy was, we are grounded in an awareness of our own transformed capacity for trust and love.

Our Dream Mentors now assist us in honing our resolve to remain centered in our own reality and authority. Our dreams often start with the same challenges as in our Quest, but now we react to these challenges with a lack of defensiveness and fear—and with consistent compassion for ourselves and others:

> I am driving toward a severe disastrous snowstorm that is burying people on the road. But I am not afraid and I continue on. My car gets stopped in the snow, but still I'm not afraid. I see a man helping others to dig out. I get out to do the same and find that the snow is neither cold, nor wet, nor heavy—in fact it has no weight at all as I shovel it out for others. Everyone is stuck in wet, heavy snow only because that is how they perceive it.

In their most fundamental sense the four phases of the Journey correspond to the seasons of nature and reflect the perennial spiritual view that our human nature—our very consciousness—participates in and is inseperable from the natural world.

For this reason, when we speak of the Journey stages we are actually describing the creative cycle that underlies the growth of human consciousness. Indeed, when our ego sleeps each night, the stories of our dreams carry us across the threshold of our limited day-world reality and tap the  greater wisdom and creativity at our core.

# A Guide to the Four Phases of Dreamwork in Your Spiritual Practice: Eddies in the River of Our Journey

I have ordered the steps in mindfulness from one to 10 because the four Journey stages—the creative cycle of growth in nature—have an innate psychological order and direction. Yet in actual practice nature is never linear. There are no straight lines to our goal, and it is important to view these steps as values we must practice time and again on our Journey. Author Anaïs Nin said it in this way: "We do not grow absolutely, chronologically. We grow sometimes in one dimension, and not in another; unevenly. We grow partially. We are relative. We are mature in one realm, childish in another. The past, present, and future mingle and pull us backward, forward, or fix us in the present."[2]

The various aspects of our lives—family, work, creativity—are always evolving in some stage of this cycle of creative growth. We may ignore the Calling of our dreams in one domain of our lives, while continuing on our journey of change in another. Even as we confront the imbalances that our dreams call us to face, our life journeys do not begin with the Calling and end with the Return, only to remain resolved or static. We are continually cycling through change, accepting or rejecting the call to follow our own heart's wisdom. And within those cycles, we often move backwards and forwards emotionally in this process.

> I've come to think of our Journey—in dreams, and in life—as a river full of eddies, where water may be captured and swirled back, and where we are often held more or less in place before flowing on.

Consider the seasons—as Spring approaches we are not surprised if one day we have cold, dry, wintry weather, and the next is warm and rainy. Yet we know that we are progressing toward Summer. Similarly, as we are part of nature, our Journey is profoundly organic, so there can be no strict linear order to our growth and the dreams that nourish it.

One night we may be deeply immersed in a Calling nightmare, while the next night receive direct guidance and support in a typical Illumination dream. However, over the course of time, when we practice dreamwork, we do have an experience of "forward movement," or evolution both in terms of the sequence of our dreams, and the experience of expanded awareness they bring us. We begin with a tendency to have mostly Calling and/or Quest dreams, which yield to more frequent Illumination dreams and then more Return dreams.

With each new day, the momentum of life requires us to move through cycle after cycle, picking up lost threads and completing lessons that we have already begun, which remain incomplete. And though our life is truly one organic whole (a single "macrocosmic Journey"), our perception of it is fragmented into different identities and challenges.

At home I may be very non-judgmental with my children, but at work feel hatred toward my boss and indulge in constant judgment. I may tell myself that "I've got a problem at work," but actually I'm simply still engaging in "judgment." The venue has changed, but the problem remains. Conversely, I may have problems releasing control at work, but receive affirmation from my dreams that I am succeeding at this task, because I have successfully released control with my wife. Can you think of any skill you've learned in life that has not required the same pattern of trial and error: practice—improvement—more practice?

Yet, when we know the stage of growth we are in, we can become more conscious of our attitude toward change, and the particular perspectives we must release to facilitate our growth. Ultimately, our psyche will assess each night what lessons we need to become more mindful of, show us when we have forgotten or not quite learned what we need to know, or alternatively, lead us on to the next step.

Therefore, in actual practice, our Journey comprises many smaller journeys occurring simultaneously throughout our life—in love and work relationships, on our career path, and in creative efforts of all kinds. The focus, theme, and content of the story is ever-changing, but the underlying lesson of our Journey, and therefore our dreams, is always the same: to become grounded in the values of our heart, and to serve them.

The endless cyclic nature of the Journey means that we are born time and again, similar to a phoenix rising from the ashes of its own past. We are Called. We answer the Call, and struggle through the lessons of the Quest, we are enlightened by the Illumination, and then we work to bring our new vision to everyday life, as we Return to the ordinary world.

The cyclical nature of dreams is in keeping with the seasonal cycle of life energy within and around us. As with the pull of tides, dreams help us to harmonize and align with the cycles of our own emotional and spiritual growth.

The spirit of *Mindful Dreaming* is to return dreamwork in our culture to its perennial place as a spiritual practice—and to guide you through the unavoidable stuck places that inevitably occur in every practice.

Dreamwork helps us to unfold the map that plots our own unique path toward healing, growth, and wholeness. The Sufi poet Rumi said it this way:

> *Humankind is being led along*
> *an evolving course...*
> *and though we seem to be sleeping,*
> *there is an inner wakefulness*
> *that directs the dream,*
> *and that will eventually startle us*
> *back to the truth of who we are.*[3]

By expanding our consciousness, and guiding us to an awareness of our true nature, dreams and dreamwork form the basis of a comprehensive spiritual practice. Dreams pull us towards and through the growth of change.

As you reflect on what you've learned about the Journey you'll notice that, despite the prevailing belief in our culture about the importance of individual effort and the value of "pulling oneself up by the bootstraps," no Journey ever succeeds without the help of allies and Mentors. Think of any story or film on any topic or a personal adventure you've experienced. You'll find that they share one common, unfailing thread: the presence of others who point the way, provide much-needed wisdom—or sufficient provocation and suffering—to start us out fresh on a new path in life. Our mentors come in many forms and flavors, but without them we never learn to walk the walk.

Indeed, whenever we travel far from home it's incumbent upon us to know as much as possible about those on whom we will depend. Otherwise we will wander through that new land lost and confused, apprehensive and alienated.

Many of us have had this experience to some degree in a foreign culture or even a strange city—and it is even more common for us to feel this predicament as we travel the twilight road of our nightly dreams. We may sense that the perspective of those we visit offers us something to enrich our waking life, but without preparation we understand little of the language they speak, the values they hold, and how they understand the universe or perceive reality.

In the next two chapters you'll find a field guide for your nightly travels so that you can better understand your Dream Mentors—allies who offer the exact guidance, motivation, and wisdom you need at the specific time you need it on your Journey. In this process, the perennial spiritual values you've heard about all your life will be enriched and renewed. Understanding more about your teachers, you will find that you are increasingly embraced and healed by them. You are ready to learn the landscape, rhythms, and language of the universe aboriginal peoples have forever called the Dreamtime.

# Chapter Practices

As any spiritual practice does, dreamwork evolves and deepens over time. Keep in mind that our dreams can, and often do, show us a view that is different from what we believe, or are consciously aware of in our waking life. Some dreams are vivid, emotional, and dramatic markers of a particular Journey stage. Others can be less clear, including elements of different stages. Your awareness of the Journey stages will increase over time, as will your ability to recognize their emotional hallmarks in your dreams. With your greater awareness, you will also see patterns and phases in your dreams—a long series of Quest dreams, for example—as your psyche flows back around to still unresolved issues.

The Mythic Journey, with its four universal stages, provides a remarkable context for understanding dreams and life. When we realize the stage of our Journey we can see our suffering, frustration, or joy as part of the larger emotional and spiritual landscapes of our lives. Locating our stage or place on the Mythic Journey map reminds us that there are no shortcuts on this universal path we all travel. Knowing the stage of our Journey, we can better accept the unavoidable cycle of change, stop resisting "what is," and come into greater alignment with our dreams and their purpose for us—our Calling.

## Determining the Stage of Your Journey Through Your Dreams

Use the following chart to reflect on the primary types of dreams you've been having during the last few weeks or months. Briefly review Hallmarks of the Journey in Waking Life on pages 42–43 to refresh your memory about the characteristics of Calling, Quest, Illumination and Return dreams. For the purpose of this practice you can rely on recall, or if you've been journaling your dreams, review them now. You may also choose to make a rough count of each type of dream.

|  | Calling | Quest | Illumination | Return |
|---|---|---|---|---|
| Nightmares: Dreams of mortal terror | | | | |
| Dreams of confusion, frustration, fear. anxiety, or guilt | | | | |
| Dreams of guidance, increased clarity, problem-solving, insight, or epiphany | | | | |
| Dreams of firm resolve without the presence of fear or anger; dreams of compassion and charity towards others | | | | |
| Your predominant type of dream | | | | |

# Determining the Stage of Your Journey Through the Nature of Your Feelings and Attitudes

After considering your current feelings about a primary relationship, your job, or a creative project, reflect on the predominant phase of the Journey you've experienced during the past three months. In the following chart, check the stage of your Journey for each of the primary areas of your life. Often your initial instincts are the best indicator. For example:

≋ Do you feel frightened or resistant to starting some change you are contemplating (*Calling*)? Are you conflicted, lost, or in turmoil (*Quest* )? As you reflect on, say, your relationship with your parents or spouse, do you feel less conflicted than you once did, experiencing more clarity and insight (*Illumination*)? Are you resolved and at peace with your new perspective (*Return*)?

≋ Have you ever felt as if you were in the same Journey stage throughout all areas of your life at once?

|  | Calling | Quest | Illumination | Return |
|---|---|---|---|---|
| Spouse or lover |  |  |  |  |
| Mother/father |  |  |  |  |
| Children |  |  |  |  |
| Work |  |  |  |  |
| Friends |  |  |  |  |
| Creative energy/ goals |  |  |  |  |
| Predominant dream types (insert result of exercise) |  |  |  |  |
| Your predominant Journey phase |  |  |  |  |

# Hallmarks of the Journey in Waking Life and Dreams

|  | Calling | Quest | Illumination | Return |
|---|---|---|---|---|
| Seasonal Time | Autumn | Winter | Spring | Summer |
| Types of Energy | Waning<br>Diminishing | Depleted<br>Blocked<br>Stuck<br>Stagnant | Blossoming<br>Healing<br>Creative<br>Radiant | Grounded<br>Present<br>Focused |
| Attitudes Toward Change in Walking Life | Limited awareness of what needs to change and reluctance to change even when challenged. We go "kicking and screaming into our Calling." | Reluctant desire to change but slowly increasing commitment to overcome the fear of change despite severe trials and challenges. | Fully open to the experience of change and knowledge that change, was worth the suffering required. | Commitment to maintain and strengthen new values in everyday life. Awareness of others' need for change, and commitment to teach and help others with the process of change. |

|  | | | |
|---|---|---|---|
| **Emotional Hallmarks** | Life feels empty, unfulfilling, and without meaning. | "Dark night of the Soul." Feelings of confusion and despair slowly yield to feelings of hopefulness. | Epiphany. Feelings of release and redemption along with influx of healing, creative energy. | Feelings of empowerment, resolve, deepened confidence and trust in one's own authority and reality. |
| **Typical Dreams** | Nightmares focus our attention on the perspectives and values that require change. Inspirational dreams give us a taste of how our lives could be different if we open to change. | Quest dreams focus on our ego's continuing resistance to values that must be released; show few signs of resolution; encourage surrender by placing us in dramas that require us to face our powerlessness to effect change on our own. | Provide us with inspiration for change from Mentors and allies. Experiences of joy, release, expanded consciousness, compassion for self and others, redemption, absolution for our past mistakes. Open us to the Present Moment in which Witnessing Consciousness resides. | Portray us as our own mentor and healer. Remind us how others will benefit from what we have learned, and encourage an attitude of charity and compassion toward all. |

# Chapter 2

## Receiving the Gift of Direct Experience From Your Dream Mentors

*The only source of knowledge is experience.*

—Albert Einstein

*Nothing ever becomes real till it is experienced—even a proverb is no proverb to you till your life has illustrated it.*

—John Keats

Travelers and early archeologists encountered the vast beauty of the pyramids, temples, and obelisks of ancient Egypt, but at first had no comprehension of what the hieroglyphic language of the ancient Egyptians meant. Without knowledge of what the tiny images expressed, they surmised that the hieroglyphs were a language of pictures and images, representing words and concepts. However, it was still many years before archaeologists were able to decipher the secrets of the Egyptian language.

In a very real sense we are what an old friend of mine calls "Dream Archeologists," because the language of dreams is also a language of pictures and images we must take time to diligently unearth. Fortunately however, each of us carries a personal Rosetta Stone of life, experiences that enable us to understand the meaning of our dream images. However, in this chapter you will learn how dream images carry more than mere meaning and are, indeed, bearers of a profound creative experience that can be plumbed for our own healing and growth.

In waking life we frequently speak in image and metaphor. In fact, images can convey both the literal and metaphorical at the same time. An image of a man bent over and sweating, with a heavy boulder strapped to his back, may tell us that there was once a man who carried a heavy stone with difficulty. However, this is a literal understanding of the image no different than a sign along the highway that depicts a curve in the road. The symbolic or metaphoric understanding of the same image might be "a long-suffering man" or "a man shouldering the weight of the world."

At first glance, dreams may seem opaque and difficult to understand to our rational wakening mind. Freud himself concluded that they must be disguised messages about information too upsetting for our conscious minds to handle.

Yet dreams speak the same simple language of metaphor we do in our everyday life. For example, let's reflect on the following conversation. Listen for the metaphors: "I'm really through with this relationship. I'm *shutting the door* behind me! You ask me what will I do now that there's no one to love me? Well, *I'll cross that bridge when I get to it.* I don't want to *miss the bus* in my life and never have the relationship I've always hoped for."

In waking life you wouldn't need to go to a dream dictionary to understand what that woman is saying—but ironically you might well find yourself puzzled by images of doors shutting, bridges, and buses in your dreams.

The events of the day and of recent weeks are often embedded in our nightly dreams as our psyche's way of providing the most metaphorically "fresh" experience. This is why I discourage people from using dream dictionaries. As the previous example illustrates, we need to understand dream metaphors as related to our own life experiences. For someone who almost drowned as a child, a dream of swimming at the beach is not necessarily about a much-needed vacation. Dream dictionaries discourage us from exploring our own associations to the metaphors in our dreams. For you, "in the swim" may mean "at the brink."

# Dreams Are Metaphor and Much More

Dream images are the same as the metaphorical images of a poem. The great 19th-century poet Rilke could just as well have been describing how to work with a dream when he spoke about poetic images as being not simply metaphors, but actual "experiences." "For the sake of a single poem," he said—and I would add for the sake of a single dream:

> [Y]ou must see many cities, many people and things…and know the gestures, which small flowers make when they open in the morning. You must be able to think back to streets in unknown neighborhoods, to unexpected encounters, and to partings you have long seen coming; to days of childhood whose mystery is still unexplained…to childhood illnesses…to mornings by the sea, to the sea itself, to seas, to nights of travel…and it is still not enough.[1]

So, too, writer Muriel Rukeyser reminds us, "Breathe-in experience, breathe-out poetry."[2] To "understand" a dream we must breathe back in the experiences bound up in its images. Mindfulness is the practice of slowing down and experiencing the sights, sounds, smells, and feelings of this present moment—and Mindful Dreaming is grounded in this practice.

# Embracing Your Dream Mentor's Experience as Your Own

Campbell understood that all myths—public and personal—used the language of metaphor to embody their life energy and that's why he described metaphor as "the mask of God through which eternity is to be *experienced.*"[3]

He also reminded us that dreams are our personal—as opposed to public—myths, and that all myths arise from the same Source. Thus, as you've read earlier, when Campbell spoke about the gods of myth he was also speaking about the images of our dreams as "personifications of the energies that inform life....They're alive and well in everybody's life."[4]

I would add that the gods of your dreams are alive and well each night in the bodies of your Dream Mentors.

And the first step in working with any dream is to practice mindfulness that your Dream Mentors are carriers of a profound gift of healing experience—expanded consciousness—that you are being called to embrace.

> To dream mindfully means that we view all dream characters, whether human, animal, angelic, demonic beings, or even impersonal forces of nature herself, as our Mentors.

In modern parlance, you might call the embrace of this dream experience a "growth factor" as powerful as any hormone our body produces. For doubters: Ask anyone who has successfully worked with a dream about the surge of healing energy and expanded awareness that becomes available when the perspective of a Dream Mentor unfolds—when we experience the world through that Mentor's eyes. As the great mystic Meister Eckhart said, "When the soul wishes to experience something, she throws an image of the experience out before her and enters into her own image."[5] In Mindful Dreaming we are called to commune with the people, animals, and other beings in our dreams and to "enter into" their image so that we can share in and learn from their experience.

The result of our efforts leads to what has been termed the AHA experience, because what is known from the dream is, known from its experience and no longer seems hypothetical or just "possible." This is the primary way to distinguish logical knowing from experiential knowing—and the *true* meaning of a dream versus someone else's idea about what your dream means. Logical conclusions are always felt to be the best among the possibilities, but all other perspectives seem potentially true.

For example, have you ever seen an acquaintance approaching whom you know you will have to introduce to a friend—but you've forgotten her name? You may run quickly through a long alphabetical list of names, all of which are objectively "possible." However, only when you hit upon the correct name do you feel that distinct sense of "knowing" that runs through your entire body, bringing with it that wonderful rush of relief. That's the "experience" of knowing.

# Dream Images Aren't Primarily Symbols

That's right. "Symbols" are what we have named experiences when we have forgotten or distanced ourselves from *what that experience feels like*—the experience of that image. For example, if I dream of riding a wild horse in early morning through a mountain pasture of wild flowers, I may look back on that dream and wonder about the symbol of a wild horse and how wild flowers symbolize something different than garden flowers. And by the time I've finished "thinking" about those symbols, looking them up in a symbol dictionary, or asking my Jungian therapist what it all meant archetypally, it would be reduced to something "quite interesting" or intriguing. Thinking creates wonderful possibilities to ponder—while flattening and drying up the experience we are contemplating. Experience is the true basis of all learning. In the language of modern science, "Experience precedes cognition." Or as the old Sicilian aphorism reminds us, "Only the spoon knows how hot the soup is." So it is best to remain mindful that every dream image stores within a rich, infinitely layered complex of life experiences, feelings, values, and attitudes.

In this sense dream images are holographic. Holograms are pictures created with laser light in which every part contains the whole picture. Though holograms are "made" by scientists, the universe itself seems constructed on this principle. For example, we can clone life because we understand that within each cell, no matter how specialized its function, lies enfolded the blueprint of the entire system. So it was that second-century Kabbalist Abot de Rabbi Nathan said, "One man is equivalent to all Creation. One man is the World in miniature."[6] Many now believe that the human brain stores the memory of every experience we've ever had holographically.

Thus the holographic image may at first appear "flat" as any normal picture or painting would. However, when you walk around it, changing your angle of focus—a holographic image such as a dream image becomes three-dimensional.

When working with a dream image of that wild horse, I may start with just the two-dimensional thought that "I am riding a wild horse," but then I may choose to enter into that image with all of my senses. (At the end of this chapter you can learn a simple method with which to move more fully into the experience that your Dream Mentors embody.)

As I circle around the visual image of that horse I can see it from above as I sit on it, from all sides, and from below; know its solid girth, feel grounded in its earthy colors; and feel the steam pour from its nostrils and heat the chilly air—experiences on that kind of crisp mountain morning that always evoke a certain hard-to-describe openness and excitement in me. As I feel into the emotional nature of that horse, I may start with the memory that horses are enjoyable to ride, but then move on to re-experience that horse more deeply, feel its strength, its quiet power, the liberating experience of hurtling over obstacles and racing through beautiful fields—confident in a way I've rarely or never before allowed myself to feel.

> This is a really mind-bending notion—that within a single image exists an entire universe of experience.

Implied in this reality is the profound fact that understanding can be obtained in two different ways—from both rational analysis and "experience." We can rationally observe a phenomenon or event, dissect and analyze its parts, deduce or infer its nature. That's what most scientists do and it's by far our culture's most preferred approach to solving all problems. Alternatively, we can learn from the experience of a thing or action. We don't need to rely on logical deduction and inference. We can learn directly from the experience enfolded in every image. Some like to call this process "intuition," but this term has come to imply a kind of indirect knowledge based on something intangible. In fact, a better term might be "experience," as in "I experience the problem in this way," implying a very direct and tangible way of knowing in one's body as well as mind.

This is how Einstein arrived at his General Theory of Relativity, arguably the single most radical shift in our Western understanding of reality ever—through experience. Those of us who have seen news clips of this wooly white-haired professorial old man at work may recall him standing in front of a blackboard filled with alien-looking mathematical equations. Some of us even heard how for years only a handful of scientists in the entire world truly understood his theory and the mathematical operations underlying it. However, although we all know the timeworn story of how Einstein failed his math course in grade school, fewer of us are aware that he actually needed other mathematicians to do the advanced math required by his theory.

So how did Einstein lead all of humanity to another level of consciousness about the nature of reality even though he couldn't do the math? The answer is that he "experienced" this deeper reality—in much the same manner as mystics insist on doing. In truth he experienced it first in a dream and then later developed a technique for focusing his experience and learning more about it. First the dream:

While still an awkward adolescent headed for a boring job at the patent office, he dreamed the dream that changed the course of human history—for better or worse. Einstein shared that it was night in his dream and he was with friends sledding down a hill and having a grand time. However, on one trip down, he became aware that he was traveling faster and faster. Realizing after a moment that the sled was approaching the speed of light, he looked up and saw the twinkling starry light of the night refracted into a brilliant spectrum of colors he had never before seen. Filled with a numinous sense of awe, wonder, and reverence, he understood this vision as one that clarified his calling in life—a vision that contained all the answers as well as questions he would need to ask. "I knew I had to understand that dream," said Einstein, "and you could say and I would say, that my entire scientific career has been a meditation on that dream."[7]

Some years later, prompted by this original experience, Einstein realized the importance of directly experiencing for himself the part of the universe he wished to study. He simply needed a more systematic way to re-create and focus his experience. Toward this end, Einstein developed his famous *gedanken or* "thought experiments," an approach now used by many theoretical physicists. The reference to "thought" you'll soon see is ironic, as these experiments actually didn't require rational thought at all.

To arrive at his General Theory of Relativity, he meditated on a beam of light as it extended out into the universe. He then visualized himself stepping onto that beam into the cosmos, taking special note of everything he saw and *experienced.*

In this way he viewed the universe from the perspective of the light wave rather than from his ego's habitual point of view. After this experience of altered consciousness Einstein wrote down his observations and, with a little help from his math tutors, arrived at the mathematical proofs that became the empirical evidence for his General Theory of Relativity.

It has often been said that there is nothing new under the sun. Indeed, since time immemorial, Shamans and mystics of all kinds have used "thought experiments" such as Einstein's to determine the nature of reality. Listen to Mayan shaman Martin Prechtel speak about how he was trained to call the primal energies of nature—the spirits and gods—to act as his allies and teachers: "A shaman had to *become nature*, not just an observer of nature….The secret was to get behind the eyes of what you wanted to call, become that being's visions, likes, and dislikes; *understand by being* what your subject wanted to go toward…."[8]

As Henry Miller wrote, "The moment one gives close attention to anything, even a blade of grass, it becomes a mysterious, awesome, indescribably magnificent world in itself."[9]

Because our Western culture favors logical thought over experience, we learn from our scientists how to analyze and dissect a

> As soon as we analyze something intellectually we distance ourselves from it and lose the opportunity of direct knowing available from the experience itself. This is both sad and ironic because the experience and "feeling" of something is a gateway to profound insight, healing, and growth.

problem. Thus, when we encounter something new we are more likely to ask first what caused it, then how it feels. In fact, we have a sense of control when we describe an experience in great detail—the more we say, the more we feel in control of what has happened.

In contrast, author Malidoma Somé, who writes of his childhood growing up as a member of the Dagara tribe in West Africa, suggests that indigenous people approach experience in a different way than those in our culture:

> *The more intense an experience, the more likely indigenous people are to leave it in the language in which it came rather than to discuss and dissect it with words. It is almost as if discussing diminishes what is being discussed. Villagers feel that words conquer experience, dislodging experience from its rightful place of power. So unless powerful experiences and ideas are addressed poetically, or with proverbs, people don't want to take the risk of losing in a fog of words what they have struggled so hard to acquire.*[10]

Somé goes on to say that for the Dagara there is a hierarchy of consciousness and intelligence, beginning with the trees and plants that are most intelligent because they do not need words to communicate and are therefore closest to the Source. Then come animals and finally human beings, who must rely so heavily on language: "Wise men and women in the indigenous world argue that humans are cursed by the language they possess, or that possess them."[11]

Thus in the language of the Dagara the word for "to utter" or "speak" has a dual meaning implying both "nostalgia" for and "exile" from the Source: "At the Source, words would not be necessary, for meaning would be produced instantly. We could see, feel, and touch the results of someone's thought instead of relying on words to give us a picture of it."[12]

The great Indian sage Ramana Maharshi, too, had little love for words. He was sought out by disciples from around the world seeking to experience awakened consciousness through merely sitting in his silent presence. When asked about his belief in silence as the greatest teacher, he spoke in terms similar to Somé's:

> *Again, how does speech arise? There is the unmanifest abstract knowledge, and from here the ego gives rise to thoughts and then words. In this order of descent, words become the great-grandchildren of the original Source. If the word can have some effect, how much more powerful will preaching through silence be? Judge for yourself.*[13]

In Zen, too, we are warned that language "fits over experience like a glove."

Again it was the poet Rilke who implored us: "Children, one earthly Thing truly experienced, even once, is enough for a lifetime."[14] So in Mindful Dreaming we are careful not to over-analyze and dissect our dreams—honoring each image as a gift of experience that offers a sacred path back to the Source.

Perhaps we can set the intention to become as the legendary Wang Fo, who understood that the wholehearted embrace of our experience in this present moment is the goal of our Journey. Here is a version of this classic Chinese tale re-told by poet and artist Steve Lautermilch:

*Wang Fo*
*(the story goes)*
*is very old,*
*his disciples*
*so devoted*
*to the painter*
*and to the greatness*
*of his art*
*that he attracts*

*the envy of the Emperor*
*who has the artist arrested*
*and sentenced*
*to death.*
*But*
*before*
*beheading him*
*the ruler*
*orders the prisoner*
*to do*
*a little painting.*
*Wang Fo*
*sets*
*to work.*
*He paints*
*a seascape*
*like so many*
*Chinese*
*seascapes,*
*trees*
*on a mountain*
*overlooking*
*a harbor*
*neighboring*
*a temple*
*and so*
*on*
*with one little boat*
*alone*
*at sea.*
*Slowly the falls*
*flow faster*
*the river*
*cuts deeper*

*the mist*
*grows*
*heavier*
*til water*
*fills*
*the room,*
*the Emperor*
*gets*
*his feet*
*wet,*
*the Court ladies*
*feel*
*the lotus blossoms*
*that hem*
*the bottoms*
*of their skirts*
*are*
*sending out*
*new shoots,*
*while, the imperial*
*guards*
*that shoulder and corner*
*the throne*
*begin to float*
*and a few*
*priests*
*go*
*under.*
*The boat*
*arrives, the master*
*steps*
*in*
*(without a ripple)*
*and disappears.*[15]

# Chapter Practices

## Finding Metaphors in a Recent Dream

🌿 Choose a dream that you recall or that you've written in your journal.

🌿 Underline any image that could be a metaphor. For example, any object in a dream can be understood as a metaphor. Is there a bridge, a garden, a door? If you are driving a car, what kind of car is it? If you feel free and relaxed in a sports car, then a sports car is a visual metaphor for how you're feeling, "like driving a sports car"—your experience in the dream. If you're driving the car that you drove when you were 22 years old, consider your experience when you drove that car at that age. Now that same car is also a metaphor for how you once felt and how you experienced your life in part, when you were 22.

🌿 **Special Note:** As implied by these examples, when attempting to understand the meaning of a metaphor in your dream, it's important to attend to the exact detail of the image. For example, if you want to understand something about a blue bike in your dream, it's not enough to say it's an image of transportation or "getting around in the world." After all, so is a train or car. Therefore, always ask what is unique about that image of a bike. How is it different from a car or train? How is its color different for you than if it were a red bike? For example, a bike may provide greater flexibility and the chance to veer off the beaten path and/or to be closer to nature, and so on. A blue bike may be the color you always wanted, but never had in waking life.

## How to Get Behind the Eyes of Your Dream Mentor: Active Imagination

You read in this chapter how scientists such as Einstein as well as Shamans have developed similar methods for gaining understanding and wisdom through identifying with or "becoming one with" any object of interest—whether a person, animal, "ray of light," or Dream Mentor. Here are some simple instructions you can follow to expand your consciousness beyond the limiting confines of your ego's perspective.

- Move to a room in which you will not be distracted by phone calls or questions from family members.

- Find a comfortable chair or pillow on which to sit.

- Breathe slowly from your abdomen for a minute or two.

- Hold in your consciousness the image of your Dream Mentor.

- Imagine yourself as this Mentor. Feel yourself in his or her clothing or, if it is an animal, allow yourself to experience the fur on (your) body.

- Slowly feel into the experience of living in your Mentor's body.

- Experience the mood and temperament of your Mentor as you felt it in your dream.

- Experience looking through your Mentor's eyes at yourself sitting in that chair.

- Feel what she or he feels about you.

- Also feel the unique energy of your Mentor, and compare and contrast it with your own. Accept this energy and perspective as a gift.

- Now in your journal, write down a question (for example, what have you come to teach me?).

- Give a name to the Mentor if it doesn't have one and write it down below your question.

- Now relax again and feel your way back into the body of the Dream Mentor.

- Wait for a few seconds or even a minute as you (your Dream Mentor) reflect upon the question. Listen for words from the Mentor or very possibly images that may arise.

- Write down the answer.

- Repeat the process with another question based on the response you have received.

# Chapter 3

# The Grammar of Co-Creation in Our Dreams

*The last of the human freedoms is to choose one's attitudes...to choose one's own way.*

—Victor Frankel

*The act of contemplation creates the thing contemplated.*

—Isaac D'Israeli

We all know how confusing our dreams can be, and this is the bane of anyone who wishes to learn dreamwork. In this chapter you'll learn how our shifting intentions within each dream create the often fragmented jumble of scenes we find so frustrating.

Our perennial spiritual traditions have consistently taught us that our conscious intentions interact with and co-create our reality and the universe in which we live. "We are what we think," said Buddha in the ancient Dhammapada. "All that we are arises through our thoughts. With our thoughts we create the world."[1]

This perennial spiritual philosophy applies to the principles of Mindful Dreamwork, which affirms that we create our own reality as we dream. Within our nightly dreams reality unfolds in direct relation to our waking attitudes and intentions. The thoughts, intentions, and attitudes we nurture in waking life determine, for better or worse, each new scene, and, ultimately, the outcome of the dream itself.

Although divination, meditation, prayer, friends, family, lovers, and counselors can help us along the way, the mirror of our dreams is what the Zohar—the ancient Kabalistic text—calls "the mirror that shines"[2]—one of the most direct sources of objective knowledge available to us. For this reason we are called to learn the beautiful language and grammar of dreams so we may fully experience the gift of conscious awakening they offer.

Carl Jung spoke a great truth when he said, "We know that the mask of the unconscious is not rigid—it reflects the face we turn towards it. Hostility lends it a threatening aspect, friendliness softens its features."[3] Consequently, our Dream Mentors mirror our inner attitudes and values—our intentions—and guide us accordingly. Even the landscape and setting of our dreams mirror our attitude and "perspective." As you'll read in the following chapters, our task as mindful dreamers in the first half of our Journey is to release our habitual perspectives so that we may experience the truth that lies embodied behind the dark cloth of projections with which we dress our Mentors. When we have learned to withdraw these projections, we realize that our Dream Mentors are the "perfect" mirror we have been seeking. Sufi scholar Llewellyn Vaughan-Lee says that the true Teacher "...is a mirror in which the seeker can first glimpse, then slowly become familiar with, and finally recognize, his Real Self."[4] This is true as well of Dream Mentors who arise from the same Source, are of the same nature and are no different than the Zen Master, Taoist Sage, or Sufi Teacher. All wait to be unveiled by the seeker.

In spiritual practice we are always called to view the world around us with an "I am that, too" attitude—to remain mindful that we are one with the world and must not judge. As a result, that which we ignore or reject in our dreams becomes hostile and that which we embrace returns the love we offer. We see this principle frequently in fairytales and fables when, for example, the repulsive frog or beast transforms into the prince only when we are willing to kiss or embrace it.

In general, Dream Mentors mirror our intentions for better or worse. Let's look first at some examples of this principle. A client of mine, Eileen, who judged herself unworthy of love, persisted in the belief that her lot in life was to feel deprived and that "good things happened to other people." Here is her simple dream:

> A friend walked into my office and headed my way with a beautiful bouquet of flowers. I thought, "Those are so beautiful they couldn't be for me." Then the flowers wilted and died in my friend's arms.

That was a powerful, life-changing dream and a major turning point for Eileen. She immediately saw and *experienced* that the belief she held—"I'll never receive love"—was depriving her of love and sustaining chronic suffering in her life. She had to ask herself how many countless times she had enacted the same drama in waking life, failing to see and respond to gifts of affection and love from others— and letting their love wither on the vine. Eileen subsequently practiced more mindfulness of her negative judgments about herself and felt more resolve to stay open to the great potential for joy in her life. "In the province of the mind," said John Lilly, "what one believes to be true either is true or becomes true."[5]

Here is another variation on the same theme: Patricia was feeling despair about ever feeling truly comfortable with herself. She shared with me her sadness: "I can't imagine what it would be like to really let go and live the authentic life. I know that won't happen because you just can't live in the zone all of the time." As we discussed how Patricia expected to suffer, she remembered this dream from the night before our session:

> I am sitting on a grassy area with five other women who are all laughing and having a wonderful time looking toward the sky and pointing out things they see: "Oh! There's a cloud shaped like a frog! There's a beautiful bird!" But I can't see anything that they see because something is blocking my view.
>
> Then I see that one woman has what looks to me like a hernia and I say that must be painful. She says no but invites me to touch it. The tip of my finger burns when I touch her and I believe then that I am feeling her own pain. Yet she says she feels no pain at all. The other women touch her too and none of them feel the pain either—just me.

In this dream, the pleasure of seeing and experiencing whatever one wants is available to all of the women, but "something" blocks Patricia's view of the possibilities in life. That "something" is her expectation or intention that there must always be some kind of suffering and emotional pain ("You just can't live in the zone all of the time."). As a result, Patricia "feels" pain and the presence of suffering even when it is absent because that is what she expects or intends—and so it is, in our dreams and waking life. "When an idea exclusively occupies the mind," said the great 20th-century yogi Sri Sivananda, "it is transformed into an actual physical or mental state."[6]

Notice that Patricia's Dream Mentors challenge her perspective. Here's a reliable dream tip. Whenever others in your dreams experience things differently than you do, give the benefit of the doubt that your own perspective needs to shift. In this case Patricia's experience of her friend's hernia pain is denied by all five women, including the friend. The main exceptions to this rule are Dreams of Illumination and Return, in which we are apprenticing as or have become our own Mentor. (You'll read more about such dreams in Sections IV and V.)

In the meantime we are called to remember the sage advice of the Queen in *Alice in Wonderland* about the limitations we impose on reality through the intentions we set:

> *"There is no use trying," said Alice. "One can't believe impossible things."*
> *"I dare say," said the Queen. "When I was your age, I always did it for half an hour a day. Why sometimes I've believed as many as six impossible things before breakfast."*

As for so many of us, the idea of feeling too good or feeling good for too long pushes the button on our fear of being self-centered or selfish—a universal fear that blocks our ability to change and grow. (You can read more about our three great fears on the Journey in Section II.)

As Patricia and I discussed how her expectations created her reality, she paused long enough to see the world through the eyes of her five female dream mentors—and when she did, her feelings of depression that had been growing during the past week, as well as the developing migraine headache with which she had awakened in the morning, dissolved within minutes. This shift was no more difficult for her than the effort it takes to see a bird or a frog in the clouds.

Rick, a friend of mine who was deeply ambivalent about things mystical and often found himself both condescending and attracted to those around him who spoke of their spiritual experiences, shared this dream with me:

A pond suddenly forms in my back yard and I watch a yellow and green leopard emerge from the deep. I am not afraid and it doesn't threaten me in any way. However, when I call it to me the leopard becomes hostile and attacks.

Whenever we see something transmute in a dream we must consider our attitude or intention toward the experience it embodies. When I asked Rick with what attitude he called to the leopard he confessed, "Well, I mean the colors and all...I thought he looked pretty silly for a leopard." He meant that he didn't intend to treat the leopard with respect. We take this fact for granted in waking life. I know that when I assume a hostile or judgmental attitude toward someone he or she will react negatively. Why shouldn't it be true in our dreams as well?

A client told me a similar dream with a noticeably different intention and outcome:

I dreamed of seeing a beautiful black panther. As I stood there I experienced a growing feeling of awe and admiration for his grace and strength. Then I became the panther and found myself sprinting through the jungle feeling the foliage against my muscled body and the power and sureness with which I—or maybe it was the panther—bounded over every obstacle.

And so it is that when we are conscious of our intentions and give the benefit of the doubt to the healing potential of our Dream Mentors, obstacles in our life begin to dissolve. As the poet Emerson once said, "A good intention clothes itself with power." Our intentions and attitudes create reality and, in so doing, each intention also creates a new dream scene or a marked shift in the story line or plot of the dream. This is called the grammar of dreams.

Let's review: In Eileen's dream *when* she sets the intention that the flowers "are not for me," *then* the flowers wilt. Similarly, *when* Rick intends to hold a disrespectful attitude toward the leopard, *then* the leopard attacks him. Once again, *when* my client holds the intention to see the black panther with "awe and admiration," *then* he becomes the panther and receives the gift of experience, the "power and sureness," that the panther brings to him.

Here are some more examples of this phenomenon.

At a time on my Journey when I assumed that I could simply ask for dreams to provide solutions to the challenges in my life, I dreamed:

> I am in a large room and algae-like plants are growing up through the floor in the shape of letters and words, which form messages from the Divine in answer to questions I have asked. I lean back, relax, and observe with genuine interest. However, soon the growth becomes so profuse that I can't read a single word or letter. I feel desperate to learn what is being presented to me. Then the scene changes and I find myself holding a huge metal hedge clipper. Immediately I know in the dream that it's my job to do the pruning.

It's easy to see how my feeling "desperate to learn" is a shift of attitude and intention from my laid-back, passive stance at the start of the dream. *When* I desperately wish to learn, *then* the scene changes radically and I'm given the guidance and the means, or tool (clippers), with which to fulfill my intentions. Our intentions literally and figuratively "set the stage" anew in our dreams and waking lives.

On another level, I was nurturing an attitude of control toward my dreams, expecting them to fulfill my wishes. It was as if I was an aristocrat in control of my servants. *When* I nurtured that attitude *then* I could no longer learn from the messages of Nature (the Source), my Dream Mentor. Yet *when* I released control and assumed the correct attitude of reverence and humility toward the Source as a respectful apprentice needing to learn, *then* I was given the tool with which to do it. In fact it wasn't even necessary to feel the desperation I felt in the dream, only to release control, intend to give the benefit of the doubt that I had something to gain from the Source and accept guidance. (You'll read more about the central importance of releasing control in Chapter 6.)

In this case I awakened having gained the insight that we are indeed co-creators of our reality with the Source. Though we may not make the seed, without the gardener there is no garden. Put another way, our life is only the garden—or jungle—we choose to make it.

Here's another dream of a client, Laura. Steeped in an oppressive sense of responsibility and desire for control she routinely relied upon her intellect rather than her heart to relate to the world around her. Not surprisingly, she felt chronically depressed and anxious. As you read through her dream notice how the scenes shift abruptly—just as in the many dreams you've probably experienced in which there are a series of disjointed and fragmented images that leave you feeling frustrated and confused.

> I am reading stories by Goya to a group of men. The pictures are great but I'm becoming increasingly bored. Finally I tell them that I'm shutting the book for good.
>
> In the next scene, I'm in a room without a desk and only a sofa and recliner to relax on and daydream. At this point I say, "I could never live in a room without a desk!
>
> Suddenly people come and clothe me in a Girl Scout uniform and I say proudly, "I'm the oldest Girl Scout alive!"
>
> Then I find myself looking in a mirror and see a bald spot that reminds me of my bald uncle who committed suicide.

Let's look at the dream scene by scene. First, Laura finds the pictures of this book about Goya fascinating, but the words dry and boring. *When* she intends to give up her heavy dependence on intellect and "shut the book for good," *then* she finds herself in a room that requires no desk and in its place a sofa and recliner on which to relax. However, she is not truly committed to letting go of her excessively intellectual and responsible attitudes and *when* she declines the opportunity to experience pleasure in life ("I could never live in a room without a desk"), voila—*then* she finds herself dressed in a Girl Scout uniform. For Laura the uniform is associated with military rules and regulations—"always acting responsibly and obeying authority." In the dream *when* she embraces excessive responsibility and proudly proclaims her identity as "the oldest Girl Scout alive," *then* she finds herself looking in a mirror and resembling a bit her depressed, balding uncle who committed suicide—that is, feeling as if life is not worth living.

When we worked with this dream (a dream of imminent loss, which you'll learn more about in Chapter 8) Laura quickly realized the self-destructive effect of holding on to her overly responsible attitudes and understood why she was feeling so depressed. In the literal and figurative "mirror" of her

Dream Mentors, she saw that her intentions were not consistently self-caring and compassionate and that they were gradually leading her down the self-destructive path her uncle had followed. She wasn't yet exactly like her uncle; just beginning to experience life as he did.

In her dream Laura experienced the outcome of each intention and, indeed, the outcome of depression in waking life was also just as she intended. Of course, she didn't want to suffer or feel depressed. However, she was not conscious or mindful of the suffering caused by her intention to "always act responsibly."

Clinging excessively to the values of intellect and responsibility meant avoiding most of the simple pleasures in life. And so it was that she felt chronically depressed—her life in control, rational, and productive, but empty of joy. Our Dream Mentors mirror our waking life intentions and the consequences of these intentions for better or worse. Listen to Rumi: "Today like every other day we wake up empty and scared. Don't open the door of your study and begin reading. Take down a musical instrument. Let the beauty we love be what we do. There are hundreds of way, to kneel and kiss the ground."[7]

A quick shorthand way to understand if we are nurturing healthy, waking life attitudes and moving in the direction that the Source is calling us, is to look at the end of our dream. Ask yourself if at the end of your dream you are feeling more or less suffering: Has your dream environment become darker or lighter? Are you feeling more or less fear? More or less joy? Are you feeling more or less resolved and clear in your vision?

> The mood of each dream, and in particular, the mood at the end of your dream, are great measures of whether you are in alignment with your Calling and acting with wisdom and compassion for your own needs—or not.

Degrees of pleasure and joy at the end of your dream reflect your embrace of the Journey's lessons in mindfulness and indicate that you are moving toward or doing the work of the Illumination and Return. Conversely, degrees of pain, anguish, confusion, guilt, or fear suggest we continue to embrace our ego's old script and remain in the time of our Calling or Quest.

You can also pay attention to how your intentions create positive and negative outcomes from scene to scene in your dreams. For example, when a scene in your dream has a more positive or negative mood than the preceding scene, search within yourself for a corresponding positive or negative intention that created that mood.

# Setting the Intention to Receive Help From Our Dream Mentors

In the field of dreamwork there is a time-honored technique called Dream Incubation for seeking guidance and healing that most Mediterranean, Asian, and indigenous cultures began practicing more than 3,000 years ago. The basis for this technique is the understanding that our dreams not only mirror our waking life intentions and attitudes, but serve to help us change and heal them as well.

Incubation is a method for receiving tangible answers to your prayers. When you awaken in the morning write down the dream or fragment thereof. Don't resist writing the dream down because it seems on the surface about a different topic than you incubated. Your dream may be comparing your marriage problem to a situation similar to one that occurred at work two years ago. Other times you may awaken with a dream that immediately speaks volumes about the problem you've asked about. While you're at it, don't be afraid to ask for a "simple dream I can understand" as part of your incubation question if the first dream feels too opaque.

To incubate a dream, just focus on an issue or concern in your life with which you have been struggling. Boil down the problem to a single sentence, write it in your journal, and repeat it as a mantra or prayer until you fall asleep (for example: "I need help understanding..., or "What's the benefit of (or problem with) this relationship I have with...?").

It's important to understand that we are always incubating our dreams every day of our lives—only we are usually doing so unconsciously. Whatever is most challenging and urgent in your life today is likely to be tonight's dream topic. One advantage of conscious Dream Incubation is that it will focus your dreams on a particular concern among many you may have. In addition, when you awaken with an incubated dream you can assume it relates in some way to your question, and that gives you a head start in grasping the dream's message.

Be careful not to demand an answer. I learned early, to my dismay, that aggressively insisting on a dream answer often can yield a full-blown nightmare. It's a matter of the old adage to "be careful of what you pray for." In truth, any dream we recall is one we're able to handle. However, nightmares occur when we're only barely ready to accept some new perspective and probably resistant to it. In my case I was receiving exactly the answer I needed *and* in the glaring light my attitude demanded. If we haven't been able to recall a dream or haven't been able to understand the ones we've received, chances are we may not be fully open to the answer. Although nightmares are packed full of juicy information and gifts we very much need, they're really not much fun.

In the face of the Divine, humility is a powerful and core spiritual practice. (See Chapter 6.) For this reason, it's best to ask humble questions such as these:

≈ How can I heal this pain I'm experiencing?

≈ What are the attitudes or intentions I hold that are causing my suffering?

≈ What is the correct view of this problem?

# Dream Grammar: An Overview

You have learned in this chapter that our intentions create consequences in dreams just as they do in waking life. The practice of Mindful Dreaming is grounded in the importance of this truth, as we cannot change or grow without awareness of the thoughts and intentions that set the stage for events to unfold in our life—for better or worse. Buddhist Master Hsing Yun puts it this way: "Intention is the core of all conscious life. It is our intentions that create karma, our intentions that help others, our intentions that lead us away from the delusions of individuality toward…enlightened awareness. Conscious intention colors and moves everything."[8]

> Only when we become conscious and aware of our ego's intentions or strategies is it possible for us to release them. This is why its so important for us to become familiar with the grammar of our dreams.

So it's a good idea to practice awareness of the simple principles of dream grammar as you write down each dream.

This same principle of intentionality underlying dream grammar is the basis for the practice of Dream Incubation. By setting the sincere intention to respect the wisdom of our Dream Mentors we set the stage to receive guidance from the Source.

Now that you are ready to "give the benefit of the doubt" to your Dream Mentors and know how to ask for help, you're ready to learn more about the first four lessons in mindfulness they teach us and how to benefit from these lessons in everyday life. But first try out some of the practices that follow.

# Chapter Practices

## *Practicing Mindfulness of the Intentions You Set in Dreams*

Remember that the importance of understanding dream grammar lies in its ability to teach us whether our dream actions are in alignment with what is in our best interest, or simply serve to nurture our old habits of thought—ego strategies. Here's one more reminder about how to determine the grammar of your dream:

- For the purpose of this practice, recall or find a dream in your journal that is short—that is, with only one or two scene shifts. In your journal write a summary of the dream story in as few words as possible, but begin with the word *when*.

- Now search for a shift in the mood of the dream, the action, or even a change in the lighting if that is relevant to the story of the dream. At the start of this shift, insert the word *then* and continue to describe what happens. Here's a simple example:

    > At the start of my dream *when* the sun is bright and its a beautiful day, a friend invites me to a party and I say that I have too much work to do. *Then* the sky turns gray and I see a homeless man walk by who looks like he doesn't have a friend in the world.

In this example, dream grammar immediately provides us with information about the presence of our old ego script at work. After all, what else would cause a beautiful day to go so wrong? And why does a lonely homeless man appear "when" I turn down an invitation to a party? Note: In Chapter 6 you'll learn that this is an example of a Control dream in which we—our ego—refuse to follow or accept guidance from a Mentor.

## Practicing Mindfulness of Your Waking Life Intentions

In the field of social psychology there is a phenomenon called the Self-Fulfilling Prophecy. Much research has shown that what we expect of others affects how they respond to us and even how they perform on tasks we may set for them—all without our conscious awareness of this process! During the coming week make a mental note of and journal about your intentions and expectations as you interact with others. Ask yourself how many events turn out "just as you expected." Practice greater mindfulness of your intentions and how they may be contributing to the outcome of events—for better or worse.

## Dream Incubation

There are numerous ways to benefit from the wisdom of our Mentors. You read in Chapter 2 about the importance of becoming one with and embodying the experience of your Dream Mentors. Consider incubating a dream based on your intention to feel more empathy for a Mentor's experience in one of your recent dreams. For example, before sleep you might say, "Help me to *experience* more fully the wisdom and perspective you wished to bring me last night in my dream."

Remember: Try not to dwell on the answer you "think" will be given, as the spirit of this practice—as with all spiritual practice—is to surrender our assumption that our ego knows more than the Source.

# Chapter 4

# The Integrative Practice of Mindful Dreaming

If you wish, you can skip this chapter for now or briefly review it, as it refers to methods of working with types of dreams that you won't begin reading about until Chapter 5. Nevertheless, the following Integrative Practice may be adapted to use with any dream, though it is designed for use with those more emotionally difficult dreams in the Calling and Quest sections that follow next in this book.

Mindful Dreaming emphasizes mindfulness practice with dreams rather than a set of "techniques" for working with them. Therefore, a myriad of other methods or techniques not mentioned here may serve the goal of mindfulness as well.

As you will see, the Practice incorporates each of the five lessons in mindfulness we learn and practice in the time of the Illumination and Return on our Journey (Solitude, Humility, Compassion, Non-Attachment, and Embrace of the Present Moment). The practice of these lessons is the medicine needed to release the ego values so prevalent in our life and dreams during the Calling and Quest. Though you will read about these lessons in greater detail in subsequent chapters, it is not necessary to do so now as you will find the Practice self-explanatory.

At the end of chapters 5 through 10 of the Calling and Quest sections of this book I will simply reference this model of practice and suggest that you return to this chapter to work with the specific type of dream you have been reading about.

# Living and Dreaming Your Practice

These simple meditation and mindfulness practices allow us to use the imagery and healing energy of our dreams for our personal guidance and spiritual growth.

# Embracing Solitude and Stillness

**Set the intention to release distraction, embrace solitude, and create sacred space.**

In your home, find or create a quiet, still space for meditation. Some people find it helpful to create art, altars, or objects as sacred practice, and to provide assistance in remaining mindful of the powerful lessons in our dreams. You may want to find or create an object—an amulet to carry the new energy you are working toward incorporating into your life. Hold it while you meditate and while practicing the methods described here. Then bring this object with you throughout your day as a means of reinforcing mindfulness of your new experience. If during the week you encounter a situation that calls for the new energy you found embodied in your dream or Dream Mentor, use the object to help you remember how that energy felt in your body during meditation.

Another equally fine way to create an altar is to imagine one during meditation. Carol Anthony, who has written extensively on the use of the *I Ching* Oracle with meditation, describes a process of imaginally placing those things or ideas to which our ego is attached on an inner altar with the intention of sacrificing or letting them go.[1] In the inner world it is our intentions that create change—not the manner in which we ritualize them.

# Embracing Humility and Accepting Guidance

**Set the intention to release control and embrace humility by following the guidance of your dreams.**

While in your place of solitude, choose a recent or recurring Calling or Quest dream—one that you feel is "reaching out to you"—and work with it in the various mindfulness practices that follow. You may also wish to incubate a dream for use in this weekly practice asking for guidance in one of many possible ways, including:

≈    What do I most need to experience at this moment in my Journey?

≈    Help me to experience the benefits of solitude, humility, compassion or non-attachment in my life.

≈    Help me to release distraction, control, judgment, or attachment)where it is most needed in my life.

≈    Help me see where the obstacles to solitude, humility, compassion or non-attachment lie in my life.

≈    Help me to understand the ego strategy that presently requires the greatest mindfulness in my life.

(Other suggestions for incubation are available as well throughout this book.)

Please keep in mind that if you can't recall a dream or if you simply can't grasp its message, it is very helpful to hold your incubation request in awareness throughout the week as a prayer, mantra, or ongoing intention that you are setting to receive help. In this way you are "preparing the ground" for the next dream to provide assistance, or to have an experience of insight or epiphany spontaneously in waking life.

# Embracing Self-Caring and Compassion

**Set the intention to release judgment and embrace self-caring and compassion.**

## Meditation

In the space of solitude and stillness that you have set aside in your home spend the next five or 10 minutes in general meditation. If you are already experienced with meditation, then by all means follow the steps of your own practice. For those of you who are inexperienced, here are some simple thoughts to keep in mind:

*Sit in a comfortable position that is relaxed: cross-legged, or if on a chair, with your feet on the floor and back upright if possible. Your mind and body should be alert, present, and quiet, opening to the breath. Set the intention to quiet your thoughts and focus on the empty, still space between them—the background rather than the foreground of your awareness. Sit with your breath, feeling it move deeply into your abdomen, your chest rising and your abdomen expanding with each inhalation. As you exhale, feel the breath leave your body, being mindful of how your body feels as the breath leaves. Be especially mindful of the moment before each inhalation—the space between the breaths. As always in meditative practice, don't admonish yourself if you become entangled in some inner drama or set of worries; just gently return your focus to the breath and the quiet space between your thoughts. This is one way to practice releasing judgment.*

# Create an Emotional Bridge From Your Dream to Waking Life

Bring to mind the entire dream you have chosen or incubated and re-enter the dream. Experience the defining negative mood of the crisis or conflict. Stay in the drama of the dream and sit with that feeling. Be mindful of what is happening in your body, your breath, and your thoughts.

Ask yourself where else in your life you feel this mood or these emotions. This method is called "emotional bridging." Take your time and "feel into" that situation in everyday life in which you have encountered the emotions in your dream (for example, restlessness or frustration, judgmentalism, insecurity, and so on) and note the suffering that is always present—just as it is in your dream. After bridging or locating that dream experience in a relationship, at work, or in some creative endeavor, reflect on other times you've felt this way in the past as well.

Having created your "emotional bridge," you now understand one aspect of suffering in your waking life that your dream—the Source—has identified as in need of healing at this very moment in your Journey. It is time to release the thoughts of your ego that are at the root of your emotional suffering.

**Set the intention to experience compassion for the suffering caused by these thoughts in waking life.**

Feel the sadness of living in this way. Refuse to engage in the thoughts of self-recrimination and blame you usually feel for being so restless or controlling, judgmental, insecure, and so on.

Toward this end, you may also wish to practice the Buddhist exercise of Tonglen that emphasizes compassion for others. This may be a helpful step, though in Mindful Dreaming true healing on our Journey is elusive until we experience compassion for our own suffering. Our experience of alienation and lack of compassion for those around us has its deep and sole source within the motives of our own ego. Try instead what is referred to as Metta practice, which begins with loving kindness toward ourselves: Breathe in compassion for the suffering created by one of your ego's five favorite habits: Distraction, Control, Judgment, Attachment, or Impatience. Breathe out judgment about these habits or the suffering they cause.

For example, here is the adapted Metta method for embracing solitude.

*I breathe in Compassion for my lack of focus and restlessness and ceaseless wanting. I breathe out the feelings of judgment I hold about them.*

Alternatively:

*I breathe in Compassion for my (lack of focus and restlessness and ceaseless wanting). I breathe out the suffering they create in me.*

When practicing other forms of release (for example, the release of Control and embrace of Humility), you may substitute the words *lack of focus, restlessness, and wanting* with words that describe controlling behavior:

- *For the release of Control:* "I breathe in Compassion for my fear of surrender and mistrust of the Source and its guidance."

- *For the release of Judgment:* "I breathe in Compassion for my self-criticism and feeling of being unlovable."

- *For the release of Attachment:* " I breathe in Compassion for my resistance to change, rigid clinging to my outworn identity, and all that is familiar."

Of course, I urge you to use your own words and to apply the adjectives that best describe your ego's own thoughts. A helpful hint: As you breathe in, imagine the breath being pulled through the chakra of your heart. There is a great deal of scientific evidence that this method of breathing has a powerful healing effect on your heart and overall physical and emotional health.

If you find it difficult to feel compassion, then in your meditation, consider opening to sadness that the feeling of compassion for yourself is so alien. In this method of practice, even if you don't experience compassion for yourself—just learning that it is absent in your everyday relationship with yourself is a major step toward expanded consciousness.

Practicing mindfulness of compassion in the midst of your suffering becomes one specific medicine to reduce your stress and most importantly, to help you embrace the Compassionate Witness within—the Grail on your Journey.

# Embracing Non-Attachment

**Set the intention to release attachment and embrace grief and letting go.**

Our dreams and Dream Mentors also assist us in practicing mindfulness of Non-Attachment. Practicing Non-Attachment means that we set the intention to fully release the limiting perspective, thoughts, and beliefs to which our ego is attached or with which it is identified.

An excellent way to accomplish this is through the practice of embodying the unique energy and new perspective of our Dream Mentors. Embracing this new energy and perspective will allow you to approach your waking life suffering more mindfully and with an entirely new consciousness of what is needed.

- ⇒ Return to your place of solitude and sacred space.

- ⇒ Practice meditation as described above for five or 10 minutes.

- ⇒ Re-enter the drama of your dream.

- ⇒ Breathe into the unique emotional essence of the primary Mentor in your dream. As you do, pay attention to your thoughts, your breath, and your body. What do you notice?

    - ⋅ How is your Mentor different from yourself?

    - ⋅ In moderation, what is good about your Mentor?

- ⇒ Give the benefit of the doubt to your Mentor: Review the crisis or conflict in your dream from your Mentor's point of view.

- ⇒ Feel into the reasons she or he is acting in that way in your dream.

* How is your Mentor's perspective different from yours?
* How could this new perspective benefit your life?

- Feel into the quality of energy in your Mentor's body.

  * How is this energy different than yours? How could this energy benefit your life?

- Make an emotional bridge to a similar emotional experience in waking life (as described previously).

- Set the intention that you will recall and hold in awareness—remain mindful of this new quality of consciousness during the week when you are in emotional situations such as the one in your dream. (Don't forget to use your amulet if you've made one.)

Now mindfulness of this new perspective and energy in the midst of your suffering in waking life becomes the specific medicine needed to reduce your stress. More importantly, through the method of embodiment you are loosening attachment to your ego's viewpoint and identity and embracing the gift of your Dream Mentor's expanded consciousness.

## An Alternative Practice of Embodiment

In this practice we move into the Mentor's energetic body as in the method described previously. This time, however, we practice moving more fully into that space and physically enacting the experience. When you know that you will have privacy try the following practice with a Dream Mentor:

- Using the method described previously, re-enter the dream and merge into the body of the Dream Mentor that feels most central to the dream story.

- Allow yourself to fully inhabit the Mentor's body. Note how your body feels as your Dream Mentor's. Speak out loud a few words that your Mentor spoke in the dream—or "seemed" to be saying. How does your voice sound? What does it bring up for you to say these words in waking life? Are there any movements or gestures in the dream that were compelling? Physically re-enact these gestures or movements. How does this feel in your body? Dialogue with yourself as this character; dance, breathe, stomp, sing, fight, or play as this Mentor. What would it be like if your Mentor was inside of you at work? While making love? While being in a relationship?

≈ If only in moderation, is there any "medicine" or healing you can receive from this Mentor?

≈ Come back to yourself and reconnect with your own body. Note how this feels.

≈ Practice moving back and forth between yourself and your Mentor, noting the changes each time you shift. What more can you learn from this?

≈ In your journal, write about this experience and note any situations over the coming week that could benefit from this new energy.

≈ If you wish, you may invite another Dream Mentor into your body, though I would recommend that you not dilute the first experience and give yourself a day or so to fully absorb its healing energy.

# Embracing the Present Moment

**Set the intention to release impatience and embrace the Present Moment without resistance.**

In the waking life situations that you've already identified through "emotional bridging," practice holding "the tension of opposites." This means that though a solution to a conflict or dilemma is not yet at hand, the time is not yet right or our goals still too difficult to attain, we refuse to yield to impatience and return to our old ego script. We practice remaining in the present moment and resist aligning ourselves with any one solution prematurely.

≈ Re-enter the dream with which you've been working and merge again with your Mentor. Set the intention to hold in consciousness the new energy and perspective of your Dream Mentor together with your ego's habitual perspective—whether it is Distraction,

Control, Judgment, or Attachment. This is called "holding the tension of opposites." For example, you may have found through merging with your Mentor's energy and perspective that she is compassionate. However, in the dream you judged her as a threat. Hold the feeling of her compassion and the feeling of judgment together in awareness simultaneously. Stay with this and see what happens.

≋ Stay attentive to any image arising within you that describes the difficulty of holding this tension. If an image or descriptive phrase arises, ask yourself what it needs or what would make it better. See what comes. Does anything shift? (This is what psychologist Eugene Ghendlin calls "Focusing."[2])

≋ If not, set the intention to wait without resistance in the present moment without indulging worries about the past or future regarding this problem. Give the Source the benefit of the doubt that you will find a way—a new, third perspective that will allow you to transcend the conflict between Distraction and Solitude; Control and Humility; Judgment and Compassion; Attachment and Letting Go. Wait for this third way that will allow you to embrace the peace you seek. (See Section III for more about this central challenge of the Quest.)

**Set the intention that you will practice mindfulness of this tension in waking life.**

During the week when you are in emotional situations like the one you "bridged to" in your dream, recall the "tension" you felt in your meditation—or any "release" you experienced. Practice mindfulness of releasing impatience and embracing what is until a new way offers itself. Tend patiently to your garden and wait for the flowers to bloom.

# Section II

## The Time of Your Calling:
### Embracing Four Lessons in Mindfulness Our Nightmares Teach Us

*Nourish beginnings, let us nourish beginnings. Not all things are blest, but the seeds of all things are blest. The blessing is in the seed.*

—Muriel Rukeyser

It's the middle of the night and I'm waking up from a horrific nightmare:

I'm in the middle of a large, sprawling city, only there are no buildings or even roads. I can tell it's actually the remains of a city because of the enormous number of bricks strewn everywhere. In fact as I turn a slow 360, I see that every inch of terrain is covered with bricks, and not one brick sits upon another. Just as I'm thinking I could never have imagined a picture of devastation so complete, I see that each and every brick lies split and fractured as well.

Yet lying at my feet there it is—the only unbroken brick apparently left in this bleak and dying universe—and it seems so clear what that brick is there to tell me. "It's all over. You gave it your best shot. There is nothing left to hold on to—no control, nothing more to hold precious. There's no sense blaming the evil in the world because there's no moral court left to hear your stale adolescent claim of a good and loving God."

I pick up the brick and hold it high over my head, and raise my knee high—intending to complete the destruction—to smash to smithereens this single, surviving brick still daring to look the way it was born. What better table then my own body for this last supper of destruction?

Throughout my life I had thought I would somehow have a pass on major suffering. Things were always going to work out—but here I was swimming along the shores of bankruptcy, in another relationship that wasn't working, and then there was the divorce before that. The shards of a once sheltered and contented life lay undeniably scattered around me.

I had to admit I was living my life in a slow sickening freefall of anxiety and dread. Everything I had built and treasured lay in pieces. It seemed the only energy I had left was to take control and feed the scenario of ruin, to plan ahead for all the ways in which chaos would soon flood the valley of despair that had become my life, to maintain some shred of dignity by giving up before I was forced to, to feel some perverse joy in being the one to break the last brick and take control of what seemed so clearly out of control.

Such is the time of the Calling—and such are its dreams. Whether in one important area of our life or all of them, we stand benumbed at the loss. The Autumn-time of the Calling is any time when we feel that our perspective about a major aspect of our life—family, intimate relationship, work, spirituality—no longer serves us, and a growing emptiness has taken its place.

> The Calling is a time when we intuitively sense that the values, which we have held precious, or simply never before questioned, are actually the source of our suffering.

Signs of the Calling are many and varied, but we feel a rumbling within—both ominous and oddly exciting—and always a deepening discontent. On the inner level we may experience feelings of emptiness, depression, anxiety, or even panic attacks. The subjective experience is one of increasing depletion of energy, emotional numbing, and greater difficulty in decision-making.

Outwardly, we may find ourselves in the midst of a pattern of losses, injuries, accidents, or deaths that ultimately leave us feeling that some important part of the blueprint of our lives has been stolen from us. We often have no idea what changes are required in us, nor how to change—and so we go kicking and screaming into our Calling.

Trembling with fear or apprehension each step of the way, we nevertheless persevere. For this reason Campbell sometimes called this task the Heroic Journey. On our Journey we each have a chance to become our own hero or heroine. This means we view our suffering as a call to make sacrifice—risk emotional pain or loss by giving up values that we and those we love or respect hold very important. We persevere in this goal without knowing that our suffering will cease—without certainty of redemption. We persevere out of commitment to our own healing, growth, and wholeness, often with relatively little social or family support. And so the hero or heroine's path in the time of the Calling is indeed a "road less traveled."

We have come to think of heroes as people who are simply good "models" for us, as in, he or she is "my hero." What we mean by this is that we admire someone for doing

> True heroism is defined by an act of sacrifice that is both conscious and willing.

something we ourselves are still too timid or fearful to do—for example, speak out about some important subject or take a risk we're afraid to take ourselves. Of course for that person, the act may not have been difficult or required any type of sacrifice, and so in fact, he or she is not acting heroically. Similarly, even the act of saving another's life may not be heroic, as these situations sometimes elicit a decision without conscious forethought: "I saw her being washed away in the flooding river and I really didn't think about it. I just jumped in and grabbed her before she went down." You may be thinking quite rightly, "Why play with words? That behavior is still so extraordinary as to deserve the description of heroic." Yet the very nature of success on the inner Journey is that we make a willing sacrifice in a knowing, conscious manner. Feeling we have no choice or that we are being forced to act may be described as obedience, submission, or reflex, but does not reflect a true change in our perception of reality or an expansion of our consciousness.

Minister Bruce Barton, well-known at the turn of the century for his work in motivating others, once made an interesting, though flawed, observation: "What a curious phenomenon it is," he said, "that you can get men to die for the liberty of the world who will not make the little sacrifice that is needed to free themselves from their own individual bondage."[1]

However, the truth is that the sacrifice necessary to free ourselves is the most difficult we will ever face.

Have you ever asked yourself what keeps you from responding to the Call and making the sacrifice necessary to explore new paths in your life? Why don't you just "follow your bliss"? You've learned that your Dream Mentors and indeed the entire dream landscape are holograms of experience alive within us, offering us the gift of increased awareness, mindfulness, and a greater capacity for experiencing life more fully and joyously. So it would seem natural that we

> When we respond to the Call to become our own heroine or hero, we make sacrifice on behalf of our own life, to rescue ourselves from emotional and spiritual death, and we commit to what is above all a *conscious* struggle—one which requires many willing leaps or sacrifices to release ourselves from suffering.

would feel eager to embrace and align ourselves with the new perspectives our dreams—and life—offer. Yet let's face it: We all start with some fear and apprehension about the spiritual search—let alone our dreams. In the time of our Calling, how do we go about making the sacrifice needed to change things when the thought of committing to change often feels dreadful and paralyzing?

# Our Three Greatest Fears in Nightmares and Waking Life

We come by our anxiety honestly. We all share in common three fears that stop us cold on our path. Ironically our most cherished goals are, at the same time, our worst fears: transcending the concerns of our ego, learning genuine self-caring, and embracing change.

## Our Fear of Transcending Ego

It's important to understand what sacrifice really means. Most often we consider sacrifice as the giving up of material possessions (for example, donating to a worthy cause or to our church). Alternatively, when we think of heroic sacrifice we may imagine choosing to risk our lives or our entire fortune for some humanitarian goal. In most cases we imagine that the heroic action will positively affect others around us.

Interestingly, the Hebrew word for sacrifice, *kerev*, means "to bring nearer." True sacrifice refers to an inner action which brings us nearer to the consciousness of the Source. In the time of our Calling, sacrifice means the willing release of our five most loved and valued ego strategies—habits of thought that block our awareness of an expanded reality: Distraction, Control, Judgment, Attachment, and Impatience.

In our nightmares, it is our beliefs about the world, our personal reality created by these unhealthy ego strategies that are washed away, consumed by raging fires, swallowed up by the quaking earth or blown to bits.

We experience our nightmares as warnings of catastrophe and bad omens, because we intuit that our ego's favorite strategies are inadequate or doomed to failure, even if once they served us well. This is because these are the same four habits of thought around which we organize our daily identity—our persona.

So in nightmares and waking life we are terrified at the thought of giving up what we think is the core of our identity, when actually we are simply called to give up or transcend the ego strategies that cloud the perception of our true identity—an identity that requires no strategizing, willing, or planning at all. As it is said in Zen:

*Sit quietly,*
*Doing nothing.*
*Spring comes,*
*And the grass grows by itself.*[2]

# Our Fear of Self-Caring

Remember that the Mythic Journey is the story of our Call to break loose from the security of old values and beliefs—our fear and resistance to that change, and the subsequent joy of finding redemption for the suffering we've endured along the way.

One of the primary reasons we resist the Call in our lives is our ingrained dread of "breaking loose" and the fear of selfishness that it evokes within us.

But to engage in the Journey is to release the well-intended everyday values of family, friends, and society that maintain our feelings of alienation from ourselves and from the common ground of consciousness we all share.

As a result, whenever we grow, some degree of fear is always present. This is because the goal of every successful Journey—to transcend the collective reality—is heresy from the perspective of our family, church, and society.

Yet how ironic that every spiritual leader who has shared with us a life-renewing or divine experience has in every case found that he or she had to break the rules and challenge the collective reality to arrive at that vision. More ironic yet is that around every such revolutionary vision there grows a deadening, judgmental, and authoritarian body of "religious" duties and rules. These we are generally asked to follow without challenge and to accept the knowledge handed down without a validating experience of our own.

> The death we fear in our nightmares is no more or less than the death of a strategy in life that has become so much a part of how we see ourselves that we think we can't survive or won't exist without it. For example, "I am a person who is always 'nice' or 'strong,' or 'who would never hurt someone I love.'"

To directly experience our true nature, we are called to reject the most central assumptions by which we have lived—the guideposts by which we have journeyed as accepted members of society. Consider Jesus' words: "For I have come to set a man against his father, a daughter against her mother, and a daughter-in-law against her mother-in-law; and a man's enemies will be those of his own household."[3] Similarly, in the ancient Hindu *Bhagavad Gita*, the Lord Krishna tells his servant Arjuna that to follow the true spiritual path he must engage in a battle in which he will have to kill family and friends. Out of his reluctance comes one of the world's greatest spiritual treatises: "I do not desire victory, nor pleasure nor Kingdom, O Krishna! I do not wish to kill my teachers, uncles, sons, grandfathers, maternal uncles, fathers-in-law, grandsons, brothers-in-law and other relatives, who are about to kill us, even...for this earthly kingdom."[4]

The Journey throws us headlong into what feels to be the most profound ethical challenge we have ever faced. How dare we see the world differently and disappoint those we love and respect? Overcoming this fear of selfishly hurting others is arguably one of the most difficult challenges of our Journey. (In Section III you'll learn more about how we are constantly feeling this pull of opposites in our daily life.)

Foremost among the collective teachings that harden our heart to our own suffering are those that teach us we are good to care for others and selfish to attend to our own pain and hurt. From society's point of view we must always serve the needs of others and the "common good," so to question the rules handed down to us is a very courageous act indeed. To question any aspect of the collective wisdom of our family or culture is to violate a major taboo, opening ourselves to accusations of selfishness and to the threat of rejection or abandonment.

> To envision and live a more meaningful, richer life it is necessary to step out of the box—to liberate ourselves from the narrow and confining reality held by parents and other authority figures who influence our values.

Our fear of selfishness is pervasive and controls us with the same power found in the spells and curses of fairytales and fables. We fear that if for the sake of our own vision we choose not to meet the needs of those we love or reject what matters to them, that we will be branded as a deeply self-centered or "bad" person.

The idea that we should care about our own pain or suffering always feels somehow alien, unwarranted—yes, selfish. We routinely assume that if we are hurt or upset that it's probably unwarranted suffering or a groundless complaint—"not as bad as I'm probably making it—probably my own fault anyway." As a result, when we are in emotional pain our first fear is that we are *just* feeling sorry for ourselves. These are always code words that mean we are feeling sad or upset "for no good reason."

> I believe that this is why in our culture we find the terms "self-caring" or "self-nurturing" so awkward, and yet the word "selfish" *slides* so easily off our tongue.

When you consider acting on behalf of your own needs, how often do you hear yourself say, "I know that I'm probably being selfish but...?" Growing up how many of us heard, "Stop crying or I'll give you something to cry about!?" Again the meaning is the same: "You have no good reason to feel sad and you deserve punishment for 'selfishly' wanting support." We can feel sad for someone else in the blink of an eye, but it just doesn't feel comfortable to say, "I feel so sad for myself." In our culture that sounds dangerously close to self-indulgence. Rather, we think that it's someone else's job to feel sad for us, and if there is no one to mirror our sadness or pain, then we question what we are feeling. Even with support from others we continue to worry and second-guess ourselves.

There's an unspoken formula we're raised with: "Doubt whatever feels very good." Yes, it's okay to feel good, but not too good or at least not all of the time. Remember Patricia's lament, "You can't stay in the zone all of the time." This is not so much an assessment of our capacity for joy as a cautionary remark about the dangers of selfishness.

We ask ourselves, "What about others—the needs of my family and friends, and the suffering humanity around me? How can I complain? Other people are hurting more than I am. I should be grateful." After all, it's true: We're born into a family and society that has kept us alive and provided a means to survive, asking only that we accept the rules as they are handed down to us. "What kind of person," we ask ourselves, "is so ungrateful and so willing to allow those who support and care for me to feel hurt?"

Yes, to practice gratitude is essential, but thoughts in which we view our emotional pain as less important than others' are simply a thinly veiled rationale for minimizing the importance of our own suffering. Yet we persist in our conviction that only "bad people" are selfish enough to let those they care about remain in pain. But wait, is that true? What if we were to ask the following questions of those who judge us selfish: "If you love me do I owe it to you to see the world through your eyes? Why do you need me to think or act in a prescribed way? Will that reassure you about the correctness of your own views? Do you really love *me* if I have to think and feel the way you do—or do you love to see your reflection in me when I seem like you?"

These are the issues with which most of us struggle on the Journey—and our failure to resolve the answers to these questions leads to a pattern of relationships that pop psychologists have named codependency. But it's an ancient and profound ethical dilemma: "How much can I care for myself without acting selfishly? Will I realize too late that I have hurt someone I love and that I've become a 'bad person'? Don't I need to keep others happy in the knowledge that someday they will return the favor and say its okay to meet my own needs?"

There is an interesting tale told by Thich Nhat Hanh and first recounted by the Buddha about the importance of self-caring: There were once two acrobats—a little girl named Meda, and an adult who was her teacher. To perform

> There's a sadly amusing joke about what happens to a codependent person before she dies: "Everyone else's life flashes before her eyes."

their act they used a tall bamboo pole, which the teacher balanced on the top of his head while the little girl sat perched on top—a challenge that required their full attention and perfect balance. One day the teacher informed his student: "Here's the best way to work. I will watch you and you watch me, so that we can help each other concentrate, stay balanced, and prevent ourselves from being hurt." But the little girl was wise and answered: "Dear Master, I think it would be better for each of us to watch ourselves. To look after oneself means to look after both of us. That way I'm sure we will avoid any accidents and will earn enough to eat." The Buddha said: "The child spoke correctly."[5]

Most of us live with an unstated belief that we should always meet the expectations of others and "watch out" for their needs before our own.

We also often harbor a double standard for ourselves versus our friends and children. Those desires that we think are bad and selfish in ourselves we view as very acceptable in those we love. This perspective we like to call "compassionate," but the irony lies in the utter lack of compassion for ourselves it implies.

Here's how poet David Whyte sees it:

> *Each human life requires a singular courage to live because each life represents a unique corner of creation which is found nowhere else. We share commonalties with one another, but our common qualities are found in me and found in you with...a particular recipe and flavor which is not found anywhere else, never has been since the beginning of time and never will be ever again.*
>
> *There is no one but our self who can live out this corner of creation, which is ours and ours alone to live. Therefore, in the matter of identity, everything is at stake....You can fail to hold up your end of the conversation and the usual consequence is to then live out someone else's life as a form of protection, mistaking it for your own. It takes tremendous courage to live out the central conversation, what we might call our destiny, no matter how small a corner of the world it might be. A good life is the one we were made for, the life that our deep psyche and our outer character are both drawn to naturally, and as long as you have this star in sight—as long as you have the happiness of being in the conversation you were made for, then it doesn't*

*matter how hard the outer circumstances are, because, despite everything, it will make sense to you. There is a faith in loving fiercely what is rightfully yours. Especially if you have waited a long time to find it....*[6]

Although we may love and respect our parents, church, and culture, the views about selfishness and compassion that they condition in us are at times one-sided, judgmental, and inhibiting of our ability to love ourselves and live our life most fully. The ancient metaphor of taking the sword to family and friends is a clear call to release our attachment to such collective truths and values.

As master artists do, our Dream Mentors constantly offer a different and more enriched view that we are free to paint on the canvas of our life—or to ignore. Emily Bronte affirms this truth from experience with her own dreams: "I've dreamt in my life dreams that have stayed with me ever after, and changed my ideas; they've gone through me, like wine through water, and altered the color of my mind."[7] Only then can we hear an older, wiser voice within us to help us find our own Grail, whether it is the spiritual insight we seek, the resolve to "be heard and understood" when in conflict with a loved one, or the affirmation of our own creativity no matter how we fear that others may judge our work. Every challenge in life requires that we remain mindful of our own sadness, pain, or suffering. In an airplane emergency with our child, we are told to place the air mask on our self before our child. What good are we as a dead parent to our child?

The unbounded life energy and fresh experience bundled in the image of every dream and Dream Mentor offers a necessary counterpoint to the restricting and ofted prejudiced attitudes about self-caring that the Collective Unconsiousness promotes.

If we do not nurture a self-caring and compassionate attitude we become drained and resentful, unable to authentically support those we love because we have not met our own needs or healed our wounds. "You can search throughout the entire universe for someone who is more deserving of your love and affection than you are yourself," said the Buddha, "and that person is not to be found anywhere. You yourself, as much as anybody in the entire universe, deserve your love and affection."[8]

## Our Fear of Change

Yet as primary as this fear of selfishness is in most of us, it is part of a larger, more general fear of change—of the new and novel. "The fastest way to make an enemy," said Woodrow Wilson, "is to change something."[9]

A friend of mine dreamed he stood with one foot on a dock, and the other on a beautiful sailboat that was slowly moving from its berth toward the open sea. His anxiety grew as he stood paralyzed, watching the arc of his legs widen beneath him and begin to tear and split the muscles of his lower torso. The dream ended right there with the pain of feeling unable or unwilling to choose the familiarity and security of the dock or the adventure of the Journey. As French author André Gide has said, "[We] cannot discover new oceans unless we have the courage to lose sight of the shore."[10]

Campbell pointed out the resistance we have in the face of change. He showed how myths and fables often depict their heroine or hero as deeply reluctant to accept their Calling.

Underlying our deep ambivalence to "take the leap" is a profound mistrust and fear of the novel and change. Religious historian Mircea Eliade tells us that interest in the "new" "is a recent discovery in the life of humanity. On the contrary, archaic humanity...defended itself to the utmost of its powers against...novelty...."[11]

> Though we seem hardwired to go out into the world, even to explore the unknown of outer space, by the time we are six months old we also cringe and recoil at the sight of a new face—terrified by all that is strange and new.

What Jung loved to call the "tension of opposites" is always with us—in this case, the opposing desires to open to new experience and the desire for permanency, stability, and the familiar comforting feeling of repetition.[12] (In Section III you'll read more about this tension as the central challenge of the Quest.)

This conflict is present in the heroic stories of myth as well as on our own Journey. Every heroine and hero begins terrified of change, wanting to hold on to what is familiar, tried, and true. We have one foot on the boat but one still on the dock. For this reason, at the start of every Mythic Journey, Campbell points out that the guardians of the threshold are always seen with apprehension and mistrust as demons, forces of evil and destruction. Only later as our fear (and ignorance) subsides do we view them as allies, diving beings and angels urging us toward growth and wholeness.

That's also why you'll recall that Jung seemed to define God in terms we save for the Devil: "(A)ll things which cross my path violently and recklessly...."[13] He was really speaking of how we (our ego) initially perceive God in the time of our Calling as a destructive rather than redeeming force, radically destroying the landscape of our life.

It is sadly ironic that in both our waking life and dreams our fear of change means that we initially see those who are offering help as threatening, or at least as highly suspect and untrustworthy. We start out on our Journey often feeling deceived and betrayed, if not attacked and mortally threatened because we are still attached to our old way of being and identity, the status quo. Indeed the presence of such feelings is usually a good indicator that we are in the midst of our Calling.

When we honor and work with our dreams we increasingly embrace change and these same threatening dream figures then transmute over time, and in the Illumination stage of our Journey, appear as Mentors and allies who help us through our greatest fears. In the time of the Calling a space must be cleared for the novel energy and perspective of the Divine, but change is always by definition a frightening event for us—that is, for "our ego."

The fear we feel at the start of our Journey and within our nightmares is a perennial concern. The ancient Chinese oracle and 4,000-year-old compendium of spiritual wisdom known as the *I Ching* or *Book of Changes* is based on hexagrams that reflect 64 archetypal times and situations. The *I Ching* provides advice as to the types of correct and incorrect attitudes we may hold at such times. The hexagram "Shock" speaks to the time of our Calling in words that at first we rarely understand: "The shock terrifies others for a hundred miles...and yet he does not let fall the sacrificial spoon and chalice."[14] The *I Ching* is telling us that, rather than reacting to loss or change with fear and confusion, the superior person "is always filled with reverence at the manifestation of God."[15]

In other words, we are required to develop sufficient respect for change and the upwelling of radically new perspectives that we always maintain our reverent attitude—mindful that out of our greatest fear and loss can come the greatest gift: "Shock comes—then laughing words," says the Oracle.[16]

Thus the *I Ching* says about times of Shock: "In fear and trembling the sage...searches (her) heart lest it harbor any secret opposition to the will of God."[17]—and indeed, the will of God most often requires a fundamental acceptance of change as unavoidable.

# The Reason We Fear Our Dream Mentors

As Nobel Laureate Elias Canetti noted, "All the things one has forgotten scream for help in dreams."[18] The help required is our loving acceptance and embrace of the change Dream Mentors bring.

In our Calling, Dream Mentors always have the same goal: to shake us loose from our old script and offer a new vision of how life can feel. Yet no matter how positive their visions, as harbingers of change our Mentors create within us a natural antipathy.

> The essential lesson of the Calling is that, from the perspective of the Source, creating a path of our own "is" the problem. The only life-promoting path is the one that is guided by our Psyche— one that serves our growth and the growth of consciousness.

For this reason during the first half of our Journey our attitude toward every Dream Mentor must be to offer the benefit of the doubt that the healing experience they embody will shift our perspectives about who we are and what new experience we need to live our life more authentically.

As the purpose of our Calling is to clear a space in waking life for the experience of renewal, our Mentors help us release our ego's attachment to the many stories we tell ourselves that stand in the way of our new growth—stories about who we think we are or ought to be—the persona we have spent our lives creating and to which we are attached with every fiber of our being. "Those who do not have power over the story that dominates their lives, the power to retell it, rethink it, deconstruct it...and change it as times change," says author Salmon Rushdie, "truly are powerless because they cannot think new thoughts."[19]

For this reason the initial three lessons in mindfulness our Mentors teach help us release the habits of thought that cement and keep our story of suffering in place. (See the Lessons in Mindfulness Throughout the Journey table on page 82.) Each of these three habits are methods of resisting change that keep us unaware, unwilling, and feeling unworthy of a fuller, richer life experience. Distraction makes us unaware of the need for change. Desire for control leaves us unwilling to surrender and embrace the humility needed to accept change and follow guidance from the Source. Self-judgment makes us feel unworthy of any change for the better that would come from the guidance we receive.

> To benefit from the wisdom of our Calling nightmares, we must appreciate that our Dream Mentors are, if anything, the embodiment of change—carrying experiences back to our conscious awareness that are long forgotten or entirely original to our waking mind.

As we discover through our Calling and Quest that these values are the cause of our suffering and not the means to avoid it, Dream Mentors teach us the fourth lesson in mindfulness: the importance of grieving—the wisdom that change and transition are an unavoidable, very necessary, and natural part of the life cycle. To grieve is to fully release our ego's story about our identity—our attachment to who we are, what we have accomplished and acquired, and what we stand for.

And contrary to what many think, to be non-attached has nothing to do

> Mentors help us to release the limitations of our waking life (ego) point of view. They do this by presenting a new vision, which, when embraced, expands our consciousness and opens us to a profoundly creative and healing experience.

with depression, a state of emotional detachment, or loss of passion for life. In fact, we are learning on our Journey to let go of those very habits of thought that cause life to feel so flat and unfulfilling. As writer Anaïs Nin wisely reminded us, "Life is a process of becoming, a combination of states we have to go through. Where people fail is that they wish to elect a state and remain in it. This is a kind of death."[20]

Ultimately when we are pushed by our life to change we are threatened to the core of our being and those we see responsible for suggesting change are viewed initially as repulsive, threatening, or as our mortal enemies. Sufi Sheikh Llewellyn Vaughan-Lee reminds us that in the Sufi tradition, the Teacher may be seen as acting "with seeming coldness, even inhumanity, but he acts from the level of the Self. He follows the laws of a world very different from the physical plane and is concerned with the real freedom of the seeker, freedom from the ego and duality of good and bad, just and unjust."[21] So, too, in Mindful Dreamwork, all dream characters are our teachers or Mentors embodying the same wisdom as the gurus of every spiritual tradition. It is simply our egos that limit our experience of their true nature.

The way Mentors appear to us depends upon our attitude of acceptance or resistance to change. And so we arrive at the following truth:

You will recall Jung's dictum that our psyche "reflects the face we turn towards it."[22]

## Lessons in Mindfulness Throughout the Journey

|  | Calling | Quest | Illumination | Return |
|---|---|---|---|---|
| **Practice** | Practice Mindfuness of Willing Sacrifice. | Practice Mindfulness of the Tension of Opposites. | Practice Open-hearted embrace of Present Moment: Find redemption. | Practice Mind-fulness of Heart-centered values: Act with Resolve and Clarity. |
| **Lessons in Mindfunless** | ✷ Release Distraction.<br>✷ Release Control.<br>✷ Release Judgement.<br>✷ Release Attachment. | ✷ Release Impatience. | ✷ Embrace Solitude.<br>✷ Embrace Humility.<br>✷ Embrace Compassion.<br>✷ Embrace the formless Witnessing Consciousness. | ✷ Share with Resolve and Heart what has been learned on our journey. |

# The Soothing Balm of Lunar Consciousness

In the time of the Calling the experience of mortal threats, death, devastation, or major loss in our waking life and dreams freezes us in what had been our unimpeded forward march. At such times we must learn from the Greek Perseus, whose job it was to kill the Gorgon Medusa. As you may recall, all those who looked upon Medusa were turned to stone. In response to this challenge Perseus knew what to do—not to look "head on" directly at her face. He used the gift of a polished bronze shield given to him by Athena as a mirror with which to see Medusa indirectly and reduce the power of her visage, and in this way succeeded in slaying her.

The popular film story of Indiana Jones and his search for the Grail highlighted a more modern version of this lesson. In one compelling scene the Nazi SS had found the Holy Ark and hoped to plunder its riches. Indiana and colleagues are tied up nearby. As the Nazis prepare to open the ark Indiana warns his friends to look down and keep her eyes closed. As the ark is opened the Nazis peer inside. First they experience ecstasy as beautiful angelic spirits emerge—then terror as the spirits incinerate them. Indiana and his friends, however, are spared by their humble attitude, just as Perseus is spared by not looking directly at Medusa. To do otherwise is to become "inflated," as Jungians like to say, and to arrogantly assert our own power and control. (See Chapter 6 about Dreams of Control.)

These two stories teach an essential lesson about the need for reverence and humility in the encounter with divine perspective—that is, in our encounter with any image that embodies great change, something very new or foreign-feeling to our waking consciousness—a lesson that if unheeded leaves us paralyzed, turned stone cold with fear.

It is said in the myth that Medusa was born in a northern area where the sun never shone. This means that one could approach her correctly only with what I call the cool, reflective attention of "lunar consciousness." The light of the sun when overhead creates a glare, washing out the subtle hues and colors, the varied textures of what we observe. Lunar light adds depth and dimension to the flatness of the landscape we study, and reveals the shadows and corners—the crevices where often lie the most precious gems.

Lunar consciousness requires us to perceive globally, the way we do with those art pieces in the mall. Their flat and uninteresting surface gives way to a luxurious three-dimensional world of color and flow when we relax our automatic attempts to focus on something specific.

Dream Mentors appear vile and threatening when we mistrust the experience of change they embody, but compassionate and wise when we are ready to embrace that change.

Lunar focus is diffuse, is attentive but without a goal, opens to the mood of a problem, and makes us aware of what knowledge is absent, what we don't know, what we aren't capable of knowing by dint of will or ego alone. This is the consciousness of contemplation, and its answers are felt as inklings, images that ebb and flow in waves of feeling rather than discreet particles or facts.

Lunar attention is playful as well as serious. We feel the answers to our questions in our body rather than in the mental space of our head. Lunar consciousness is what we need to unfold the meaning of a dream and especially Calling dreams, which so often fill us with mortal fear, dread, or loathing—dreams that upon awakening send us running, heart pounding to find the solar light of the waking world.

Our ego habitually engages any perceived crisis with a kind of thinking and attention we can call solar consciousness—a frontal assault or "head-on" kind of approach. Solar thinking is intended to shed as much light as possible on what lies in the dark. We pull out of our ego's tool bag all sorts of rational strategies. First we may try to distract ourselves. When distraction fails, we may recall the similar problems we've encountered in the past and, hating that we are powerless, plot to regain control. We judge ourselves for even having the problem, or judge others for creating it. We obsess about the intolerable losses we will endure if we don't fix it. Worse, we realize our mother had this problem and we vowed we'd never be like her.

Just in the nick of time, we find ourselves endowed with the gift of prescience and foresight into the course of our life, knowing now with certainty how this crisis, if unsolved, will lead to a miserable future whose barren landscape we mentally review in the minutest detail. We step into that future and suffer the indignities hurled upon us by loved ones and friends who will be and no doubt are withdrawing in pity or disgust at our failure to overcome the problem.

It's in this moment—perhaps four or five minutes into the onset of the crisis—that we begin to feel the cold, numbing fear, the embalming fluid of despair, begin to course through every vein and artery as we slowly turn to a semi-lifeless lump of clay. Solar consciousness is always powerless in a face-off with Medusa, and all that is new and foreign to our ego's consciousness.

Of course, solar thinking is a process in which we can engage at the mere threat of being fired at work, rejected by our lover, or lacking funds to pay our bills. The concerns of our ego—fear, anxiety, and survival—are what create solar consciousness. We zero in on the threat, relying on our ego's favorite defenses against change, become overwhelmed, and feel paralyzed. This is why it's important not to look straight at what we fear most, just as those of us with a fear of heights know not to look down. "There is one art of which man should be master," said Samuel Coleridge, "the art of reflection."[23]

In this section you've learned about the hallmarks of the Calling in your life, this time of profound change, the three universal fears we encounter, and how to respond to fear with a reverent and reflective attitude.

So read on now about how our Dream Mentors teach us the four lessons in mindfulness needed to "save our lives" and embrace our Calling. You'll also be reading about the types of dreams that correspond to each lesson in mindfulness. Each has a predominant and identifiable mood and set of emotions that you will find summarized in the table on page 87.

# Section Practices

Recall a time and journal about when you felt called to change or grow in your life.

≈   How has the story of your life changed?

≈   What identity or image of yourself did you have to release?

≈   In retrospect, despite the suffering you experienced, in what way are you better off for having let that part of you go?

In your journal, write a paragraph or two about the main ways in which your life was once quite different than it is now.

≈   Create a title for your two stories—one to describe your old identity, and one to describe your new image of yourself.

- Has anyone difficult in your life proved to be a "teacher" with regard to providing life lessons?

In the past or currently, recall a fear of selfishness that has held you back from what you desired or from making an important change in your life?

- Consider what aspect of that "selfish" wish may be an expression of self-caring.

- If a friend were to share the same wish with you, would you consider her selfish? If not, why is it all right to have a double standard for yourself?

- Why is it okay for others to have their needs met, but not yourself?

## Practicing Lunar Consciousness

Recall the last time you felt in "shock" about some loss or threatening situation.

- How did you approach the problem?

- Was there a moment in which you wondered what gift might lie in this experience?

- If so, did you wonder about that gift right away or was it days or weeks later?

- If not, how did you handle the problem? Did you magnify the problem and focus exclusively on all the worst possibilities? Did you imagine how bad your future would be?

- How long did it take you to truly "reflect upon" the problem?

- How much more productive was that reflective or "lunar" approach to your fear?

Recall a nightmare or frightening dream and journal about the threatening Mentor in that dream.

If you prefer to draw or paint, that's great, too. In either case, do so with a "lunar" approach—that is, assume a playful attitude and get some distance on the image as if you were in a contest to see who could write the most campy screenplay for a horror movie. Include little details, mention the colors, the lighting, and any sounds you may have heard in the dream. Set the intention to have fun and be creative. Above all remain mindful that those who frighten us in dreams seem threatening only because our ego is not yet comfortable with the experience of healing change that our Dream Mentors embody.

**Predominant Mood and Emotion of Calling and Quest Dreams**

| | Dreams of Distraction | Dreams of Control | Dreams of Judgment | Dreams of Attachment |
|---|---|---|---|---|
| **Predominant Mood, Emotion, Imagery, or Behavior** | Feelings of emptiness; unfocused; restless searching; wanting; isolated, hurried; wandering; confused; disoriented; feeling distracted | Frustrated; powerless; immobilized; arrogant; stubborn; manipulative; rigid; reckless; refusing advice; paralyzed; feeling "out of control" | Fearful; terrified; emotionally or physically attacked; escaping; mistrustful; perceived malevolence in others; in battle of good vs. evil; feeling judged and criticized | Feeling of loss; apprehension about loss; resistance to loss; anger at loss; deep insecurity and grief |

# Chapter 5

# Dreams of Distraction: Nightmares That Teach Us Mindfulness of Solitude

*Ten thousand flowers in spring, the moon in autumn,*
*A cool breeze in summer, snow in winter.*
*If your mind isn't clouded by unnecessary things,*
*This is the best season of your life.*

—Wu-men

*Without going outside*
*you can know the ways of the world.*
*Without looking through the window*
*you can see the way of heaven.*
*The farther you go*
*the less you know.*

—Lao Tsu

# Our Intent to Distract Ourselves

Taoist Lao Tsu was the first to articulate the philosophy of wuwei, or "non-doing," as a means to transcend our habit of indulging in distractions created by our scattered and unfocused thoughts. It was for this reason he counseled us that "the farther you go, the less you know."[1]

Poet David Whyte tells the story of a time when he felt exhausted by the demands of his life and asked his friend David Steindl-Rast, a Benedictine monk and well-known author, for the antidote. Steindl-Rast told him that it wasn't rest he needed but wholeheartedness—that we exhaust ourselves by doing so many things, but eventually none wholeheartedly.[2]

We rarely question our "monkey mind" life. As though we're trapeze artists, we live our days swinging from place to place and thought to thought. Ironically, we rationalize this constant movement—our love of distraction—as a means to find the peace and rest that will soothe our souls. Even when we take time to rest we do so half-heartedly, guilty that we are wasting time and being unproductive, or as a means to recuperate—a prelude to a new round of exhaustion.

Our restless yearning—our ceaseless wanting—is never quenched because we are seeking what cannot be found inside the box of conditioned thoughts in which we've been raised. The great sage J. Krishnamurti asks us if we have ever reflected on our automatic habits of thought and action:

> *Have you ever sat very quietly with closed eyes and watched the movement of your own thinking? Have you watched your mind working—or rather, has your mind watched itself in operation, just to see what your thoughts are, what your feelings are, how you look at the trees, at the flowers, at the birds, at people, how you respond to a suggestion or react to a new idea? Have you ever done this?*[3]

The challenge of the Illumination for every heroine and hero on the Journey is to create a space for the experience of stillness that opens us to the profound wisdom found only here and now in this Present Moment. If we want to find relief from our suffering we cannot depend on the paradigm of reality offered by our family or culture for the answer. Einstein too reminded us, "We can't solve problems by using the same kind of thinking we used when we created them."[4] We must look outside the box.

In response to our feelings of emptiness and need for fulfillment our culture prescribes half-hearted remedies. Similar to the way a mother who responds to her child's tears by suggesting, "Let's have something yummy to eat" or "You need some sleep. Take a nap and you'll feel better," our culture prescribes a multitude of irrelevant solutions for our miseries—smell better, have more fun, do something new and exciting, get back to work, take a break, try this new pill.

Nothing works because the solutions *are* the problem, and simply adding more of them makes matters worse, not better. It's up to us to step out of the box. If we want to experience life wholeheartedly we must first find solitude—the only condition that allows us to find the stillness and silence that are the first step to inner peace. Contemporary sage Eckhart Tolle describes the thoughts that distract us as the universal disease of the ego: "Not to be able to stop thinking is a dreadful affliction, but we don't realize this because almost everyone is suffering from it, so it is considered normal. This incessant mental noise prevents you from finding that realm of inner stillness that is inseparable from Being."[5]

Yet in our culture there is little support or sanction for the perennial value of solitude. In the 10th century A.D. there were no less than 40,000 monasteries in Western Europe. Remarkably, today in our culture even the word *monastery* sounds strange and unfamiliar, and in its place the weekend "retreat" is now in vogue for a small minority of us.

Ours is an extremely extroverted culture. If you are naturally introverted you know how out of place and odd you have felt all your life. On the popular Myers-Briggs Type Indicator, those who score as introverted, feeling types comprise between 1 and 5 percent of the population. The idea that there are "inner" issues to work on still conjures up the stigma of terms such as inadequate, odd, crazy, eccentric, and weird in many parts of our society. In the corporate world of health insurance, work on the inner world is paid at half price, and then only when we submit to labeling as "disease," the natural turmoil of spiritual growth.

So it is that there is precious little support for stepping out of the box. The hard truth, says Lama Thubten Yeshe, is that "just as we are responsible for our own suffering, so are we solely responsible for our own cure. We have created the situation in which we find ourselves, and it is up to us to create the circumstances for our release."[6]

That release is found when we honor solitude through mindfulness of the pervasive distractions in our life. Joseph Campbell put it this way:

> *You must have a room, or a certain hour or so in a day, where you don't know what was in the newspapers that morning, you don't know who your friends are, you don't know what you owe anybody. This is a place where you*

*can simply experience and bring forth what you are and what you might be. This is the place of creative incubation. At first you may find that nothing happens there. But if you have a sacred place and use it, something eventually will happen.*[7]

Ramana Maharshi, called by some the greatest Sage of the 20th century, had this to say about solitude: "The happiness of solitude is not found in retreats. It may be had even in busy centers. Happiness is not to be taught in solitude or in busy centers. It is in the Self."[8] Yet solitude is not simply an external place we set aside, separate from the distractions of the mundane world. The essence that all places of sanctuary or solitude share is that they are inward space.

This means that we refuse to engage in the view that the sacred is somehow separate from the ordinary world. The Divine is not limited to the main sanctuary of a church or an earth altar in the rain forest. Neither solitude nor sacred space has an external location. We may sit cross-legged in the forest but remain conscious only of the outer world from which we just came. There is no solitude in that consciousness.

Solitary or "lunar" consciousness requires an attitude that daily honors and affirms awareness of our inner world. Ultimately, in the reflective inner space of solitude we develop lunar consciousness and, through dreamwork, meditation, prayer, or other ritual, create a gateway through which we expand our awareness beyond the constraints of our everyday sensory world. In the Gospel of Thomas, Jesus says, "Many stand outside the door, but it is only the solitaries who will enter the bridal chamber."[9]

> Within the quiet between our thoughts, between our breaths and the beat of our heart we find our greatest teacher—the silent witness that stands at the threshold of awakened consciousness.

The practice of mindfulness depends upon and requires the silence of solitude. Where else are we to release the incessant thoughts and endless stories we tell, but in the cleansing silence?

To embrace silence is to leave no counterpoint for our ego's shouts of anger and despair. In solitude we create a space in which to step back from our compulsive thoughts, our plotting to control, relentless judging and grasping—a space which to witness our own suffering with compassion.

"Silence," says Ramana Maharshi, "is the most potent form of work. However vast and emphatic the *Sastras* [scriptures] may be, they fail in their effect. The guru is quiet and peace prevails in all his silence, vaster and more emphatic than all the Sastras put together."[10]

Within the sacred vessel of silence lies the experience of the present moment, the Grail on our Journey. Silence is the ever-present threshold to a consciousness that transcends the warring opposites within—a clear space in which to choose to act or not act; to distract ourselves or remain centered in solitude; to seek control or embrace humility; to judge or to witness compassionately; to rigidly identify with what we have or to let go, grieve our losses and welcome change without pre-conditions. This is why Justice William Douglas suggested that "solitude is the beginning of all freedom."[11]

Yet although we can learn to live in solitude, we cannot always engage in silence. So it's important to be mindful of what we say and how we say it. When we speak carelessly it is as if we live on the edge of a beautiful, quiet pond, but let our motorboat run in it day and night. "Before you speak," says the great Hindu sage Sai Baba, "ask yourself is it necessary, is it true, does it improve on the silence?"[12]

When we are mindful of solitude we set the intention to embrace the compassionate witness that lies quietly within us all.

# Nightmares: Dreams of Distraction and the Loss of Solitude

When we are not devoting enough time to create a still and quiet healing space within, we may become aware of outward symptoms of emotional distress or physical injuries that require us to slow down and look inward. Our dreams, too, may be painful, as they bring with them an experience of change that we mightily resist. However, we must remember in Mindful Dreaming the axiom that the more resistant we are, the more frightening our dreams and Dream Mentors appear.

Mike, a very outgoing, extroverted young man in his 30s, had spent most of his life in a devoted effort to be among as many friends, colleagues, and family members as he could—always with the hope that he could bring a little cheer into their lives and be of help whenever they were in need. To do otherwise, he thought, hinted at great selfishness.

The symptoms that signaled the need for change in Mike's relentless extroversion and a more inward focus came in the form of panic attacks—strong feelings of anxiety, a pounding heart, difficulty breathing, and a crushing feeling in his chest. As you'll recall, all kinds of intense emotional pain are hallmarks heralding the time of our Calling. Mike dreamed:

> I am taking a leisurely walk out in nature, see a cave, and decide to go inside. I'm surprised it's actually a very nice place and has some interesting lighting and features. I'm aware of how peaceful I am just being alone in the cave, and that this could even be a great place to live if I wanted to. But I start feeling restless. Its kind of lonely and I'm not comfortable here. My friends are waiting and anyway, I need to get home and back to work.
>
> I see a natural ladder of stone that leads up and out of the cave. Through a hole in its roof, I can see the sky and the sun is shining brightly. But as I climb out fine grains of sand pile up at my feet. With each upward step, the sand piles higher until it presses down on my chest, creating a crushing feeling so I can't breathe. When I step downward into the cave, the sand recedes. This cycle continues for the rest of the dream as I try to climb up and then have to climb down over and over. Every time I want to go back outside the sand piles up, I get that crushing feeling again and I can't breathe. I wake up terrified.

This is a classic example of how our dreams both diagnose our problem and suggest the healing lesson in mindfulness that is needed. As is the case for most of us in this culture, Mike's perception of what is okay in life does not include solitude. Climbing up and down the ladder is a compelling snapshot of his ambivalence about the solitary life. In the initial scene of his dream Mike voluntarily enters the cave and finds comfort there. When we spoke together about his dream, Mike described the fine grains of sand as the perfect image of the many concerns and responsibilities he habitually drew into his life. Indeed, the more he steps toward the bright light of solar consciousness within his dream, the more he feels the crushing burden of life-depleting responsibilities and the more his waking life symptoms of panic attack return (the crushing fear in his chest and inability to breathe). In his dream it is clear to Mike that he can be symptom-free in the solitude of the cave, but he tries again and again to leave. The old Chinese proverb goes: "I dreamed a thousand new paths...I woke and walked my old one."

However, in Mike's instance, he honored the message of his dream. Mike realized that that he wasn't required to give up his old path—his social life—to embrace the solitude needed to end his suffering. The goal of wholeheartedness does not require us to choose one experience over the other, but to achieve a balance and resolve to explore the "cave" as well. Mike invested more energy and interest in his dream life, joined a dreamsharing group, and in this way created sacred space in his daily life. His symptoms steadily abated and then disappeared, never to return. "All of man's miseries," said French philosopher Blaise Pascal, "stem from his inability to sit quietly in a room and do nothing."[13]

In Chapter 6 you'll learn next about Dreams of Control in which we find that we can never achieve the goals our ego sets—only those our Self views as promoting our growth. In this dream, too, Mike cannot get out of the cave because to do so would not be in his best interests. Yet this remains a dream of distraction. Why? Because the predominant mood upon which the dream story is based is one of being "restless," "lonely," and isolated: "I miss my friends who are waiting.... I need to get home and back to work." To paraphrase the grammar of this dream: "I can find peace in solitude, but *when* I feel lonely, isolated and restless, *then* I try to return to the distractions of my everyday life—and begin to suffer once again." In Control dreams the predominant mood around which the story unfolds is one of helplessness and frustration about not having what it is we want—when we want it. In Dreams of Distraction it is apparent that the solution lies in solitude, whereas in Dreams of Control the solution lies in greater humility and the willingness to be led.

Whereas Mike's distraction nightmare conveniently provided a narrative story about his resistance to solitude, we often dream or at least recall only fragments or single images. Yet a picture is worth a thousand words.

Years ago my client Beth had the wisdom to quit an amazingly toxic 80-hours-per-week, always-on-call career as a high-tech, high-powered sales-person. She retreated to a relatively quiet life trading in stocks and managing her financial assets from a computer in her own home. She got together often with her many friends. However, Beth began to experience numerous physical problems that required a series of surgical procedures. She understood intellec-tually that to heal required acceptance of greater solitude, but she resisted this change and continued to make plans for parties and to maintain her social life. This is Beth's nightmare:

> I'm in a room with one of those old telephone switchboards that they used to use in the early 1900s. Some very aggressive men terrify me by breaking into the room and tearing out all of the wires on the switch-board. I wake up with my heart pounding.

Upon later reflection in the cooler light of lunar consciousness, Beth easily grasped that her Dream Mentors—the vandals—broke into her awareness to impose on her the gift of solitude and silence—in this case one of those gifts "we can't refuse." Her connections to the outer world were severed in the dream, and with them the habit of indulging the many distractions in life that stood in the way of her healing.

It's true that her Mentors might have chosen to throw her cell phone against the wall to impart the same message, but for Beth the early-20th-century technology, with its numerous overflowing tangled set of lines, served as a graphic visual image of her many social involvements that the seemingly vicious and uncaring Mentors wished to separate her from. Plato once said, "Whoever is delighted in solitude is either a wild beast or a god."[14] Dream Mentors in our Distraction nightmares often seem to be both.

Yet we truly understand a nightmare only when our experience of terror or loathing of the beasts who plague us has transformed into one of gratitude and appreciation for the guidance we have received from the Divine. Our final dream provides a great example of this transformation.

Melinda had spent the majority of her life denying her emotional pain and her favorite anesthetic was the practice of distraction. In response to a minor fight with her husband or the painful memories of emotional rejection by her parents, nothing beat shopping. There was always something new to see or buy at the mall. Shopping and staying distracted, she said, was always the greatest way to strengthen "my hard shell." For years Melinda's favorite song was Simon and Garfunkel's "I am a Rock." Even when she fell ill with cancer she never worried too much about dying. After all, what was there to lose when she felt so numb to life anyway?

Yet Melinda had an inkling that there was indeed something more, and entered therapy to find out. She did attempt to reclaim her long-suppressed feelings and the joys that had been buried with them. She even began to meditate, but found it difficult to follow through with any new practice or approach to life. She reported dreams in which she played and won at the computer game *Tetris*, but returned each time to her former playing level rather than move on to the next. She quit meditating and continued to cling to any distractions that life threw her way. Melinda would often say that perhaps she was just being selfish for wanting to enjoy life more fully when her family still had needs of their own. She continued to vacillate and then was shaken by this Distraction nightmare:

> I am facing a busy and confusing crowd in a downtown area anticipating my usual mindless escape into shopping. Someone with gentle and loving hands turns me around so my back faces the crowd. Then I'm shot and I know that I'll die. I'm terrified. I keep wishing that I won't die and will stay alive. But then I realize that I'm in no pain at all. I'm very relieved, but now I want my family to know that I'm not in pain. I see now that I was only shot in the legs by the shotgun and not in the center core of my body. But the dream ends as I keep repeating this single phrase: I want to live. I want to live.

Melinda identified the busy downtown shopping scene as a perfect image of her life as she lived it and quickly grasped that she was being prompted to turn her back once and for all on her chronic habit of distraction. But three other things stood out as well for her.

First, the hands of the person who turned her away from the busy scene were protective and loving hands that "somehow softened me as I turned. I actually felt in the nightmare as if I was softening. I guess there goes the 'hard shell of distractions' I hide in!"

Second, Melinda was relieved in the dream that she was not in any pain, but felt it was more important—in fact, essential—that her family know that as well. Indeed, when we choose to move inward and to embrace solitude the first thing we often fear is that our loved ones will believe our withdrawal is a sign of loneliness and suffering. So Melinda is preoccupied in this dream with the need to let her family know "I'm not in pain." In truth, as Lord Byron reminded us, "In solitude we are the least alone."[15]

Finally, Melinda understood that her mantra in the dream, "I want to live," was the realization that living behind the hard shell of her distractions was no life at all. Despite the many years of "shopping for life," her "core" was still intact and she could move on to live life more wholeheartedly. And that she did. Since that dream Melinda's life and relationships have taken on new texture, color, and depth. "Our noisy years," said Wordsworth, "seem moments in the being of the eternal silence."[16]

Keep in mind that in the time of our Calling these dreams are experienced as nightmares. Later in the Journey our Mentors gradually lose their threatening quality, and in fact, the issues they address later become the source of deep feelings of joy, resolve, and mastery. You'll read more about Mike's, Beth's, and Melinda's dreams and see how they transform through the Journey in coming chapters.

As we learn that our dreams always prescribe the medicinal experience we need, we gradually release the view of ourselves as powerless victims of fate in a less than loving world. We can view our suffering as a simple reflection of the choices we make, for better of worse. When we resist change and choose values that inhibit our growth, then we suffer the pain of standstill in our lives.

# The Healing Power of Distraction Dreams: An Overview

The predominant mood in Dreams of Distraction is an incessant wanting and searching, a restlessness and emptiness that is never filled by the objects of our distraction. Distraction dreams call us instead to the healing balm of solitude— the sacred space and silence of a consciousness freed of the "dreadful affliction" of words and thoughts. Within that living silence we start our Journey home, leaving behind the emptiness of a world where ceaseless yearning never fills our soul.

As Lao Tsu says, the healing nature of solitude is that "without going outside…you can see the ways of heaven."[17]

We do not need to search the world for answers to the problems we face, for in solitude we nurture our receptivity to the answers available from a wiser, guiding consciousness within. It is necessary to give only the "benefit of the doubt" and to hold a serious intention to receive guidance.

The practice of dreamwork itself is a superb means to draw the experience of solitude into your life. Even the resolve to take our dreams seriously, to read about them, write them down, and reflect upon them is an important way to release distraction, honor solitude, and engage in an act of profound respect for the Source.

Practicing mindfulness of a dream from the previous evening and holding it in awareness is a form of communion with the Source—a way to nurture that quiet inner space from which we receive guidance. Simply setting the intention each evening to receive a guiding dream (incubation) is a form of active communion with the still space of wisdom and solitude within.

However, at the start we must be content with more questions than answers. It is as the poet Rilke implores us:

*Be patient toward all that is unsolved in your heart.*
*And try to love the questions themselves*
*Like locked rooms*
*And like books that are written*
*In a very foreign tongue.*
*Do not seek the answers*
*Which cannot be given you*
*Because you would not be able to live them.*
*And the point is to live everything.*
*Live the questions now.*
*Perhaps you will then gradually*
*Without noticing it, live along*
*Some distant day into the answer.*[18]

At the beginning of our Journey, we are not always called to solitude by our dreams; only if that is what is needed. It may be that we are naturally introverted, exploring our inner life in counseling, or simply practicing meditation. However, once we have created a quiet space of solitude—a space in which to hear, as Emerson says, "the whispers of the gods"[20]—we are often called to release other ego strategies as well. Although there is no set order to the dreams that teach us release, we'll look next at our love of "control."

But before you read on, heighten your consciousness of solitude and distraction with the following practice.

# Practicing Mindfulness of Distraction in Dreams and Everyday Life

To work with your Distraction Dream return now to Chapter 4 and choose one or more of the mindfulness practices described there.

This week, journal about your thoughts of indulging distraction and the ways in which these thoughts and actions create suffering in your life.

- ⅋ Notice how often you engaged in distractions or made plans to distract yourself. Alternatively, notice how often you have embraced solitude during the past week.

- ⅋ Take note of how easy or difficult it is to release the impulse to distract yourself—or to stop and pause long enough to practice solitude.

- ⅋ Reflect on how you would feel if you would allow yourself to simply sit quietly and remain still inside.

- ⅋ Incubate a dream for help in embracing solitude.

# Chapter 6

# Dreams of Control: Nightmares That Teach Us Mindfulness of Humility

*Demand not that events should happen as you wish, but wish them to happen as they do, and you will go on well.*

—Epictetus

*Do not struggle. Go with the flow of things, and you will find yourself at one with the mysterious unity of the Universe.*

—Chuang Tzu

## Our Intent to Control

When we regularly honor solitude in our daily life, we clear a space to experience the sacred. This is a space in which we embrace and nurture a new, more receptive quality of consciousness—one already present within us, but as yet mostly unnoticed. Learning to release distraction is necessary, though not sufficient on our Journey.

A primary block to accessing this expanded consciousness is our intent to control the people and events in our life. Learning to release control is a central tenet in most spiritual practices, and prayer, meditation, and dream-work are the primary methods to assist us in the willing sacrifice of this ego strategy.

In prayer it is often advised that we avoid setting an intention for what we wish to occur, release control, and pray instead for what is in our best interest or the best interest of others. The act of praying correctly is actually a practice in releasing our love of control, surrendering our willfulness, and placing our energy into harmony and alignment with what is possible now in this moment. There is a Chinese parable of a rainmaker told to Carl Jung by his friend and *I Ching* scholar Richard Wilhelm that beautifully illustrates this principle:

> *There was a great drought where Wilhelm lived (Kiao-chau); for months there had not been a drop of rain and the situation became catastrophic. The Catholics made processions, the Protestants made prayers, and the Chinese burned joss-sticks and shot off guns to frighten away the demons of the drought, but with no result.*
>
> *Finally the Chinese said, We will fetch the rain-maker. And from another province a dried-up old man appeared. The only thing he asked for was a quiet little house somewhere, and there he locked himself in for three days. On the fourth day, the clouds gathered and there was a great snow-storm at a time of the year when no snow was expected, an unusual amount, and the town was so full of rumors about the wonderful rainmaker that Wilhelm went to ask the man how he did it.*
>
> *In true European fashion he said, "They call you the rainmaker. Will you tell me how you made the snow?"*
>
> *And the Chinese man said, "I did not make the snow; I am not responsible."*
>
> *"But what have you done these three days?"*
>
> *"Oh I can explain that. I come from another country where things are in order. Here they are out of order. They are not as they should be by the ordinance of heaven. Therefore the whole country is not in Tao, and I also am not in the natural order of things because I am in a disordered country. So I had to wait three days until I was back in Tao and then naturally the rain came."*[1]

In truth, as guru David Hawkins tells us, "We change the world not by what we say or do, but as a consequence of what we have become."[2]

Similarly, the great 19th-century sage Gandhi implored us to "be the change"[3] that we want to see in the world.

As is prayer, dream incubation is grounded in the benefits of releasing control. As you read in Chapter 3, to incubate a dream, we pray or meditate on an open-ended question we wish our dreams to address. The ideal attitude underlying any incubation question is one in which we are saying, "I have no earthly idea how to understand or solve this problem. Please help." In this way whenever we incubate a dream or pray we are practicing the release of control and the mindfulness of humility.

· In our culture, humility is viewed as something akin to a character flaw. The very word itself connotes a kind of self-effacing passivity about which we ought to feel somewhat embarrassed.

To say that a man you know is humble raises for many the specter of someone a bit "broken" or at least ineffectual. Ironically, in most other Eastern and indigenous cultures humility is considered a supreme virtue. The *I Ching* or *Book of Changes* is a compilation of Buddhist, Taoist, and Confucian thought and holds the attitude that humility or modesty is the supreme virtue. Modesty, says the *I Ching*, "is not to be confused with weak good nature that lets things take their own course."[4]

In fact, of the 64 hexagrams in the *Book of Changes* none is considered more auspicious to receive than the hexagram of modesty: "It is the law of heaven to make fullness empty and to make full what is modest; High mountains are worn down by the water and valleys are filled up. It is the law of fate to undermine what is full and to prosper the modest."[5]

The Old and New Testaments of our own past culture view humility in the same positive light. In the Book of Matthew it is said, "And whoever shall exalt himself shall be abased and he that shall humble himself shall be exalted."[6]

Humbling appears to be the driving spirit and central dynamic of Nature. This means that nature works against the arrogant presumption of our ego that we should be in control. In Jungian psychology, fullness is referred to as "ego inflation."

On a very practical level we find repeatedly that our greatest insights come when we successfully release our attempts to be in control through rational analysis. It is commonplace to hear scientists and inventors say that their discovery came when they had virtually given up seeking an answer—"forcing a solution." Indeed, the richness of our culture is due in large part to the epiphanies that artists, researchers, and inventors have experienced in their dreams— when their ego was consigned to a subordinate position in which control was impossible. If you've heard of George Frederick Handel, Richard Wagner, Robert Louis Stevenson, Charlotte and Emily Bronte, René Descartes, Orson Welles, Ingmar Bergman, Elias Howe, James Watt, Billy Joel, D. H. Lawrence, or Dmitri Mendelev, you've heard of people whose amazing works of art, symphonies, and inventions arose from the control-free environment of their nightly dreams. As author and artist Larry Eisenberg said, "For peace of mind, we need to resign as general manager of the universe."[7]

When we engage in control our strategy is to attempt by dint of will alone to create conditions in which we will no longer suffer: "If I don't take charge, nothing will happen." "If I don't convince her to do this, everything will be screwed up." "He's going to change if I have anything to say about it—and that's that!"

Yet we cannot relate to the Source in the same way that we habitually relate to our waking world. To insist on control is to neglect the humility needed to open to the Source and allow ourselves to be led.

To seek control is to insure there will be little help forthcoming, and we slow the progress on our Journey. Equally important, to persist in our worship of control is to contribute to a waking life that feels perpetually frustrating at best, and at worst filled with a nagging sense of inadequacy and failure that we have not succeeded at having the control "we should." "Life is what happens to you," said John Lennon, "when you're busy making other plans."[8]

In the end, we must learn to approach waking life as we approach the Source—with reverence and humility—without rigid plans and controlling agenda. Yet, this is very difficult, because in our culture control is virtually a sacred value worshipped as a way to build self-esteem and receive the admiration and praise of others. We want to control our feelings, the weather, what others think of us, what they buy and wear, how they act, how we act, and how long we can live.

Each day of our life we nurture plans to struggle for what we want, to make things turn out our way, and influence others—forcefully or diplomatically—to achieve the goals we desire. This is the approach our culture sanctions and which we all take for granted as entirely sane. From the moment we awaken we rarely question the need to be feeling on guard, expecting criticism, planning our defense, and feeding our suspicions.

In his poem "What to Remember when Waking," David Whyte prompts us to reflect on what we are missing when we live life in this way:

*In that first*
*Hardly noticed moment*
*In which you wake,*
*Coming back*
*To this life*
*From the other*
*More secret,*
*Moveable*
*And frighteningly*
*honest*
*world*
*where everything*
*began,*
*there is a small*
*opening*
*into the new day*
*which closes*
*the moment*
*you begin*
*your plans.*

*What you can plan*
*is too small*
*For you to live.*

*What you can live*
*Wholeheartedly*
*Will make plans enough*
*For the vitality*
*Hidden*
*In your sleep.*[9]

We lack trust that life will provide us what we need if we don't nurture constant control. Sadly, we no longer have any deep sense of Divine Order, but rather only that order that we ourselves create. We fear that without constant planning and effort chaos will ensue. We believe we have nothing to depend on but our personal will and rationality, our logic, and ourselves.

We want to be the master of our world or, at the very least, to be seen as in control of what happens to us in our lives. When we feel in control, we feel proud of ourselves safe, secure, and successful.

Some of us don't feel comfortable if we appear too controlling and may even loathe the thought that others would see us that way. Consequently, to save face we often choose less-explicit methods to have things the way we want. We may passively resist others' wishes, and find a way to "persuade" people that we are right and that *they* should change" or "dissuade" them from what they intend "for their own good." Even when no one is offended by our controlling ways we must remain mindful and honest with ourselves about our subtle efforts to stay in control.

Perennial traditions have always insisted that our growth depends on surrendering our willfulness. In so doing we practice giving the benefit of the doubt that there is an underlying ground of intelligence and order on which we can stand even more confidently than the fabricated world created by our egos.

Of course this is the reason why AA (Alcoholics Anonymous) and other 12-step programs have been so successful. People who have been addicted to alcohol are able to stop drinking—sometimes for a lifetime—through nurturing a humble attitude toward their Higher Power. Until that time no attempts at control from others, no pleading or tears from friends and loved ones, no loss of job or family, and no psychotherapy can slow their self-destructive plunge. All that is required is to open to the possibility of something greater than one's own ego and, as it is said in the Serenity prayer, "to accept the things I (my ego) cannot change."

It is purely illusion when we think we can change someone else. In my 33 years as a therapist I've never changed anyone. When someone seems to respond to our suggestions, persuasiveness, or superior logic, it seems as if we have influenced him or her, but in truth that person was ready to change and was seeking out the information or perspective we happened to offer. If you hadn't said a word, that person would have soon enough found his or her new direction from another similar source of guidance.

You can know that you are slipping into efforts at control whenever you feel some degree of frustration, tension, or irritation about the person or situation that is resistant to your most heartfelt and "reasonable" attempts at influence. To feel frustrated is to be ego-involved, which means that in some way we have a personal investment in the outcome—perhaps a fear that some harm will result if that person doesn't follow our own vision of what is safest and best for him or her. As human beings it seems impossible to avoid feeling such fears and it is at such times that we take out of our ego's bag of tricks every subtle or not-so-subtle manipulation and demand. But again, the time must be right and the person ready if any change is to occur. We can only hope to be present, to remain open and supportive to the usually small steps of change and growth that we make as human beings. In nature we never expect the seed to blossom before the plant has grown.

Often we attempt to control a relationship because we fear that our own needs won't be met. For example, we may wish to empower our spouse or partner, but withhold our support: "What if she starts to become more independent and spends less time with the children?" "What if he takes this new Journey of his so seriously that he looks for a more fulfilling career and we don't have the income we once did?"

Ironically, the attempt to control others leads us to place limits on our own freedom of action. For example, to avoid more conflict a wife controls her anger and hides her feelings when her husband is upset with her. Eventually she comes to feel stuck in the identity of perpetual victim. What we wish to control ends up controlling us.

Even when we succeed at controlling those around us our success is a pyrrhic and empty victory, as we have created in the other only a mirror of ourselves, and what they do for us is without affection. "The beginning of love," says Christian mystic Thomas Merton, "is to let those we love be perfectly themselves, and not to twist them to fit our own image. Otherwise we love only the reflection of our selves we find in them."[10] A difficult challenge, indeed!

Psychologist Victor Frankel reminds us, "When we are no longer able to change a situation…we are challenged to change ourselves."[11] Yet even efforts to change within are often misguided because they are still based on our ego's value of control—for example, the over-responsible eldest child who wishes to "get better control of herself" and to become "stronger" when she feels she wants to cry. She fears that her vulnerability—the really healthy and authentic part of herself—may show, and she controls it whenever she can.

In Chinese the words *I Ching* mean "the easy way" because the ancient book's central axiom is that we must know and respect the "time" in which we plan to act. When we know the time, we swim with and not against the daily currents of life. This means that for every decision that confronts us we are mindful that, though our goal may be a heartfelt and worthy one, it remains wrong—indeed fraught with obstacles or not possible to achieve at all—if the time for its fulfillment is wrong. As it is said in Ecclesiastes, "To everything there is a season, and a time to every purpose under the heaven."[12] When we act at the right time we never feel as if we are forcing ourselves or others. There is always a sense of the barriers to action simply dissolving.

So although you may not choose to consult the *I Ching* to determine the best time to act, you can learn the language of your dreams, which always indicate whether an action you are taking or plan to take—your intention to take control—is correct for the time and in alignment with your highest interests.

# Nightmares: Dreams of Losing Control

Despite our culture's belief that we can control and rise above nature, our own nature is inextricably and seamlessly woven into the fabric of life on this Earth. We are on this Earth to find our place and role in service of the Natural Order and not as its masters. Indeed in the Natural Order, the time of our Calling is the Autumn time when the control we once seemed to wield in our lives is fast fading and we intuit that this favorite strategy must be released. Sadly we are so identified with our ability to be in control that we feel mortally threatened, hopeless, and unlikely to survive without it. We ask, "Who am I if not someone in control?" Our resistance leads to nightmares in which we experience control slipping fast between our fingers. Yet when we examine each of these Control Dreams with the reflective focus of lunar consciousness, we find that there is a more intelligent and wise source that is leading—working toward what is best for us and our highest interest.

If you look closely at any nightmare, in addition to raw fear you may find elements of multiple ego strategies. For example, in Distraction nightmares the predominant mood or experience is isolation and aloneness, but one might find elements as well of judgment, attachment, or control. Similarly, in Judgment nightmares the predominant experience is that of being chased or attacked, but within such dreams one may easily see evidence of the refusal to grieve characteristic of Attachment nightmares. (See the Predominant Mood and Emotion of Calling and Quest Dreams table on page 87 to review the predominant moods of each dream motif.)

In Control nightmares we find ourselves unable to exercise our will, and we awaken in profound anxiety or fear that we are without any way to save ourselves and about to die. It's important to keep in mind that in nightmares the death we fear is the loss of an ego strategy with which we are completely identified—an approach to life that has become so much a part of how we see ourselves that we think we can't survive or won't exist without it.

> In Control nightmares, the common element is that we have no control, and the predominant experience one of frustration and helplessness.

There are five types of nightmares that prompt us to accept our utter lack of control and push us to surrender in the Autumn time of our Journey. I have named the five types of control nightmares as dreams of:

- Abduction.
- Command.
- Powerlessness.
- Immobilization.
- Looping (moving in circles).

## Abduction Dreams

**Lesson: Trust the Force. You are being guided.**

Remember the old Roman adage you read earlier: In the time of our Calling, "The fates lead those who will and drag those who won't." In dreams of abduction we find ourselves being dragged and carried away against our will, virtually abducted by an impersonal force. In either case the impersonal or alien nature of the abducting force—our Mentor—points to the fact that what is occurring has its source in something neither personal nor familiar—something clearly "other" than our own ego. This is a common theme in fairytales and fables such as *The Wizard of Oz*, wherein a tornado lifts Dorothy straight out of Kansas and drops her off just where she needs to be to learn what she needs to learn. This is a dream mentioned by Campbell in his book, *Hero with a Thousand Faces*:

*I was in a blossoming garden; the sun was just going down with a blood-red glow. Then there appeared before me a black noble knight who spoke to me with a very serious, deep and frightening voice: "Wilt thou go with me?" Without attending my answer he took me by the hand and carried me away.*[13]

Here's another similar example. A woman about to embark on what turned out to be a life-changing experience of psychotherapy dreamed at the beginning of her work:

> I am on a ship and there is no one piloting or navigating. It's dark and the water is rough and choppy. The ship and I are being pulled out to sea by some force that's beyond my control. I don't understand. I wake up sweating and very afraid.

A "lunar" look at the dream shows the woman indeed terrified by her lack of control. However, "upon reflection," the ship is being guided, pulled out to sea, and there is a distinct direction in which the ship is moving—it's not floundering. Within the dream there is no evidence of imminent danger, only the dreamer's presumption that the lack of a human captain (that is, her ego) must be catastrophic. However, the cool light of lunar consciousness tells us that the threat is to our ego strategy—in this case, the wish to be in control—and not our true self. We are not our ego strategies—but we think we are.

## Command Dreams

**Lesson: When the Goddess or God speaks, listen. You are being Called.**

These dreams might be better named "offers we can't refuse." A powerful force or Voice sometimes experienced as "God" makes a suggestion in a way that "leaves us no choice" as to whether we will follow our own will or that of the Divine.

At the start of Section II I shared with you part of a Calling nightmare in which I saw that an entire city around me had been demolished and destroyed—not one brick was left standing or intact, and indeed, that was how I viewed my waking life at the time.

In that dream I spot at my feet the last remaining whole brick in my broken and shattered world. I hold it high over my head, poised to smash it across my knee and add it to the rubble that had become my life. However, the dream goes on when a voice breaks the eerie silence: STOP! DO NOT DO THAT.

For those of you who haven't yet heard that voice, when you hear it, you'll know it—it sounds as no other does. It's a voice that ushers from the marrow of your existence—from before you had a name—a voice to which there is never any possible retort. Sometimes the voice is quiet and resolved, but the simplicity of the words spoken belies the power they carry. In this case its booming bass filled every space in my despairing body. And at once I knew there was a guiding energy—a presence that knew more about this situation than I did. Even though I didn't want to listen in the worst way, to resist the raw power of the Voice would be to try to stop a train speeding full boar down the track.

The healing energy in this Calling dream partly resides in the knowing certainty that comes with the experience of that Voice—the knowing that I am not alone and that there is a future—a plan I am not aware of that awaits me. The Voice shifts my consciousness itself from a paralyzing solar focus on the pervasive external devastation within the dream to a powerful intuition that there is something I don't know, don't understand, and can't control—something that will explain, and make meaning of my suffering, and offer redemption.

When I give the benefit of the doubt to that intuitive hope of redemption, then the scene shifts in accord with that intention. (See Chapter 3.) Now I am with the producer of a public radio show. In waking life I recently have met this woman who asked me if I wanted to host a weekly call-in show on dreams. I had been feeling great reluctance to accept her offer due to my lifelong fear of public speaking. My sister is an amateur actress who has loved the stage since she was a child. As for myself, with each new presentation I scheduled, no matter how small the audience, I would suffer nearly disabling anxiety for weeks beforehand. It was true that my passion in life was dreamwork, and I had no problem leading experiential dream groups. However, in those I rarely gave formal presentations, preferring to teach by example. How could I sit in front of a microphone while thousands of people hung on my every word?

Now in the dream, there she is: the producer, handing me a contract—indeed a narrow rectangular piece of paper suspiciously the size and shape of the one surviving brick I was just holding in my hand a moment before. I take the contract in my hands, ready to politely refuse, perversely proud that I was someone who knew and respected my own limitations. As my public speaking anxiety begins to rise in the dream I am relieved to see that there are few words printed on the contract and I have my excuse. I hand it back, turn my back on her, and begin to walk away when the voice returns: "Sign the contract!" I try to resist and keep walking, but again: "Sign the contract!" I take the contract back, my dream ends—and a new life begins.

I awaken feeling deep in my bones that I am being Called—in this case, to release control—and the devastation in my life has been a lesson in humility for my ego. The fruit of that lesson—the opportunity of a forum to do what I most loved to do. Equally important was the feeling of reverence I experienced for a ground of greater wisdom and guidance, which my proud ego had spurned in favor of having things under my own control.

The show was a great success, and to my amazement I found myself looking forward with excitement to share my knowledge of dreams with thousands of people each week. Once disparaging of extroverted values, I became a devotee of this mode of being in the world and felt at home with myself as never before.

While hosting that call-in radio show, a man shared with me a dream that he had at a time in his life when he knew he was avoiding his lifelong calling to become a minister. Despite the fulfillment it might bring, he saw the ministry as a life of hardship. He felt overwhelmed by the work that it would take to be trained and the financial difficulties entailed by such a life. He dreamed:

> I'm having a wonderful time paddling around in a small, pretty lake playing games in the water with friends. The day starts out delightfully, but after a while clouds start to form on the horizon and move slowly toward us. Soon everything's becoming dark like when a tornado is about to touch down. The water starts to churn and, to get away from the storm, I reluctantly start to climb uphill along the shore of a creek that feeds the lake. As I had hoped, the sky gets lighter and less ominous the farther up I climb. When I look back nostalgically at the beautiful lake, thinking of returning to swim once again, the sky gets very dark again, the wind starts to whip up, and the lake waters become even rougher. I'm very frightened and then a voice—clearly God's voice—booms out "DO AS YOU ARE CALLED TO DO." I awaken in terror. However, as I reflect on the nightmare I'm in awe that God has spoken to me! I realize that I really must give up my fantasy of the "easy life," stop paddling around, and pursue my life's passion.

## Powerlessness Dreams

**Lesson: "The best laid plans of mice and men oft go astray." When the time is not right, action is useless.**

In these dreams we have a clear goal in mind, we know what we want, and we believe that we know how to achieve it. However, in dreams of powerlessness we find ourselves trying to achieve these goals but failing miserably. In fact, the failure is experienced in the form of emotional or physical pain, or alternatively as extraordinary frustration that leaves our sense of control devastated and we have no choice but to surrender. In every case we feel our ego's lack of control as an utterly devastating powerlessness without hope or remedy of any kind. We are perhaps most familiar with these dreams in their more benign and less frightening form in the time of our Quest: It seems as if most people I've talked to have had this kind of dream in which, for example, we are trying to run from a situation and find ourselves moving in slow motion "like in molasses" or unable to move at all. Alternatively, we are attempting to drive to an appointment and end up lost or back where we started, unable to get through to someone on the phone, unable to hear the operator or she won't put us through, and so on.

In all these cases the strategy we have chosen to solve our problem is experienced in our dream as ineffective and we feel immensely frustrated and helpless. The reason for our "failure" in every case is that our ego's plan is the wrong one for the situation or for the time in which we are acting. Contrary to what Freud has said, dreams only fulfill our wishes when what we desire is in our best interests.

Let's look now though at the same principle at work in nightmares. There is only one difference in these dreams versus the previously discussed Quest dreams of lacking control: The greater degree of fear present in our Calling dreams is due to the greater resistance our ego experiences about having to release control in the time of our Calling.

Tony, a client of mine who was admittedly "headstrong" and stubbornly resistant to his wife's direct pleas for greater sensitivity and support, described himself as "getting way too angry" at her and rarely allowing her to point him in a new direction. This is his dream of powerlessness:

> I'm driving down a road at 125 mph. Suddenly I lose complete control and my car veers off the road and we crash in an inferno. I wake up in shock.

We often awaken from such dreams resolved to get our life "back in control." But these nightmares are not counseling us to develop better control. Rather, they are stories of how our attempts to be *in control* are reckless and leading to great danger in our life. Our desperate need is not to regain control, but to practice mindfulness of humility—to learn to follow instead of lead. As you read earlier, in Jungian jargon, we say that we have become "inflated" with power when we become too identified with control—acting as if we can do whatever we want when we want and as fast as we want. Our ego is drunk on control, driving recklessly down a dead-end road, and the end is near.

Practicing mindfulness always means giving attention to life-sustaining values, and Tony's behavior in the dream has none of these. A side note: After we discussed his dream, Tony became aware, as never before, of the destructive path of control he was traveling in life. In fact, upon reflection he felt much fear about losing a precious relationship with his wife if he continued to revel in control. Had he felt this grief in his dream, we would have understood it as an Attachment nightmare, prompting him to let go of his identity or attachment to the macho image of a man in control. However, in Tony's dream, the only conscious experience was one of devastating helplessness and frustration as he careened off the road. This was exactly the medicine he needed. Before he could yield to grief and letting go, Tony needed to experience the futility of control in a way so undeniable that he would consider releasing—and grieving for—this very favorite strategy of his.

A client, Janine, began therapy by sharing the story of an acutely painful childhood, being raised by a mother who was extraordinarily detached emotionally from Janine and deeply jealous of her daughter's close bond with her own mother—Janine's grandmother. In contrast with Janine's disorganized, sloppy, and negligent mother, her grandmother modeled a compulsive degree of organization, neatness, and rigid rule-keeping. At the end of the night even her dog had learned to sit up on its haunches at the side of the bed with its paws together in prayer. It was no surprise that Janine felt deeply cared-for by her grandmother who, in contrast to her mother, paid so much attention to the details of her life. Over time of course, Janine's self-esteem came to be based on her ability to live an orderly and clean life. Most of her energy each day was consumed by her efforts to keep her house clean and spotless. Rarely could she enjoy guests that visited, as she worried before, during, and after these visits about the cleanliness of her home. It was no surprise then that one of the first dreams Janine shared with me was this Control nightmare of Powerlessness:

I am walking out of my house toward my car, intending to get some errands done. As I turn the corner I see a very dark-skinned man inside my car laughing out loud as he throws very black dirt all over and inside my brand-new car. I tell him to stop over and over again, but he won't listen and, in fact, laughs even louder. I'm horrified and wake up.

When she told me this dream a week later she was still upset as we began to unfold her Dream Mentor's message about the benefits of relaxing control, laughing, and playing in the dirt as we love to do in childhood—before we develop the deadening rules and strategies needed to feel loved in one's family. A side note: In the next chapter you'll learn that Dreams of Judgment are defined by our perception that a Dream Mentor is attacking or chasing the dreamer with the intent to harm her. The main mood is fear. In Janine's dream she certainly sees the dark man as threatening, if not attacking, her property. However, the main mood of her dream is that of helplessness and frustration as she demands "again and again" that the man stop what he is doing. Even in the telling of her dream she emphasizes her anger—not fear—about the arrogance with which he laughs at her.

You'll hear more about Janine's success in releasing control and finding compassion for her own suffering in later chapters.

Betty, a woman with whom I worked in therapy, lived in anger at her cold, rejecting mother and wished her mother would finally die and leave her alone. She woke up very frightened from this dream of impotence:

My mother has died and I am working hard on the funeral plans. I make a list of family and friends to notify. I contact the funeral parlor and arrange for the kind of coffin that will be used and the time of the funeral. I've decided on what I'll say to the mourners and what songs will be sung. Though I'm not a musician, I even compose a dirge to be played at the end of the funeral. I finish the dirge just in time for the start of the funeral. I walk up to my mother's open casket to say my "goodbyes" and look inside. At first she seems in peace, but then she opens her eyes, looks at me and smiles. I wake up with my heart pounding and in a sweat.

Initially deeply disturbed by this dream, Betty realized upon reflection that the "best laid plans of mice and men oft go astray." As much as she may have wished for her mother's early demise, and for freedom from her cold, critical grip, the time of the Calling for Betty required that she first release her own grip on the wish to control.

With perseverance she could indeed find freedom from the oppressive relationship with her mother. This occurs not by wishing for the control to plan her death, but through the profound healing that comes when we accept that those we perceive as our enemies are the greatest teachers on our spiritual path. In Betty's case the gift she received from her very controlling mother—her Dream Mentor—was the importance of releasing control. Betty had been telling herself that she just wasn't going to let herself be upset anymore and had to take matters into her own hands. She was done with the relationship, would cut herself off from her mother, and didn't need to continue therapy. Reflecting upon her dream, she realized that if the image of her mother smiling alive and well, could cause such fear, then she needed a more compassionate attitude to heal her remaining wounds—not more control over her mother. She found the humility to follow guidance, remained in therapy, and continued on her path of healing.

Contrary to Freud's notion that our dreams are simply wish fulfillments, dreams of Powerlessness teach us that the Divine gives little weight even to our most heartfelt desires if they serve our ego's needs. Betty's dream is a nightmare because in waking life she is strongly identified with the intention to control. The fear she experiences at the end of the dream reflects her intense resistance to releasing this intention and the terror we—our ego—always feel when our greatest act of resistance fails.

Rita's problem was quite the opposite of Betty's. Her husband had physically abused Rita for many years. When he fell ill and died unexpectedly, she was immensely relieved, but very ashamed that she felt so good about his passing. Her very conservative religious upbringing contributed to her feelings of shame, as did the flood of hostile thoughts toward him that she was now entertaining even as he lay cold in the ground. She wished, indeed prayed, for memories that would transform her anger into feelings of love for this man. This was the nightmare dream of Powerlessness that called her to release control:

I am carrying a huge bouquet of beautiful flowers to my husband's grave. I place them on his tombstone and make it quite beautiful. I pray to simply love him and forget the past abuse. Suddenly, the sun is gone and it's getting darker and the wind begins to blow—I mean like a hurricane. My husband's tombstone and the beautiful flowers I have laid on it are blown away.

Rita was frightened and very shaken by this dream. It's not that the Divine is opposed to our love and compassion for those who have hurt us—quite the contrary. Rather, Rita's problem lay in the fact that she wanted to use "love" to forget and deny the painful reality of her past relationship—and learn nothing from her suffering. From the point of view of the Source, this is just another example of how we think we can control reality and shape it into what we want it to be. The same impersonal force of Nature or Mentor we saw in the dreams of Abduction and Command manifests as a storm that blows away the flowers and all that is not in our higher interest—in this case her intention to remain in control.

## Immobilization Dreams

**Lesson: You are being restrained for your own good. Reflect on your wish to escape and allow yourself to be led.**

These nightmares are very common, if not universal. Generally they include the experience of trying to escape but being unable to move or take some desired action. The lesson here as in all dreams of Immobilization and Paralysis is that we are not meant to be in control and that our strategy for "getting away" from what frightens us is the problem. Thus we are not merely frustrated in our effort to flee, but kept from moving altogether.

Remember Mike (from Chapter 5), who discovered the importance of living in the "cave" and releasing distraction? Sometime later he dreamed that he was in a room high up in a castle-like building: An archer is shooting arrows at him as he stands backed against a wall. He resists mightily as each arrow pins him tighter to the wall. Though he feels no pain where each arrow enters his body, Mike does feel increasing anxiety as he realizes that the last arrow will pierce his forehead and fully immobilize him. The arrow hits its mark.

Notably, Mike's last memory is that his head is held in such a position that he has no choice but to stare out the small window in front of him. What he is made to see out this window is a beautiful, lush green landscape of rolling hills.

When we explored Mike's associations to this scene he acknowledged that despite his new emphasis on creating solitude in his life, he continued to work long hours and took little time to relax and enjoy life. The green, rolling hills evoked for Mike just such an experience of relaxation and much-needed escape from the world of work.

This is a classic example of how such frightening experiences as Immobilization in our dreams serve to get our attention—make us look at what is needed—when all else fails.

Consider the fascinating case of President Lyndon Johnson, whose dreams arguably led to the end of the Vietnam War. Johnson's biographer, Doris Kearns Goodwin, has written about a number of the president's dreams.[14] She describes how Johnson would come to visit her each morning at 5:30 a.m., and while she sat at the window seat he would climb into her bed in his robe and pajamas, snuggle up under the covers and reminisce about his life.

The president recounted to her a number of recurring nightmares about immobilization and paralysis beginning in his childhood, when he would dream of sitting paralyzed while a herd of cattle stampeded toward him. Later, as president, his dream paralysis became immobilization, and he found his legs shackled with heavy chains to his Oval Office chair when he wanted to leave work after signing a stack of mail. He then resigned himself to signing more mail. If those were my dreams, I would want to consider the common thread or theme in which I am trying unsuccessfully and without hope to escape from a situation. In the first dream, perhaps there is a virtual stampede of collective opinion that I need to honor and acknowledge rather than to run from. In the second, I may be wanting to avoid or escape from the task of responding to those who seek my opinions and thoughts, and from the perspective of my dream or Source, this would be very unwise—and is not permitted.

Then, after the infamous Tet Offensive in Vietnam, Johnson dreamed of himself in the paralyzed body of Woodrow Wilson—immobilized and without a voice. Profoundly frightened by this recurring nightmare, he would leave his bed and walk the dark halls of the White House with a flashlight until he came to Woodrow Wilson's portrait, which he would touch to reassure himself that it was Wilson who was dead and incapable of movement—not himself.

Typical of these dreams, we may awaken feeling inadequate, and interpret such experiences from our ego's point of view as a confirmation of the need to be more assertive and in control. However, the message from the Source is quite to the contrary. We require more humility and deference. For example, there was likely a hidden gift in Johnson's dream of being in Woodrow Wilson's paralyzed body. At the time of the dream, his war was failing, and Johnson found himself truly ineffective and impotent in his efforts. If that were my dream I would want to ask myself: Is there a way in which I need to learn from someone—in this case, my Dream Mentor—who had a life experience similar to mine? Is there a way in which President Wilson effectively dealt with his physical paralysis and lack of influence that would help me in this situation? For example, Wilson may have succeeded by being more yielding or by having a finer sense of "when to hold them and when to fold them." Perhaps President Johnson needed to see him as a model of someone who could succeed well in life and effectively exercise power while accepting major limitations in his ability to be in full control and to do everything he wanted.

No dream implies that we are truly impotent. It is just that our ego strategy is impotent and doomed to fail—and we are not our ego. When we persist in the arrogant attitude of forcing our will to achieve something not in our best interests or when the time is not right for action, the Source literally straps us down, paralyzes, and immobilizes us.

## Looping Dreams

**Lesson: When going around in circles, consider stopping. Ask for directions and a better map.**

President Johnson also experienced another similar kind of Control nightmare in the form of a Looping dream that probably had major consequences for all of us.

Looping dreams occur when we persist in a course of action that is unproductive or objectively impossible to achieve. In these dreams we experience ourselves in an endless loop, the Divine's way of implying that our wish for control is causing us to "go around in circles" or "spin our wheels" endlessly. In dreams of powerlessness we may end up where we started, but in looping dreams we end up back where we started over and over again, without end—and so it was for Lyndon Johnson.

As the war casualties continued to mount he dreamed that he was struggling to swim from the center of a river toward one shore and then the other—

failing every time. He finally realized that he was going in an endless circle. Soon after this dream Johnson accepted that he could not survive the stampede of opposition to his policies and concluded that by imposing his will at all costs he could expect to swim only in endless circles and accomplish nothing. His subsequent withdrawal from office led to an even greater groundswell of popular opposition and the beginning of the end of that impossible and tragic war. Makes one wonder how history might be affected if all our presidents listened to their dreams.

We also have Looping dreams that seem less dramatic than Johnson's, but which can still have a major impact on our lives. For example, my friend Tim, who insisted on staying in his stressful profession long after it stopped offering any real benefits for his life, dreamed:

> I'm a jogger running on an indoor track. I'm getting tired and look for the door to leave. I'm getting more and more exhausted, but for some reason I keep running around the track. I can't stop. I finally wake up really scared and in a panic.

Looping dreams are a message from the Source encouraging us not only to know, but also to "experience" the futility of our course of action. Tim was now able to "experience" the real suffering in his life caused by staying in a job that "was going nowhere." Remaining in his fruitless job provided Tim with a sense of control over all the possible things that "might" go wrong if he quit. But having become more aware of the suffering he imposed on himself by holding on to control, he accepted guidance from his dream, stopped running in circles, and searched in earnest for a new kind of work.

# The Healing Power of Control Dreams: An Overview

The predominant mood and imagery of Control dreams reflects frustration, immobilization, powerlessness, stubbornness, and at times, arrogant efforts to manipulate others.

When we pause and reflect on Control nightmares their message is clear: Give up your striving for control and understand that your goals are not necessarily those of the Source. In the time of the Calling the goals and values we once found worthy are, from the point of view of the Source, no longer helpful or even healthy for us to retain.

In the stillness and quiet of inner solitude we must release control, humbly open to and call forth guidance. We can meditate, pray, consult oracles, or learn the language of our dreams to understand what we are called to do—and when. However, we must be willing to view our lack of control not as failure, but as the first sign that the Source has other plans.

> We are not asked to accept a life of floundering, only to release enough control that we may be led.

The wisest approach is always to swim with the current, not flail uselessly against it. As was the case with the woman whose abduction dream placed her on a boat without a captain, we are called to step up to the helm, and give the benefit of the doubt that we are in the safe hands of an intelligence greater than our own. As it has been said, we may not be able to change the direction of the wind, but we can control the setting of the sails.

# Practicing Mindfulness of Control in Dreams and Everyday Life

To work with your Control dream return now to Chapter 4 and choose one or more of the mindfulness practices described there.

This week journal about your thoughts of indulging control and the ways in which these thoughts and actions create suffering in your life.

- Notice how often you made plans this past week to control others. This includes trying to change others' minds, influence them to accept your perspective, do what you think is in their best interest, and so on. Alternatively, notice how often you have embraced humility and listened for that quiet voice of guidance during the past week.

- Take note of how easy or difficult it is to release the impulse to take control—or to stop and pause long enough to practice humility and follow guidance.

- Incubate a dream for help in embracing humility.

# Chapter 7

## Dreams of Judgment: Nightmares That Teach Us Mindfulness of Compassion

*I dreamed I had a child, and even in the dream I saw it was my life, and it was an idiot, and I ran away. But it always crept on to my lap again, clutched at my clothes. Until I thought, if I could kiss it, whatever in it is my own, perhaps I could sleep. And I bent to its broken face, and it was horrible—but I kissed it. I think one must finally take one's life in one's arms.*

—Arthur Miller from *After the Fall*

*There is no rule more invariable than that we are paid for our suspicions by finding what we suspect.*

—Thoreau

## Our Intent to Judge

"I shall tell you a great secret, my friend," wrote famed existentialist Albert Camus. "Do not wait for the last judgment, it takes place every day."[1]

The intention to judge is ever-present when we interact with others—no matter whether friend or foe. We judge how people believe, speak, look, act, and laugh. We judge their political party, their clothing, their hair (today), their color, their height, and their weight (as it surely will increase if they keep eating that way). They're probably too smart for their own good, probably too beautiful to have brains, too ugly to have so many dates, no doubt too good to be true. We are even less kind to ourselves.

Make a mental count today of how many mean and judgmental things you say about yourself. After you're done, ask yourself whether you'd ever talk that way to your children or lover.

How long would you keep a friend who spoke to you that way, even half the time? No matter how hurtful our secret assessments of others, they rarely hold a candle to the cruelty we reserve for ourselves.

We say its impossible not to judge, but that's because we confuse discernment with judgment. "To observe without evaluating is the highest form of intelligence," says Indian scholar and sage J. Krishnamurti.[2] I may discern that artists are a different breed, but it takes judgment to weed them out as my friends. Discernment is a perception about the qualities of a person or thing. Judgment is a decision, an assessment about whether to accept or reject another based on what we've discerned. The problem is, as Mother Teresa has said, "If you judge someone, you have no time to love them."[3]

The world around us is nothing if not infinitely diverse, but it is so difficult to love diversity—to accept others because of all that makes them unique rather than despite what makes them different. Most of all we find it so difficult to love what is unique in ourselves. Our past wounds and rejections dog us every day as we compare ourselves with others and find ourselves lacking. More importantly, we're taught that there is little compassion in life, and what there is should usually go toward others' suffering, not our own.

We fear selfishness as we would the plague. The result is that we treat ourselves as the hanging judges of the Old West. We ask ourselves, "Did I do it—or not?" "Hang 'em!" (See Section II for a more in-depth discussion of self-caring versus selfishness.)

And so it goes that what we secretly reject in ourselves, we see and despise in others—whether present or not.

If I've had to deny my needs as a child raised in an uncaring alcoholic family, then I may well find those of you who think its okay to have whatever you want to be, really quite selfish. People like you are so "entitled." Why don't you act the way responsible adults do and think about other people for a change?!

Similarly, if I grew up feeling guilt that my anger would hurt my sensitive mother, then I may believe that most people are (as is my bad self) too aggressive and hurtful. As the Hebrew Talmud reminds us: "We do not see things as they are. We see them as we are."[4] The problem is within—just the place that we last think to look.

It wasn't only Jesus who warned us about the problems of judgment. Most wisdom traditions recognize this profound truth. Listen to the Buddha as he speaks to his disciple Ananda in the Anguttara Nikaya of the *Pali Canon*: "The results of karma cannot be known by thought, and so should not be speculated about. ...Therefore, Ananda, do not be the judge of people; do not make assumptions about others. A person is destroyed by holding judgments about others."[5]

Perennial wisdom suggests that in the place of judgment we honor our interconnectedness, to see others in ourselves and to everything say, "I am that." In Jesus' famed words, "Truly, I say to you as you did it to one of the least of these my brethren, you did it to me."[6]

Perhaps, suggests Sage Neem Karoli Baba, "It is better to see God in everything than to try and figure it out."[7] Or as poet and mystic Kabir says, "As the river surrenders itself to the ocean what is inside me moves inside you."[8]

However, in our culture's love of dualistic thinking and in its conviction about the fundamental split between man, God, and nature, it's difficult for us to accept the notion that we are all one. Embracing this reality presents a most difficult challenge.

> The ground of our own suffering is the breeding ground of projection—that universal habit of hating in others what we can't stand—and won't look at in ourselves.

How do we learn to love our enemy? How do we withdraw our projections?

This is the task psychologists term *shadow work*. Unfortunately, shadow work has been widely misunderstood to imply coming to terms with the negative—or even evil—within us. Rather, the perennial philosophy is one of the "pearl in the mud," and holds that we are born innocent and later learn the habits of mind and attitudes—ego strategies—that create

> How do we experience the common ground of life we share with others when it is so difficult to stop disliking them—so hard to acknowledge as our own what we loathe in them?

the "mud," cast the shadow, and cloud the perception of our true unblemished nature. The perennial spiritual lesson is that the entire world—all of creation—"the very least of us"—is part of the same divine source. The demons that we see residing in our psyche are just the ephemeral shadows we ourselves cast upon its depths by our own self-critical attitudes. As Gandhi has said, "The only devils in this world are those running around inside our own hearts, and that is where all our battles should be fought." [9]

To work on our "shadow" simply means to discover how our judgmental thoughts and intentions create our own darkness—emptied of the light of compassion. Buddha's words mentioned earlier bear repeating: "You yourself as much as anybody in the entire universe deserve your love and affection." [10]

Until we do that shadow work, however, we continue to judge, and it is this intention perhaps more than any other that creates the dark veil of illusion that separates and alienates us from the world around us.

Whenever we judge any part of creation, including ourselves, as unacceptable or unworthy, we create a hard shell or wall between ourselves and others. In this way we close ourselves off from the flow of vital heart energy—the compassion that is the Grail on our Journey. Dreamwork and shadow work serve the same goal—all bring light to the darkness that we create through our judgment and other misguided ego strategies.

Put simply: To release judgment we must practice mindfulness of compassion. This is the message of our most popular fairytales and fables—stories that would be nightmares if we dreamed them. Think of all the tales in which the hero or heroine is called to love something ugly or repulsive. How about *Beauty and the Beast*, in which Beauty kisses and embraces the beast? In every case, when the hero or heroine fully accepts what appears repulsive—finds compassion for what is suffering—it transforms into a prince or princess—something of inestimable value. As poet Rainer Maria Rilke said:

> *We have no reason to harbor any mistrust against our world, for it is not against us. If it has terrors, they are our terrors. If it has abysses, these abysses belong to us. If there are dangers, we must try to love them…then what now*

*appears to us to be alien will become our most intimate and trusted experience. How could we forget those ancient myths that stand at the beginning of all races—the myths about dragons that at the last moment are transformed into princesses. Perhaps all the dragons in our lives are only princesses waiting for us to act, just once, with beauty and courage. Perhaps everything that frightens us is, in its deepest essence, something helpless that wants our love.*[10]

The message is clear: If we expect to find our princess or prince—that is, if we expect to change our lives for the better—we must stay mindful that the Mentors who seem in our dreams so frightening to our egos, actually offer us the compassion we most need for our suffering at this moment in our Journey—and in turn they need our embrace.

# Finding the Healing Medicine in Your Judgment Nightmares

Nightmares are among our most transformative dreams, so it's incumbent upon us to know the most fruitful way to work with them. Our Journey is the journey of the heart so knowledge and education won't take you far. But knowing how to transform our fears does help to mitigate them.

Judgment nightmares are often particularly harrowing, as their hallmark is the experience of being chased or attacked. But don't let your fear, terror, or disgust steer you away from learning the lesson of compassion such dreams offer. There is always, without exception, a pearl in the mud.

This means that the man who keeps chasing you in that recurrent dream wants your attention and has something to offer you—an experience—so important that he simply won't quit trying.

Therefore, when a Dream Mentor at first feels too threatening or repulsive to let yourself embrace, ask instead, "If I had to say—upon pain of death—what good this

> As you learned earlier, it is a central tenet of Mindful Dreaming that we view each Dream Mentor—no matter how repulsive or threatening to our waking life ego—as the bearer of a profound gift of healing.

disgusting, frightening, character embodies, what would it be?" Or ask, "In moderation what good might there be in experiencing life as this character does?"

For example, a friend of mine, Sam, felt that his life was suffocating due to the many rules laid down by his authoritarian father. He dreamed repeatedly of being chased by a psychopath whom he was sure was going to kill him. First Sam felt too terrified of his Mentor to feel comfortable experiencing his world through the psychopath's eyes. So he asked himself what the good part of living as a psychopath might be (in moderation). The answer came quickly: "I get to do whatever I want to do." Aha! The Mentor pursuing him embodied an experience of feeling free to do as one wants. This idea seemed great and relevant in the context of his smothering relationship with his father. Yet no matter how great this insight was, it didn't amount to an actual full-bodied experience.

To deepen the healing experience offered by his psychopathic Dream Mentor, Sam used Jung's method of Active Imagination. (See the instructions for this and similar techniques at the end of Chapter 2.) He allowed himself first to imagine being in the Mentor's body. He gave a voice to his psychopathic Mentor by writing a question to him in his journal: "Why are you treating me this way?" (An even better, less judgmental question is: "What have you come to teach me?") After writing down his question, he set the intention not to edit or judge whatever he was about to hear.

Sam closed his eyes, breathed deeply and slowly, and for a moment, allowed himself to "feel into" the experience of merging and living inside that Dream Mentor's body, only to hear the "psychopath" say, "Find joy and pleasure right now. Don't waste a beautiful life in prison with your father."

Hearing these words and literally feeling the compassionate energy of his Dream Mentor, Sam felt a new flow of life-giving energy throughout his body—an energy needed to get out from under the suffocating, oppressive rules that governed his every action in life—to do more of what he wanted to do. It's one thing to think that freedom feels good and another to feel free! Of course, it is this same freedom that his ego viewed correctly as a mortal threat to its rules. And so it is that with our sincere embrace our most demonic and reviled Mentors transform into angels.

Just as some people think of such images as mere metaphor, others say a dream Mentor embodies an old memory. In this case, that old memory is of being liberated. People very often have such memories, and it's extremely helpful to remember back to a time implied by your dream when life felt more whole. For example, if the psychopath in your own dream was 20 years old, it is more than likely that this was the last time in your life that you felt so free. Alternatively, it may have been 20 years ago. In either case, allow yourself to *experience* once again how you felt at that age.

The essential act in Mindful Dreaming is not to "recall," but to grant ourselves permission to be our Dream Mentor and to re-experience his or her perspective. And in judgment dreams, despite the fearful visage of your Mentors, their perspective is always a deeply compassionate one.

Most of us are familiar with the premise of acupuncture as a technique for curing illness by restoring the flow of vital *chi* energy. Mindful dreamwork has an effect similar to acupuncture or to shamanic healing methods. The Shaman views the absence of such life energy as "soul loss" and works to retrieve that part of the soul. We do the same when we embrace the frightful Mentors in our Judgment dreams—by experiencing life through their eyes we retrieve and "re-claim" their perspective as having always been our own. In this way we taste firsthand the fruit of compassion for our greatest wounds.

There are two types of Judgment nightmares: Chase dreams and Attack dreams. We'll begin by exploring Chase dreams.

## Chase Dreams

Your Calling is a time when solar consciousness amplifies fear and dread in proportion to the many possibilities it draws into its glaring light. (See Section II for a review of solar and lunar consciousness.) Indeed, I've heard numerous judgment nightmares and frightening dreams recounted with attention locked and focused in a narrow, solar way on the threat experienced. In these dreams solar consciousness blinds us to what are almost always extremely powerful healing images subsequent to the threat at the very end of the dream.

> Think right now about some frightening Dream Mentor of your own and consider for yourself what good that person or animal might bring to your life if you shared their energy or perspective *in moderation.*

Here's a characteristic example of a dialogue I had with a woman in a dreamsharing group about her nightmare. In her dream she was being chased by a witch-like woman, whom she was certain wanted to kill her: "All I remember," said Anne, "is that I woke up with my heart pounding and with this horrible sinking feeling."

I asked her if she would tell me the last image she recalled. I always ask this question about every dream, but it's especially important in nightmares because in our fear we frequently ignore that final detail. Ironically, the final image in our nightmares, particularly Judgment dreams, is the exact medicinal experience we are needing in this present moment of our life. "Well," she said, "I ran into this attic and then that's where I woke up." I asked Anne if the attic was frightening too.

"No," she said. "Actually it was where I used to play as a child. Those were some of the best times of my life. It was when I could go and just completely relax, play, and be creative, and no one would laugh at me."

An axiom of Mindful Dreamwork is that in Judgment nightmares our Dream Mentors always chase or point us to what it is we most need. I asked Anne what was most needed right now in her life.

"Well, all I do these days for the last two or three years now," she said, "is work. I can't even relax. So yes, having playtime and getting back to all the things that I used to have so much fun at and love would be great. The image of my attic brings that all back to me and sums it up perfectly. Now I understand why she chased me there. I guess she's just going to stay a witch until she feels like she has a life!"

Anne then added, "But it's scary for me to let go and relax. I'm always feeling afraid that I'll go overboard with it—you know, play too much and then all hell will break loose and I'll probably be fired and won't be able to support myself." This is a very frequent phenomenon that arises when we work with nightmares, because they evoke in us not only an image of the medicinal experience we need—in Anne's case, the benefits of play and creativity, but also the fear we feel about that change ("I'll probably be fired."). When you think about it, why else would we have to be terrorized and chased into doing what we most need?

Recall a dream of your own in which you ran from or were chased to some old or new location. Ask yourself how the experience of being in that place might be medicinal.

## Attack Dreams

You've just read an example of one type of Judgment dream in which we find ourselves being chased. The second very common Judgment motif are themes of perceived attack. The attack may come in any manner, but not infrequently it's in the form of an encounter with an intruder. Often the intruder doesn't act in a directly aggressive way. Our presumption of attack lies in the fact that someone or something has crossed a threshold into our personal space—as when we dream that a person is breaking into our house.

For example, a few years ago my friend Bill, who was a rather laissez-faire and laid-back businessperson, considered how it might help to tighten up the rules with his employees and develop a more traditional approach to doing business. He hadn't been "putting his all" into the business for some time. "Mind you," Bill said, "I probably won't even do it, because that's just not me. You know—too high-powered and slick for my tastes."

The next day he called me to ask about the nightmare he had. The dream was quite simple:

> I'm sitting in my living room and I hear noise at the front door. I get up to see who's there and a man has already walked into the foyer. As soon as I see him I know he's up to no good and is going to hurt me. I'm almost paralyzed—like you know how you get in nightmares?! Anyway I try to scream at him to get out but nothing comes out of my mouth. I wake up really terrified.

Dreams of attack, as all nightmares, are frightening because in the dream we actually feel that our life is threatened in that very moment. Yet as you've read, the problem is that we confuse our ego identity with our greater self—our waking life role with our true Self or Being. "The mask given time," says author Marguerite Yourcenar, "comes to be the face itself."[12]

And what is it that makes us feel on the verge of annihilation? Something new breaking into our conscious awareness, something our ego judges as alien—as Bill said, something that's "just not me." And in Bill's dream the something new is not even waiting at the door to be invited in. It's here in the present moment. I asked Bill to describe the man. "That's the funny thing about it," he said. "The guy was wearing an Armani suit. Really dressed to the hilt."

"Well, Bill, if you were wearing that suit, how would you describe the experience?"

"Ha! I'd be the consummate businessman!" he blurted out. "That's horrible! I told you I'm really not comfortable with being that kind of person."

As you've read, our challenge is to remember that all dream figures are our Mentors and all offer the gift of healing experience. Due to his conscious repulsion about being a slick businessman, I asked Bill to consider a different perspective:

"If you had to say something positive about wearing that Armani—if only in moderation—what would it be?"

He paused for a few moments. "Well, actually it would be a kind of good feeling. I'm surprised. Its like I'm really confident—no, actually, more than that—competent. I guess it boils down to feeling more respect for myself."

Bill understood right away that the dream wasn't prescribing a new wardrobe. Nor was his Armani Dream Mentor a "symbol" in Bill's psyche. Rather, he was an image of the experience Bill had dreamed that night—a much-needed experience of self-respect and competence that his ego had been judging as "too high-powered and slick." Though some businesspeople do act that way, *in moderation* these were just the attitudes of confidence, competence, and self-respect that Bill needed to embrace. And to do so was to act with compassion for the suffering his ego's limited perspective on the topic had created.

Notice that our dreams do not require us to "reinvent the wheel." Bill did not have to "figure out" how to become more confident. He merely had to be willing to override his ego's rules and re-enter or re-embrace the experience evoked by his Dream Mentor's clothing—to "let that in the door" of consciousness not with fear, but with gratitude for his Mentor's compassionate and healing gift.

Finally, recall that when his Mentor walked in the door of his home, Bill tried to get him to leave by screaming, but "couldn't say a word." That's a very common experience many of us have known in a dream. As you learned in Chapter 6, whenever we attempt to take an action in a dream but fail, it's because the control we seek is not in our best interest. Our discussion of Bill's dream makes that quite clear.

Yet Bill's helplessness and frustration—his "lack of control," loss of voice, and "paralysis" in this dream—is not the predominant experience. The predominant experience is the perception of attack by someone whom Bill assumes would hurt him: "As soon as I see him I know he's up to no good and is going to hurt me." There is a presumption of malevolence or evil in Judgment dreams that is not present in dreams of Control.

In Control dreams the primary focus is on how we are frustrated and feel ineffectual in doing what we desire, whereas in Judgment dreams the focus is on the perception of malevolence or evil from which we may not be able, or permitted, to protect ourselves. In Bill's case he first perceives a man who embodies an alien energy of competence and confidence—an attitude about power that he judges as a "bad thing"—a threat to his identity as a laid-back, easygoing, nice guy. That presumption of evil is Bill's motive for attempting to force him out of the house. If someone who seemed similar to himself had walked in the front door, Bill wouldn't have tried to make him leave. The fact that he couldn't force the man out and had no "control" is simply another tip that, despite his resistance, what is occurring is indeed in Bill's best interest.

To identify the lesson in mindfulness that your Dream Mentor is teaching, always consider the most powerful emotion or mood in your dream. (See the Predominant Mood and Emotion of Calling and Quest Dreams table on page 87 for a review of dream moods associated with lessons in mindfulness.)

Here's another brief example of an attack dream shared by my client Charles, an intellectual man and academic who over-relied on his intellect as a source of self-esteem and worth, and who was burning out under the pressures he placed on himself to meet deadlines and produce. This is his dream:

> I'm on a college campus and I've just left class, carrying all of my books and papers. Suddenly a huge, foreign-looking man comes out of no-where and tackles me, knocking me to the ground, where I end up rolling on the grass. Before I even get up I see that half of my books and papers are missing. I wake up really scared and upset.

When I asked Charles about the last image he saw in his dream and what importance it might have for him, he said, "That's easy. I saw the green grass I'd been rolling in. It's weird but it takes me back to when I was a kid and when I would lay back on the grass in the summertime, watch the clouds, and just relax without any pressures or deadlines."

Charles was able to see clearly at that moment that his Dream Mentor had tackled him not as a punishment, but as a means to provide him with the medicine of "rolling around" in the summer grass of his childhood once again. To make a space for this experience in his life, however, he would have to lose, so to speak "half of his books and papers."

# The Healing Power of Judgment Dreams: An Overview

The predominant mood and imagery of Judgment dreams is that of fearfulness, perceived attack, desire to escape, mistrust, and the perception of malevolence in others. In these dreams there is one simple story: We are good people protecting ourselves from bad people. Yet, as Longfellow reminded us: "If we could read the secret history of our enemies, we should find in each person's life, sorrow and suffering enough to drain all hostilities."[13]

Dreams of judgment call us to withdraw our projections and find the offending attitude within ourselves—within the shadow of our own consciousness. More radical yet, we are asked to embrace this once cast-out part with compassion—to "kiss the beast," to attend to what we hate in ourselves with compassionate consciousness. And in the alchemy of unconditional acceptance, we find, as Campbell said, that where "we have thought to find an abomination, we will find a God."[14] Herein lies the sacred, redeeming nature of our most frightening nightmares.

# Practicing Mindfulness of Judgment in Dreams and Everyday Life

As always, redemption requires mindfulness.

To work with your Judgment Dream return now to Chapter 4 and choose one or more of the mindfulness practices described there. This week journal about your judgmental thoughts and the ways in which these thoughts and actions create suffering in your life.

- ≋ Notice how often you nurtured judgments about others and especially yourself. Alternatively, notice how often you have embraced compassion for your mistakes, careless errors, or shortcomings during the past week. Be careful not to angrily "judge" yourself for being too judgmental! Respond with compassion when thinking about how difficult it is to change.

- ≋ Take note of how easy or difficult it is to release judgment—or to stop and pause long enough to practice compassion for the experience of being so harshly judged by yourself.

- ≋ Incubate a dream for help in embracing Compassion.

# Chapter 8

# Dreams of Attachment: Nightmares That Teach Us Mindfulness of Grief and Letting Go

*There is no coming to heaven with dry eyes.*

—Thomas Fuller

*As long as you don't know how to die and come back to life again you are a sorry traveler on this dark earth.*

— Goethe

Charles Tart, famous for his research in the field of consciousness studies, conducted a simple little experiment with groups of students. He would place a paper cup in the middle of the room and ask everyone to gather around it in a circle. Their task was to observe the cup and closely study its features. Then after less than 30 seconds, one of the students, on cue, broke rank from the group and stomped the cup flat. Participants in the experiment would routinely become upset, "feel pain," and "suffer" in response to the loss of the cup![1]

We are sensual beings. We can love and desire just about anything we hear, feel, touch, smell, or see—even a paper cup.

In this respect we are very similar to our distant relative, the chimpanzee. Hunters in Africa have a preferred way of capturing monkeys. They place food in a hollowed-out gourd. The monkey can slide its hand through a hole in the gourd to grasp the food. However, with its fist closed around the food the hole is not large enough for the monkey to pull its hand out. Unwilling to release the food, the monkey remains absorbed in his problem. The hunter approaches with his net and with ease carries the monkey off. Just as these animals do, we humans will often hold on too long to what we think is important, and as a result, sacrifice our freedom and joy in life.

The perennial moral to this story is that we are bound to suffer in life unless we are willing to let go and to accept impermanence at a deep level within us. "Renunciation," said Aitken Roshi, "is not getting rid of the things of this world, but accepting that they pass away."[2]

This is the principle underlying the ritual of Tibetan monks, who spend weeks constructing the most elaborate and beautiful mandalas made of brightly colored grains of sand only to destroy their creation once it is complete. Their goal is to remain mindful and to enjoy fully in the moment what they are creating—and not remain attached to what is done. What would life be like for us if we could apply this principle on a daily basis? What if we enjoyed every present moment and never lived in the past, longing for what we once had, nor in the future, planning what we intend to acquire?

Our dreams are infinitely creative in their efforts to teach us the answers to those questions, and with those answers, the lessons necessary for our consciousness to evolve. The various types of loss or attachment nightmares are among the most painful and frightening because we so desperately cling to what we have come to value. The power of our wish to attach and identify with an infinite variety of people and things is quite remarkable.

Yet from the perspective of the Source our suffering throughout life results from our identification with our ego and its legions of attachments—whether money, property, status, role, our prized self-image, or sincere ideals. All of these "things," or thoughts, constitute forms that the Buddhists remind us are impermanent.

This is why our ego is so fearful. We intuit that virtually everything by which we define ourselves is slipping away, if only imperceptibly. To release attachments is, from our ego's view, tantamount to self-annihilation. We must remind ourselves again and again that we are not our ego or the accoutrements with which it is identified.

A friend of mine who suffered "road rage" for many years after a number of nearly fatal car accidents went to a meditation retreat and achieved such inner stillness and peace that on her car trip home realized she no longer felt anger at virtually everyone who drove by her. Initially she was overjoyed and then fell into a momentary—though intense—panic as she wondered who it was that was driving her car! Who was she if not that woman who everybody knew as the cursing sailor when they rode with her? Who, if not the person that knew how to defend herself against all of the crazy jerks on the road? The panic was short-lived. Later she returned to the feeling of spaciousness achieved at the retreat where she had released attachment to the identity of "road rage queen." The often blissful and joyous experience of spaciousness always fills the void where our old identity once imprisoned us.

Here was a loss that everyone, including my friend, could agree was for the better and yet one that still felt initially frightening because it constituted a diminishment of her ego—her identity as she had known it.

Yet whether in small ways or large, and even in the virtual destruction of everything we hold dear, there is a Divine message: We are being Called to experience something far more profound and infinitely spacious than our limiting identity and attachments.

This is a perennial lesson emphasized by many of our spiritual traditions as well as by our nightly dreams.

Often our dreams instruct us in the lesson of releasing attachments and letting go by casting us in dramas of loss, death, and destruction. This is why in our nightmares so many things are burned down, blown up, or washed away. Those are pictures of the things and thoughts to which we are attached or identified. We are being prompted to grieve and release our losses and, in so doing, awaken to a deeper contentment and fuller peace than we ever imagined. This is because after each major loss that is *successfully grieved*, we move a step closer to formless consciousness, a mode of being that shows us there is no need to strive and grasp, and that allows us to better appreciate life's simplicity, its simple beauty. "If you haven't wept deeply," said Ajhan Chah, "you haven't begun to meditate."[3] (You'll read more about formless consciousness in Sections III and IV.)

But there are problems that stand in the way of successful grieving. You've already learned that the greatest impediment to releasing our attachments is that, from our ego's perspective, those attachments *are what I am*. I am a mother, teacher, sister, "good person," victim, rescuer of those in need, or road rage queen. To release the thoughts and things upon which we have built our identity feels as if we will dissolve and disappear. We confuse who we are with our ego and body.

There are other obstacles as well to grieving. Grief is an emotion rarely honored in our culture and, indeed, mostly reviled. How many of us hide our tears of sadness in embarrassment or shame? Sadly, the cultural myth by which we live neither understands nor accepts that most of what happens in life is outside of our ego's control. It is considered a failure to "surrender" and accept our various losses and rejections. Sadness and grief are rarely affirmed, and indeed are often treated as a sign of emotional illness. When our loved one dies it is not infrequent that physicians or even family members will suggest medication for the survivor who is in sorrow. Intense emotions, especially those that acknowledge our hopelessness about the inevitability of change, loss, and death, are threatening.

We view the experience of loss as a "personal failure," a sign of our inadequacy, a reason to feel shame and so refuse to allow ourselves compassion for our own pain. "You made your bed—now lie in it!" These attitudes of self-recrimination—lacking in compassion—are in fact the formula for depression, which is rampant in our society.

However, there is a world of difference between depression and the sadness of grief as we release attachment. We are depressed because at bottom, we angrily blame ourselves for what has been lost—for not having control—while in grief we sadly accept the loss over which we know we have no control.

> From my own experience and those of friends and clients, the experience of crying in depression feels torturous, whereas crying in true sadness feels paradoxically "good."

People often tell me, "When I'm sad and crying I feel like I've come home to my real self." That is the experience of compassion for our own suffering. The paradox of grief is that, when we allow ourselves to feel sadness and loss without self-recrimination, we feel better, not worse.

To grieve—that is to fully accept loss—is not to engage in nihilism and despair. When we cry in true sorrow—not in the self-blame of depression—we are letting go of the old identities, values, and attachments that block the natural flow of energy and fresh perspective that then arise spontaneously without our understanding or willing it. We have forgotten that life in its infinite complexity developed on this Earth without a single effort, strategy, or conscious plan on our part. We need learn only to stand out of the way of the natural healing energy inherent in our Source and grieve what was never "ours." What is most important is never lost.

Are there any of us as adults who haven't dreamed that somebody was trying to kill us, that we were trying to kill someone else, or simply that someone we loved had died? On average 25 percent of children's dreams are nightmares, and in most of these, of course, our child awakens in fear for his or her life—or someone else's.[4]

To understand Attachment dreams we must accept that our dreams are rooted in the reality of nature's laws, not those of society. What is natural law? The laws of nature are, from our ego's perspective, amoral. For example, there's usually a part of us that feels badly when we see a film of a young deer attacked by a pack of wolves. We're always choosing sides, trying to understand right from wrong, good from bad. Yet in nature the wolves are not bad or evil, but simply a part of the natural system.

The law or lesson we learn from nature is that all life—the hunters and the hunted—plays a necessary role in the endless cycle of birth, death, and rebirth.

Mirroring our individual lives, each wave in the ocean is unique, yet each comes and goes while the ocean—their source—remains. Our task is to align with this reality by seeing through the illusion of permanence and understanding that if life is anything, it is growth and change.

> The ground of life and consciousness is eternal, but its shape and form are ever-changing.

Even more than adults, children are in a very accelerated process of change and growth emotionally. This is why so many dreams of children are about being attacked or of their life being threatened. For every frequent step of growth they are called to take, there is a loss, an ending their ego must deal with. A classic example is in adolescence when we find it so hard to lose our prized status as children in order to gain the privileges of adulthood.

> When we dream about death, we are dreaming about a process of change—an ending that makes way for a new beginning.

Thus children have many threatening dreams of loss and death, in part because their egos are required more often than adults' are to give up what is secure and familiar and continually fashion a new identity. Children's dreams reflect the natural fear that we each have in the face of change: the fear of losing what we have identified with—even when we suspect that the change is clearly for the better. To paraphrase an old maxim: Life is a hard teacher. First she gives us the test and then the lesson.

Many times dreams of death include intense feelings of grief as we hold the dying person in our arms or "hear the news" that a loved one has been killed. In both cases we may awaken in horror and grief. Although there is always the possibility that such dreams are pre-cognitive and foreshadow a waking life loss, most often the Mentors in our dreams—friends, family, strangers, or pets—are embodiments of attitudes or thoughts our ego cherishes most. Therefore, when we dream of a dear friend's death the Source is calling us to let go and grieve some cherished way of viewing ourselves—some value to which our ego is attached—one that stands in the way of our growth. When a person dies or is killed in your dream, ask yourself, "What values or attitudes are *unique* to that person and how have I been identifying with him or her?" That is the part that may be dying or radically changing. (You can refresh your memory about this approach by reviewing the Chapter Practices section in Chapter 2.)

Also, you'll notice that often a loss, murder, or even suicide may occur, and within the dream our reaction is relatively non-emotional or even blasé. However, once we awaken our old ego values take over again and we feel a rush of guilt or shame about how we acted or failed to react in our dream. Our attitude *within the dream* is often a clue that we may be more accepting of the impending change in our life than we feel comfortable acknowledging to ourselves in waking life.

In contrast, there are many dreams of loss in which we feel beaten, demoralized, or defeated, and awaken feeling the same. At such times we must acknowledge our own stubborn resistance to change.

# Nightmares of Attachment

Attachment dreams are as infinitely varied in their content and story line as other dreams, but closer study of these dreams has shown me that they are best grouped by the degree of resistance our ego displays to the impending loss that must be accepted.

> As our ego's resistance to the guidance of our Dream Mentors increases, so does the intensity of fear we experience in the dream.

I'll address examples of these, starting with dreams that reflect the least resistance. Keep in mind, however, that any dream we experience as a nightmare reflects by definition considerable ego resistance, and consequently, fear.

I've named these attachment nightmares as follows and in order of increasing ego resistance, fear, and agitation:

- Dreams of Grieving (yielding to grief).

- Dreams of Forgotten Love (being helped to grieve).

- Dreams of Anticipating Loss (being reassured).

- Dreams of Imminent Loss (being warned).

- Dreams of Suicide and Murder (assisting the source).

- Dreams of Refusal (being coerced).

- Dreams of Defeat (being murdered).

These categories represent illustrative examples and not an exhaustive list of all possible motifs. Also, in this chapter the discussion ignores the possibility of precognition. Precognitive dreams are a scientifically established fact and, indeed, are often about loss and death. Yet they are relatively infrequent and very difficult to distinguish from so-called "symbolic" dreams. I mention this simply to point out that one must always consider the possibility of precognition, but in the meantime work with the dream as a reflection of your own inner drama.

# Dreams of Grieving (Yielding to Grief)

**Lesson: It is time to let go.**

Dreams of Grieving are about our ego's readiness to yield to grief. They are straightforward, direct messages from the Source that some identity to which we've been attached is ready to be grieved for and released. The cause of death is not as important in these dreams as the fact that we accept rather than resist the need to grieve.

Because our ego is in a state of *relative* acceptance and readiness to let go, these dreams are more intensely heartrending and emotionally painful than they are frightening. For example:

> My dearest friend has died. I sit down with her dead body in my lap. As I hold her close to me I sob from the deepest part of myself and in a way that I've never done before. After I woke up I felt somehow lighter. I cried so much in the dream that there was a feeling of release.

This was Ria's dream at a time when she had concluded it was necessary to end her 15-year marriage to a man with whom she had been deeply in love. Ria thought she would never be divorced. However, in the dream it wasn't her husband who died in her arms. The "best friend" who died in the dream was in waking life a woman whom Ria viewed as having an ideal relationship with her own husband. Thus the best friend's death in the dream was the death of Ria's identification with her—the ending of Ria's attachment to the identity of "successful wife"—and most importantly, an ending she was ready to accept and grieve for. Indeed, she did so within the dream itself. In fact the work of grieving was done so completely in the dream that Ria awoke feeling "lighter," "released," and liberated—always the end result of wholehearted grieving.

Such dreams also address the common notion that "it's only a dream." In our dreams we can and do feel the entire range of life emotions, and we may fully process these feelings as well—sometimes even without the help of friends or therapists. In fact, when we dream that we are running or scared, our physical heart pounds, and when we dream we are having sex, our body responds with arousal. Within our dreams we experience a reality just as powerful and at times even more graphic and vivid than waking life. This means that when we grieve in our dreams we are doing the actual work of healing.

## Dreams of Forgotten Love (Being Helped to Grieve)

**Lesson: To reaffirm life we must grieve, and honor the love we have lost.**

Dreams of Forgotten Love help us first to face the reality of a loss we have been avoiding or denying. Despite our ego's resistance they call us to embrace our sadness and grieve for the love once given us. In these dreams our Dream Mentors ask us to honor the importance of that love in our present and future life.

When we deny or avoid our grief we may shut down emotionally in many areas of our life. By doing so we actually create more suffering by closing ourselves off from the loving experience and wisdom gained in those relationships.

When we embrace grief and acknowledge the great value of the love we have lost, that loving feeling re-inspires us and affirms life itself. We may continue to miss the one whom we have lost, but the experience of his or her love is now present again in our consciousness and provides the guiding vision for a new life.

For example, Ron had been raised in a home in which his grandmother also resided. His mother was cold and distant, and Ron felt much closer to his grandmother, who treated him in a warm, maternal, and unconditionally loving way. However, his grandmother died when he was 14 years old. The trauma of this loss was made worse by the fact that he did not learn of his grandmother's death until he arrived home from school one afternoon to see her being carried out in a body bag. His mother said nothing to him until he asked. Subsequently, Ron walled off his hope for love and focused exclusively on outer goals, gradually becoming a workaholic adult. This was his very simple and very powerful dream of forgotten love:

> I am back in my childhood home and surveying the photographs that my parents always had on our living room piano. There is one large family portrait in which I am about 10 years old. I study the portrait closely only to find that my grandmother is missing from the picture.

Ron awoke from this dream extremely upset and overwhelmed. Painful memories of his grandmother's death and their mutual love for each other flooded his consciousness. The dream ushered in a period of intense grief and sadness (not depression) in which Ron allowed himself to feel how much he missed his grandmother and the love she embodied. He realized that by the time of her death he had shut off any hope of unearned and unconditional love in his life. Instead he took on his parents' values and compulsively sought praise and approval through constant achievement and work-related goals. Recalling his grandmother's love helped Ron find the resolve to live his life differently and in a more passionate and self-caring manner.

One more thought about Ron's dream: Notice that in the family portrait Ron is 10 years old, though his grandmother died when he was 14. Ron recalled that by the age of 10 years, he had given up most hope of love from his parents. His grandmother's death at age 14 was simply the "last straw." Again, our age or the age of a Dream Mentor usually reflects the time when we last felt the experience that we are being called to reclaim.

Here's another example of how the Source prompts us to honor our losses. A client of mine, Missy, told me of a recurring nightmare she experienced over a period of many years on a weekly or monthly basis. Before beginning her work with me, she had spent the last five years in a state of chronic depression with frequent panic attacks controlled only with medication.

During one session Missy shared a recurring nightmare that her house and neighborhood were flooding and the waters rising inexorably in an ominous tide. There were no sewers to carry away the water. When I asked her to reflect on how in her life it felt as if the waters were always rising without relief, she spoke about an ongoing series of losses including the deaths of loved friends and relatives. "Why," I asked, "didn't you mention these experiences before?" Missy expressed what I've come to realize is a universal confusion in our culture about the difference between the healing waters of grief and the mire of depression: "If I let myself start to feel sad, I'll get depressed again. I don't want to wallow in it."

I reassured her that sadness was the healing agent for her depression and not its cause. When we feel sad for our own losses rather than angry at ourselves for needing support, we engage the healing balm of compassion. From the time of our first discussion, when she let herself experience and feel some of those losses, Missy has never had another flooding or even the threat of rain in her dreams. On a waking life level her healing began in earnest, her fear of depression waned and she began slowly to wean herself off medication. As grief becomes possible so does more joyful energy.

## Dreams of Anticipating Loss (Being Reassured)

**Lesson: Don't panic. The loss that seems catastrophic now is more manageable than you think.**

Attachment dreams often occur because we resist releasing some part of our ego identity, whereas dreams of Anticipating Loss respond with reassurance to our waking life ego's needless feelings of panic and anticipation of suffering. Many times, rather than denying or refusing to deal with the loss of love in our lives, our ego panics and exaggerates the impact that a perceived loss will create. However, our Dream Mentors are always ready to compensate for our limited conscious point of view. It is common to have dreams, for example, of being caught in the path of a highly destructive force such as a hurricane or tornado that does little or no significant damage.

A friend of mine, Roseanne, became aware that she had symptoms consistent with breast cancer and was extremely upset. She dreamed:

> I am riding my bike in front of my old high school when I see a storm approaching. I duck inside the school to protect myself and hide beneath a desk. Now, it's a tornado bearing right down on the school. It hits and things are flying and breaking all around me. I think I'm going to die for sure. However, when the tornado passes I'm left without any wounds except a small scratch.

Despite her subsequent diagnosis of cancer and recommendations for a partial mastectomy and chemotherapy, she found another doctor who supported a lumpectomy and simple radiation. Deeply frightened and anxious, she did a great deal of research on the subject about which treatment regimen to follow. In part, because of her intuitive sense about the nightmare, she chose the least invasive care plan. Following this treatment regimen Roseanne made it through the entire grueling and terrifying ordeal without a recurrence of cancer and with only a "scratch" where the small incision was made. Perhaps, too, the "school" in which she protected herself in the dream was the time spent learning about and researching the best approach to her problem.

# Dreams of Imminent Loss (Being Warned)

**Lesson: Avoid having to grieve unnecessarily in waking life. Make the right choice now.**

Kahlil Gibran once wrote: "And ever has it been known that love knows not its own depth until the hour of separation."[5] Dreams of Imminent Loss operate on the time-honored principle that "absence makes the heart grow fonder." These dreams allow us to experience the loss of something or someone we dearly treasure so that we will reflect upon the destructive choices we have been making and the path we've been on. Typically, within the dream we have made a choice that is short-sighted. That is, we have affirmed a value that is destructive to the growth and well-being of ourselves and loved ones. Through the experience of pain, suffering, and loss in our dream we are encouraged to release some damaging ego value to which we are attached. Conversely, we are encouraged to affirm an important life value such as compassion for ourselves or others before it is too late.

Common examples of Imminent Loss nightmares are those dreams of alcoholics and substance abusers who have been sober for many years. Typically they include full-blown experiences of drunkenness and destructive behavior identical to the waking life episodes from the distant past. The standard response to waking from these dreams is a great sigh of relief and the thought: "Thank God it was only a dream!" Such experiences remind the dreamer who has been unconsciously sliding back into old ego strategies about how much will be lost if they continue to remain attached to their old destructive identity and ego values.

Jules was a client of mine who had smoked heavily all of his life. Now seeing his health deteriorate, he was determined to quit, and with the help of a 12-step program, did just that. However, stresses began to build in his life and the taste of a cigarette again became seductive. This was his nightmare warning about the damage he was inflicting on his body and the loss that it would entail:

> I am pushing a spreader across the most beautiful, lush green lawn I have ever seen. As I walk back and forth I'm just enjoying the richness of the experience. For some reason I feel compelled to look inside the spreader, which I see is filled to the brim with nicotine.
>
> I wake up with a jolt. My heart is pounding and I'm feeling sickened by what I've done to the lawn—followed instantly by the realization that it's what I'm doing to my body. That dream made a huge difference in my resolve to stop smoking.

Avery, a friend of mine, who had let himself become overly involved in his work to the detriment of his family life, dreamed:

> I am climbing to the top of a 30-foot wall and my 6-year-old son is climbing right beneath me. I see he's having a problem climbing. I'm faced with the challenge of whether to first get a grip on the wall to stabilize myself or to reach down to help my son. When I choose to get my own grip, my son falls off the wall. I watch him as he falls. I wake up in horror.

The experience of profound pain at the loss of his son stayed with Avery many days after the dream. It's not hard to understand how that dream helped him to create a different set of priorities for his life. As a result Avery let go of his "tight grip" or single-minded preoccupation with achievement and career advancement, and gave more loving time and attention to his son. In these dreams we always learn not only what is about to be lost, but also what healing experience needs to take its place—in this case, the loving energy Avery and his son could thrive on.

Here's another similar "do or die" dream of Imminent Loss: Lawrence had spent a lifetime working on releasing his attachment to or identification with his mom, Maria, and her conservative values. Growing up she enforced the values of security, passivity, compliance, and non-assertiveness. Thus, while Lawrence lived an outwardly successful life, he continued to feel trapped in a less than fulfilling existence not unlike his mother's—one that lacked the open, adventurous spirit and passion he desired from life. Many years after his mother's death he dreamed:

> I am in a car sitting peacefully and calmly with some men on my way to what I understand will be my death. They have planned to murder me when the car reaches its destination. To my horror I realize I have for some reason fully consented to this plan without protest. Now I'm feeling complete panic, though I feel that I am helpless to do anything about my plight. We're pulling up to a cemetery and I see the site where my dead body will be buried. The tombstone that will be used sits next to the grave and I know that soon I will actually become that stone. I believe I can see my name being spelled out on it. But on second thought, its not my name being carved after all. I'm wondering whose name it is as the letters slowly appear one after the other: M-A-R-I-A. My mother's name. I'm going to die, and for the rest of eternity I will be known by my mother's name. I wake up in a sweat.

In Lawrence's nightmare his resistance to releasing his grip on his mother's expectations is presented as a dark and disturbing tragedy. Initially he is so attached to his mom's values—so compliant and rule-bound—that he fully accepts the plan for his own murder—the complete loss of his identity. Not surprisingly, when he becomes conscious that he has colluded in his own death he is terrified to see that the life about to be terminated has never even been his own.

After working with the dream Lawrence realized how close he was to letting his life slip by without having followed his own bliss. The Source treats our growth and unfolding as the supreme value and, through dreams, will teach us what we need to know regardless of how disturbing the information is to us—as if our egos are, as Lao Tsu says, "straw dogs."[6]

In fact, when we worked with the nightmare, Lawrence became more mindful of the need to fight for his life—that is, fight to have a life of his own. Feeling more aligned with the goal of releasing his attachment to his mother, he told me of a subsequent Illumination Dream of Embrace (see Chapter 12) soon after, in which he found ancient gold coins buried in the earth beneath the dead leaves of a tree: "The coins had been rained on and covered by dead leaves. The more I dig the more I find." Lawrence understood this dream as an affirmation of the ancient wealth within—beneath the tears and dead debris of his life—that was his if he would continue to unshackle his mother's chains, dig deeper to the roots of life, and live more passionately. The work was of course still unfinished, but finding the gold was an affirmation that he had understood well the message of his nightmare. (You'll read more about Lawrence's Journey in Chapter 14.)

# Dreams of Suicide and Murder (Assisting the Source)

**Lesson: It's time to take responsibility for letting go.**

## Dreams of Murder

In dreams of murder we or a Mentor enact violence against another person or animal. In these instances the one murdered embodies an ego value to which we are attached. As with Dreams of Suicide, the act of murder reflects our ego's realization that a very decisive action is needed to release the value that is destructive or no longer useful. Later in this chapter you'll read about Dreams of Refusal in which the dreamer is so reluctant to release a destructive value that he or she is either mortally threatened or harshly coerced to do so by a Dream Mentor. Here, however, the dreamer or Dream Mentor takes responsibility for "killing" or releasing some value to which they were attached in much the same way as in Dreams of Suicide.

For example, my friend Chuck shared an upsetting nightmare in which his own very loyal dog was murdered by a man who stated that he was "putting the dog out of his misery." In waking life Chuck had ended a long and painful relationship with a woman. Nevertheless, he was very ambivalent about having ended the relationship. He felt that the letting-go process, even if needed, was at its core unacceptable, hurtful, and emotionally violent.

The dream clue for Chuck was the rationale for the killing provided by the murderer: "to put the dog out of his misery." Chuck was indeed long-suffering in his own loyalty and reluctantly realized that the pain and misery of the relationship had become too intense to live with. He just had to "put down" his loyal self, so to speak. Had Chuck been less ambivalent about his decision to separate from his wife, his dream dog might have been experienced as dying more peacefully of natural causes.

Chuck's dream suggests the need to look more deeply into the necessity of the separation and perhaps to find more compassion for his own suffering in the relationship. So often guilt dominates our consciousness because we are more aware of others' pain than our own. A significant lesson on our Journey is to develop greater mindfulness of the compassion needed for our own suffering (and not just that of others). This is never a matter of caring less about others, but of learning to care as much about ourselves as we do about those we love.

## Dreams of Suicide

In contrast to Dreams of Murder, to kill oneself is a more inclusive and comprehensive ending of one's reality than to kill someone else who may be "like me, but not me."

When one intends one's own death or witnesses someone else's suicidal intent in a dream it is clear that some very important attachment—a very major aspect of our identity—is being released. A suicidal action in our dream reflects our ego's consciousness that this release is necessary. Our ego is willing to take responsibility for assisting the Source in expanding our consciousness.

Whereas Dreams of Grieving, mentioned previously, are heart-rending, these dreams are more disturbing or frightening to our ego, as we are engaging in or witnessing an act of violence to achieve the desired end. More importantly, the need for violence suggests a degree of resistance by our ego that must be overcome with resolute action.

Maury, a member of one of my dreamsharing groups, became acutely aware of how his chronically intellectual and rational approach to relationships was blocking any chance for living his life passionately. Maury's detached, analytical mode of responding to most life situations and relationships was so much a part of him that he had difficulty imagining himself in any other way. But as he worked with his dreams he felt increasingly connected to his heart's values and felt a deep shift taking place within. He dreamed:

> I am in a futuristic setting. Everything is chrome and shiny and the furniture and buildings all look ultra-modern, clean, and efficient. A man walks through the door and immediately I see he is cold, calculating, and totally in control of himself. He pulls a gun out of his pocket, puts it to his head, and shoots himself. He is dead instantly. I am blown away by the shocking abruptness of this act and wake up sickened and horrified.

In Maury's dream the shiny chrome, clean, and efficient futuristic setting corresponds with the Dream Mentor's cold, calculating behavior. In fact, his Mentor's suicidal act is made in a similarly unemotional and efficient way. Maury was easily able to see in his Mentor a mirror of his own cerebral and rational mode of being in the world. Though he awoke feeling deeply disturbed and frightened, he did not need to reflect very long upon the details to feel greatly relieved that he was, in fact, ready to divest himself of his burden of excessive rationality.

Note that within the dream Maury's ego feels resistance to the act of suicide—sickened and horrified—after the fact of its occurrence. He could have dreamed that he tried and failed to stop his Dream Mentor, but instead he dreamed that he simply watched without resistance. We do not dream what our ego is not ready to accept. And Maury was very much ready to let go of his attachment to his cold and rational persona.

Let's take a moment to distinguish dream suicide from waking-life suicide. First, the occurrence of a self-destructive dream act does not necessarily imply depression or the presence of a wish to commit suicide in waking life. However, when we feel suicidal we mistakenly believe that the only way to find release is through giving up our body. In truth we need to grieve and release some attachment—some belief or perspective to which we are attached—an identity that is draining every bit of joy from our life.

In the broadest sense, whether through natural causes, murder, or suicide, at bottom any type of dream death is a necessary death required for the sake of our emotional and spiritual growth.

## Dreams of Refusal (Being Coerced)

**Lesson: You have no reasonable choice. Let go and grieve.**

Author Herman Hesse wrote: "Some of us think holding on makes us strong; but sometimes it is letting go."[7] There are times in our life when our refusal to grieve has been too entrenched. We have held on too long and have been willing—maybe even proud of our ability—to bear the negative consequences that have ensued. Now our Dream Mentors tell us that we must sever completely our continuing attachment to some value or attitude that is destructive to our growth and to our life. These dreams show us it's not really even a choice we should think about and that our stubborn attachment needs release. Our Dream Mentors either threaten our lives or rely on intense coercion to shake us loose from our ego's attachments. It is as if we are being told: "The nature of your attachment is so destructive that there is no longer any choice but to let go and grieve." We are forced to face the futility of our attachment in such a blunt and urgent way that it is difficult to remain in denial. Dreams of Refusal show us the potential loss of our own life or create such a devastating or noxious experience that we are usually—though not always—shocked into letting go of our attachment in the dream (and waking life).

Louise grew up in a family rife with misery and suffering. Her mom was a flagrant alcoholic and her dad an authoritarian and brutally insensitive man. Even she and her sister were in constant conflict. When she entered therapy she was soon struggling with intense conflict about detaching from them. She realized that by remaining in the family drama she was attempting to do the impossible—that is, to please them and to fit in. Yet this was the only family she had, and to detach from it seemed to be a loss too painful to bear. Louise then experienced this Dream of Refusal:

I am in a car with my entire family. My father is driving and I'm in the back seat with my sister. I see that my father is heading toward the ocean and I begin to feel anxious, but really start to panic when he continues to drive us right into the water. I say nothing as the car fills with water and we sink to the bottom. At the end of the dream I'm sitting there with everyone and the air is about to run out. We're all just sitting there. I don't want to leave because I know they won't follow me.

This was a turning point in Louise's journey as her dream forced her to experience how loyalty to her family's behavior was virtually suffocating and killing her. She was giving up her life to be part of the family—a dying family. The dream experience succeeded, as could no words from me, her husband, or her friends, in dislodging her attachment to the value of going down with her family's ship. As she loosened her own death-like grip on the family, her panic attacks abated and she began to express creative energies as an artist that she had let wither for some time.

Here's another vivid example of the lengths our Dream Mentors will go to get our attention: John was invested in holding on to his own childhood identity as the overly responsible and self-denying eldest son of a timid mother and a brutally intimidating father who had placed him "in charge" of controlling his many siblings. By the time he came to see me he had been in the midst of a severe depression for some time, punctuated by periods of manic-like energy and grand plans for success in life. In therapy John remained stubbornly attached to his childhood role in the family as the son who was expected to make his father proud by his grand and visionary accomplishments. Sadly, his father had never been able to express affection or love for John no matter how much he achieved and accomplished.

In fact, John was very successful, and by anyone's standards he had risen to the upper ranks of his profession. However, he could never feel content or fulfilled because no worldly achievement would ever translate as the love he missed from his father or as an experience of being lovable simply for himself. Pushing ever upwards and onwards John would increasingly crash and burn in the pits of depression—only to pick himself up and shoot for the moon once again.

His out-of-balance attachment to worldly achievement and the medicine needed is reflected in John's nightmare:

I am on the top of a mountain and have been captured by Native Americans, who have tied me naked to stakes under the hot, broiling sun. I understand in the dream that I will have all of my organs pecked out by vultures that line the boulders around me. However, I will be spared if I can hold out my arm in such a way that a sparrow will land in my open hand."

For John, who had been living his life as an eagle, the humility required to draw the trust of a tiny sparrow was indeed an ego sacrifice of immense proportion. Sparrows for John were birds with very modest goals in life who rarely venture far from their own backyard, so to speak. This was the healing perspective that his Native American Dream Mentors had in mind for John: to let go of his grand visions and to come down closer to earth. The stakes were more than clear. If he continued to remain attached to his eagle-like aspirations he would be eaten alive by the vulturous world around him that cared not at all about his achievements—or perhaps by his own vulturous hunger for more and more in life.

Needless to say, the sparrow became the metaphor for his Journey, and we frequently considered whether his behavior and attitudes were sufficiently sparrow-like to avoid the imminent loss of everything precious in his life.

## Dreams of Defeat (Being Murdered)

**Lesson: The choice is no longer yours.**

Dreams of being murdered are quite different in principle than dreams in which we act as the murderer. In these dreams our ego is not consenting, and as a result such dream experiences are often quite harrowing as we battle with or succumb to our assassin.

A friend of my family, Samantha, had endured a deeply empty and unhappy marriage while allowing her husband to believe that she was fulfilled and content. For years she refused to consider any alternative to the miserable life she was leading and would not listen to the advice of friends and family suggesting that she was deserving of more. This was her dream:

I'm in my house and look up to see a man pointing a large gun at me. He shoots me point blank in the face and I die. I wake up horrified.

In all dreams of death we must ask not just who but *what* has died. And the answer is always the same: the identity to which our ego is attached. In her marriage, Samantha—her ego—was invested in keeping up the pretense of happiness, or as we say in everyday life, "putting on a face" for her husband. She was strongly attached to this identity, her persona—the face she wore for him. So it was that her Dream Mentor used great force to, as it were, "wipe the smile off of her face." Indeed, the whole "face" had to go. It's important to note here that our dreams and Dream Mentors have no motive to punish us. Indeed, the losses we incur in dreams have the purpose of saving our life, not creating more suffering.

Samantha's "face" was more than just the lie it told. It was a prison of her own making in which her soul was dying. Just as a modern-day physician would amputate a foot with gangrene, our Self—the ancient Healer within—is ready to sever what is draining us of life and threatening our growth. Yes, in dreams such as Samantha's we—our ego—do suffer, but in the space cleared by our ego's loss, renewed life energy flows.

As we spoke about her nightmare, Samantha reflected on the great suffering in her life caused by her willingness to give up her needs for love and intimacy. Now, no longer willing to smile through her pain, she became more honest first with herself, and then with her husband and made plans to end a marriage that had died emotionally years ago.

# The Healing Power of Attachment Dreams: An Overview

The predominant mood of Attachment dreams is the feeling of loss, apprehension about loss, resistance to loss, anger at loss, deep insecurity, and grief.

The central teaching of the Buddha was that the only permanent and certain experience in this world is loss and change. It is our ego's attachment to all things impermanent that causes our suffering. It is most

> To grieve is to accept what is without resistance and to immerse ourselves in the waters of sadness, sorrow, and compassion for our own hurt and pain.

human of us—our egos—to attach ourselves, to hold on and identify with what we value, but this is the "illusion" of which Buddha spoke.

A primary goal of the Calling is to release our attachments and let our grief dissolve the hardened walls we have built around our heart.

We do so by being mindful of self-recrimination. We reject the arrogant self-blame that tells us we have failed to maintain full personal control over the forces of life, death, loss, and rejection. When we make this willing sacrifice and yield to the compassionate and healing energy of grief, we see that our insecurity and suffering comes from a sense of self (ego) that is built on all that is transient and ephemeral. We return to humility, follow a wiser path, and stand ready to embrace the undying ground of consciousness that is our true Self.

# Practicing Mindfulness of Attachment in Dreams and Everyday Life

To work with your Attachment dream return now to Chapter 4 and choose one or more of the mindfulness practices described there.

This week journal about how you create attachments, whether in the form of material objects or images of yourself that strengthen your ego. Consider the ways in which these thoughts and actions create suffering in your life.

- Notice how often this week you engaged in creating attachments, defining yourself by what you bought or own or by your family, social or professional role, and identity. This includes all of the small and large ways in which we indulge in thoughts about our special or, for that matter, inferior attributes—all are thoughts with which we have identified and to which we are attached.

- Alternatively, notice how often you have embraced non-attachment and grieved or simply let go of what you know is passing and impermanent during the past week.

- Take note of how easy or difficult it is to release the impulse to attach or alternatively to embrace grief and letting go.

- Incubate a dream for help in embracing Non-Attachment.

# Chapter 9

# Inspirational Dreams in the Time of Our Calling

*A flash of enlightenment offers a preview of coming attractions, but when it fades, you will see more clearly what separates you from that state—your compulsive habits, outmoded beliefs, false associations, and other mental structures. Just when our lives are starting to get better, we may feel like things are getting worse—because for the first time we see clearly what needs to be done.*

—Dan Millman

Not all dreams in the time of our Calling are frightening nightmares. Although nightmares show us the suffering in which we will remain if we don't change our old script, I've heard many Calling dreams that are remarkably hopeful and inspiring—in fact often life-changing. These dreams have the same goal of shaking us loose from our old script, but in addition offer a new vision of what life can become for us.

They offer us a sneak preview of a new and more joyful life perspective. Inspirational dreams show us that the solution to our problems and release from suffering is clearly possible. In so doing, they leave us more humble about

> Inspirational dreams provide an incentive to change by offering a picture of how much better our life can be if we would trust the universe to care for us and allow ourselves to be guided.

the limits of our ego's own limited vision, and thus, more aware that our old ego strategies must be released. They also spur us on, reinforce important pieces of inner work we have done, and affirm the profound importance and nature of that work.

Inspirational dreams, however, are not the same as Illumination Dreams, which we will discuss in more detail in Section IV.

They encourage in us a distinct sense that our routine way of life must undergo radical change and that none of the ways our ego has yet devised will get us to this place. They simply show us it's possible, and in so doing they offer a profound experience of hope.

A classic example of such dreams is one reported by Albert Einstein, which you read in Chapter 2. Einstein said that his dream in adolescence of sledding down a hill at the speed of light had become the continuing object of contemplation throughout his professional life. These are his words in an interview with famed reporter Edwin Newman: "[Y]ou could say and I would say, that my entire scientific career has been a meditation on that dream."[1] His eventual understanding of that dream resulted in what we now know as the Theory of Relativity that changed the world—for better or worse. But notice that his dream didn't include the formula $E=MC^2$—just the promise of its existence.

In 1985 on a lark I set off to a conference on dreamwork sponsored by what is now known as the International Association for the Study of Dreams (IASD), where I learned to my surprise I could ask for guidance from my dreams. I saw my life as so full, I never felt the arrogance of the first question I posed for my waiting psyche: "How can dreams possibly help me?" That night I had a dream that changed my life, though it wasn't the type that totally knocks you off your feet or the kind that rocks you

> Illumination dreams provide the solution to our problem or at least specific instructions on how to arrive at the solution. Inspirational Calling dreams allow us to observe as if from a distance the end effect, the outcome we desire, without knowing how in the world we will arrive at that place in life.

at your core right then and there. Rather this was one of those insidious, seductive tales—a freshwater brook trickling through your toes on a stifling hot day, whispering for you to stay awhile, wade into its coolness, and get your ankles wet.

> I am walking through a deteriorating neighborhood and against my better judgment feel compelled to enter an old, boarded-up house. On its last legs, it's wrecked and empty—a musty, dank place—the only chimera of warmth an ancient blanket of dust tucked into every webbed and lonely corner. But I begin to feel "that feeling"—that chilly wind that always paralyzed me on reluctant errands to the basement for my mother—that imminent dark presence that grabbed and squeezed organs I didn't know I had—liquid nitrogen coursing through my veins—that feeling.
>
> I'm standing there stoned with fear and in a moment either of grace or certain insanity, I refuse fear's blissful offer of escape: I hear myself announce aloud to the moldy walls: "I'm tired of being afraid all the time. I'm just sick of it. I'm staying."

Many of us have had those times in our dreams when we become the magician, the master alchemist in complete alignment with the powers that be, and whatever we intend just materializes. So it was with my resolve to stay. The old house began to change—and without yet knowing it—so did the *Pleasantville*-esque life I had crafted since I was a child:

> The sea of dust parts, clearing a path to where the boarded windows have politely now taken up home in some other dimension. Dumbstruck, I stand staring at a huge picture window—now a timeless portal of sunny energy—brilliant, warm sprinkles of light fluttering down in joyful dance around my proverbial cold feet.
>
> The house is reborn. Alive. I can almost feel it breathe. It's as if someone's home now. The woodwork is that richly carved kind, burnished mahogany tiered along the edge of both ceiling and floor. It's just a leisurely spiral climb to room after room of what I see now is an incredibly spacious, rich, and inviting place.
>
> But more profound is the question that begins to form as I awaken from the dream: "Why would somebody abandon a place like this?"

Now I'm awake, eyes wide, and I'm thinking, "Okay. Cool! This is easy. Great, there's a whole me that can be really rich and warm and inviting that I must have abandoned a long time ago. I've just got to fix up the place, so to speak. They're right about dreams—but how could my great life be like an empty, decaying, old house?" I dragged myself out of bed a little let down— dreams really could be ridiculous sometimes, I thought.

Fully 20 years later, I'm still fixing up the place, but I know now that the work of the heart—the work of awakening our consciousness—is worth the suffering we endure. I'm grateful for a dream about a moldering life I had no idea I was living, a dream that opened a portal to a deeper ground of creativity and spiritual meaning in my life—one that rescued me from the stagnant waters of a kind and nice existence that knew little of passion and true heart.

Yet it was a dream that gave me no answers or solutions, just hope and an affirmation that my life could be, and indeed, needed to be lived very differently.

That's how Inspirational Dreams work.

Here's another example: Remember Melinda in Chapter 5 who found in her Distraction nightmare that when she turned away from the distractions of the busy shoppers, she knew for the first time that she wanted to live? At the start of her therapy, she was intent on finding a way out of her many lifelong conflicts and a chronic experience of stagnation in her life. Subsequently, she shared with me the following dream:

> I am in a classroom and see an elegant mathematical equation on the blackboard. I realize that I understand fully the meaning of this equation and what it is saying, but have no idea of how to arrive at it—how to obtain the answer. However, in my dream the answer is so beautiful and profound that I resolve to make it my task in life to know how that equation is solved. I get up and walk out the door. It's raining and I step in a puddle as soon as I walk out but I am undaunted.

In waking life Melinda did indeed feel that she was living under a constant cloud and could relate easily to the rain as an image of her chronic sadness in not finding the answers she had been seeking in life. I should add that, in her profession, Melinda had always viewed mathematical equations as the essence of problem-solving. She felt equations offered the best and "simplest possible solution along with open-ended possibilities for the future." Now she was feeling for the first time that there was indeed a solution, and she was determined to find out how to apply it to her own life. Notice how her dream provided an incentive, but the solution required her to be proactive, take the initiative, and find it for herself: "God helps those who help themselves."

A friend was inspired by this dream, which is self-explanatory:

> I am wandering in a barren landscape and feeling totally lost. Suddenly, Captain Kirk appears with the entire crew of the *Enterprise*. At first I think they're going to hurt me, but then I see they're turning toward the horizon. I look up and see two incredibly beautiful constellations so rich with stars that the sheer beauty takes my breath away. Then I realize those stars are my goal and I have to walk hundreds of miles to that horizon. I feel deep disappointment and weariness and question whether I can even survive the trek—but I take the first step and keep going.

Finally, I worked with Nina, a client of mine more than 20 years ago. She had felt depressed most of her life, was unsupported by her family, and was deeply unhappy in her marriage. I'll let Nina describe what happened to her:

> *I had felt spiritually dead for a number of years. I searched for a connection to God in my teens. My father kidded me about all of the faiths I tried. I couldn't say that anything was the truth for me, and envied those people who had a strong faith. By the time I was in my mid-30s I had given up on finding God. I wasn't even searching for happiness, just a way to get through the day.*
>
> *I did have one friend, Jeanne, my pastor's wife, who represented the closest connection I knew to God. She is a wonderful woman—quiet, loving, understanding, benevolent, and humble. And although some would think the pastor would be closer to God, I believe her spirit may have appealed to me more than the masculine, assertive preacher.*
>
> *Therapy was hard work. I would go, talk, feel better, and by the next appointment feel that I needed to be there again. Dreams had been discussed in many sessions and, although they were interesting, I didn't really get it and felt separated from them. I remember asking David, "Will you tell me when I'm well?" I was looking for an answer from someone else.*
>
> *Then I had this dream that really did change my life. The dream itself is wonderfully brief and simple, which is part of its beauty:*

It is dark—night. I'm going up a hill to a window-lit farmhouse at the top of a knoll. While my focus is on the house itself, Jeanne, my old pastor's wife, comes out and meets me. She takes my hand and leads me away from the house to the top of the hill. The stars surround us...everywhere. She says, "Nancy, this is what it is all about."

*I remember suddenly feeling overwhelmed and flooded with love. In tears at my next appointment, I asked David: "How did I know to dream this dream? What was this feeling gripping me?" A feeling was already stirring in me that maybe my dreams had some answers that even David didn't have. I still wanted his guidance and it would take me several more years of therapy off and on and many more dreams that spoke to me, to fully trust that I did have the answers within me—but my life now started coming together. I was able to confront the negativity in my marriage and trust that I could find happiness on my own path.*

*And yes, with what I've learned about dreams, if I had that dream today I might be tempted to take it apart and look at the symbols—"the farmhouse...why a farmhouse?"—that sort of thing. But at the time I didn't look at it symbolically. I accepted it for the literal experience and feeling it graced me with. This is where I want to leave this dream—in my heart.*

The lesson of our Inspirational Calling Dreams can be summed up in this simple way: Accept the hopelessness of your own plans and the limits of your own vision. There is another entirely different version of reality you have never before let yourself imagine. Open to a broader, richer vision of life.

# Chapter Practices

Look back on your life and recall whether you may have experienced one or more Inspirational Dreams. You may also reflect on experiences you've had that served the same purpose—experiences that motivated and encouraged you to persevere through hard times.

Alternatively, reflect and journal about a story you may have read, an inspiring event in someone else's life or a particular song or melody that deeply touches you. You may also incubate a dream requesting inspiration or greater openness to inspiration on your Journey.

# Section III

# The Time of Your Quest:
## Practicing Mindfulness of Impatience and the Art of Waiting in the Present Moment

*Perhaps there is only one cardinal sin: impatience. Because of impatience we are driven out of Paradise; because of impatience we cannot return.*

—Franz Kafka

*Do you have the patience to wait till the mud settles and the water is clear? Can you remain unmoving till the right action arises by itself?*

—Lao Tzu

A few years ago, I dreamed:

I am being shown two immense pillars. On my left there is a cylindrical pillar, which is filled with an infinite number of boxes. Each of these boxes contains—or simply is—set of ethical or moral codes created by some culture at some time in the history of the world. In fact, the pillar is composed of every one of these ethical systems ever created throughout time. On my right stands another pillar comprising raw, unfettered primal life energy and consciousness flowing unbounded upwards eternally.

As I stand between the two pillars, a voice (which I have come to know in my dreams as "The Voice") tells me: "**In the middle...therein lies the fire.**" Now I see a raging fire between the pillars and seem to be observing it from a distance as well as standing in it. In that moment I find that the temperature is cool, but awaken knowing just how intolerable the heat can become for us all on our Journey.

I have pondered this dream now for some time and have come to understand that it speaks to the most difficult and crucial phase of our Journey: the Quest. The central challenge posed by the Quest is what Jung called "holding the tension of opposites." Buddha referred to this task as finding the Middle Way.

Indeed, from our ego's perspective, the world is nothing but an amalgam of opposites. Hard as you might try you cannot think of anything in this world that does not seem to have its opposite.

In fact, it is this world of opposites that is the left-hand pillar in my dream—the world of opposing forms and ideas that creates a need for ethical rules that tell us the "right and wrong" way to act in every situation. This is the same world as well that Eastern philosophy implores us to see as Maya—all that is illusion. But the Sanskrit word that we usually translate as "illusion" is better understood as "nearly real"—in other words, as an actual part of reality that is without objective substance because it is impermanent.

> The time of the Quest in our lives is the time in which a new, deeper consciousness is forged in the furnace of opposites.

In seeming opposition to the world of forms, rules, and laws is the experience of the Source, the Divine, the eternal, unbounded, formless consciousness that is the right-hand pillar of my dream. Yet this, too, can be turned into a mental construct by our ego—made into a set of words and images, describing an experience. And so in my dream, the "idea" and vision of formless consciousness is also "nearly real."

So what is real? What is objective and unchanging and where do I find it? The dream suggests that I should "stand in the middle," centered but not aligned with either "idea" of reality. Why the middle? Because in the middle I am neither for the consciousness of forms or against it—nor for the consciousness of formlessness or against it. In that middle place—the center—is the Present Moment in which both realities can be embraced and experienced.

How is this possible?

In this middle place lies a third, more inclusive witnessing consciousness in which reside both realities.

Another way to say this is that there are two kinds of consciousness. Our ego's perspective reflects a limited quality of consciousness in which the world appears as forms in contrast and opposition to each other. Out of this limited ego consciousness are born our subjective ideas of good and bad, right and wrong—the "ethical systems" of all cultures contained in the left-hand pillar of the dream. Witnessing Consciousness is an expanded awareness in which the same world of forms is seen as arising in the context of a background of all-encompassing consciousness, empty of forms and so unchanging and absolute—itself never born and never dying—the right hand pillar of eternal life energy in the dream.

> In Witnessing Consciousness we *experience* the world as both form and formless.

Consequently, when asked about the nature of reality, those with "enlightened" consciousness say that reality is the impermanent world of forms—and is not—and that reality is the formless world—and is not. This is the same paradox that our quantum physicists point to. Listen to the modern quantum view of reality as described by famed physicist J. Robert Oppenheimer:

> *If we ask for instance whether the position of the electron remains the same, we must say "no."' If we ask whether the electron's position changes with time we must say "no."' If we ask whether the electron is at rest we must say 'no.' If we ask whether it is in motion we must say "no."'*[1]

Now compare Oppenheimer's reality with Buddha's view in a dialogue with his student Vacha, reported in the Buddhist *Pali Canon*:

Vacha: *Do you hold that the soul of the saint exists after death?*
Buddha: *I do not hold that the soul of the saint exists after death.*
Vacha: *Do you hold that the soul of the saint does not exist after death?*
Buddha: *I do not hold that the soul of the saint does not exist after death.*
Vacha: *Where is the saint reborn?*
Buddha: *To say he is reborn would not fit the case.*
Vacha: *Then he is not reborn.*
Buddha: *To say he is not reborn would not fit the case.*[2]

For both Oppenheimer and the Buddha, reality cannot be described as or reduced to a pair of opposites. Rather than opposites, form and formlessness are complementary realities within a larger witnessing consciousness. Zen Master Lin-chi puts all of this quite succinctly: "If you live in the sacred and despise the ordinary, you are still bobbing in the ocean of delusion."[3]

To understand formless consciousness it is helpful to reflect on the stories many of us have heard about those who have returned from a near-death experience—the ultimate experience of loss—to lead a much simpler life, but paradoxically one that feels fuller and more abundant in its joys. How can this be in the face of what these people would have thought earlier to be the worst possible waking life nightmare? Such experiences of peace and joy result from the initiation of complete surrender into a radically different quality of consciousness emptied of forms and the thoughts that create them. This is consciousness of the formless described by our ancient wisdom traditions and sages thousands of years ago and more recently by our quantum physicists, who assure us now that there is not a single solid thing or true form in this universe. Physicist and astronomer Sir James Jeans as far back as 1932 attempted to explain the discoveries of quantum science, referring here to consciousness as "mind": "The universe begins to look more like a great thought than a great machine. Mind no longer appears as an accidental intruder into the realm of matter; we are beginning to suspect that we ought rather to hail it as the creator and governor of the realm of matter."[4]

Our ego's consciousness knows or perceives only forms and so believes that with the end of the body comes the end of life. Awakened sages tell us that there is a greater overarching or Witnessing Consciousness into which our attachment to the forms with which our ego identifies are dissolved—as in the experiences mentioned previously of those whose near-death events have allowed them to experience consciousness as existing independently of the body. In that timeless consciousness the impermanence of form is obvious, but so is the eternal nature of consciousness out of which forms arise.

So it's not that the material world is an illusion. "To deny the reality of things is to miss their reality," says Zen sage Sosan, "To assert the emptiness of things is again to miss their reality...."[5] The poet Kabir said it this way: "The formless Absolute is my Father, and God with form is my Mother."[6]

# Witnessing Consciousness: Nurturing the Third Perspective

A primary goal of the Quest is to transcend our ego's loyalty to the world of opposites and to "experience" a third unifying perspective. This is why in fairytales and fables the number three is magical. Knock three times and the door will open. In modern language there is the thesis, antithesis, and finally synthesis.

Yet the third—synthesis—is not a bland compromise, but rather an entirely new perspective that releases us from the box of our ego's imprisoning—indeed deadening—abstractions and expands the paradigm in which we have been living.

Buddhists refer to the philosophy and practice of "non-action" that creates a stillness in the center of our being, out of which arises this expanded consciousness. In this new experience what first appeared to us as opposites are simply facets of something larger.

My friend Hillary dreamed:

> I was standing exactly in the middle between two shining objects and felt that I must choose one of them. At the same time I thought, "Well that's impossible because these are total opposites of one another and there's no way I can choose one over the other." Suddenly, I was sucked straight into the air and when I looked down, saw a huge multi-faceted, mirrored globe like those they used to use on dance floors. From this new third vantage point I could now see these two objects as actually two of thousands of gleaming facets on an immense sphere—no longer opposite of each other at all. In fact on the surface of the sphere, none of the facets could be said to be opposites. My reality had been distorted by my limited point of view.

This dream describes the third perspective—Witnessing Consciousness—that redeems us from the conflict of opposites. As you can see from my friend's dream, the third perspective is not a thought or idea but rather a new experience of reality—an expansion of consciousness: an epiphany. Living in the background in the quiet between our thoughts, in the still center between all opposites, is the direct experience of the Present Moment, the pure sensation of life, consciousness without words or thoughts, the simple bliss of being.

Campbell was known for his pithy saying, "Follow your bliss." This was just a shorthand way of expressing the importance of directly experiencing life rather than rationally analyzing it. In his own words: "People say that what we are all seeking is a meaning for life. I don't think that's (true). I think that what we're seeking is an experience of being alive, so that our life experiences on the purely physical plane will have resonances within our own innermost being...so that we actually feel the rapture of being alive."[7]

The third perspective enables an expansion of awareness because it is a Witnessing Consciousness that affirms the value of both opposing sides. Listen again to Martin Prechtel speak about the importance of this perspective as he recounts his experience as an apprentice under the tutelage of his shaman and mentor Chiv. In this description Prechtel refers to our ego's consciousness as the "mind of self-preservation" and to the Source as the "mind of natural instinct":

> A current began to pulse between the mind of self-preservation and the mind of natural instinct to become part of the life around me. After a year of practice, that pulse became so fast that it took on the character of a unique 'third thing.' That third thing that appeared was what I would need to have in order to survive my initiation as a shaman. While immersed in nature, not analyzing, not understanding exactly but becoming nature, one really did begin seeing how vast the human soul can be. It was this middle place, this third thing, Chiv and I were after, the place of shamans in the middle of the world.[8]

Notice that Prechtel doesn't say that he's detached and no longer interested in the world or that he ascends to heaven. Rather he says that he "becomes part of the life around him"—experiences himself as one with creation.

A client of mine, Patricia, shared this dream in which the scent of wisteria leads her into an expanded awareness of her universe:

> I am making a unique mosaic tile design on the floor. I realize that I've made it asymmetrical because I haven't perfectly calculated "center." Then I sit yoga-style, and by visualizing the entire room I make it more symmetrical and find the center. I begin to feel anxious when I see that there are no doors or windows. Then I smell the wisteria outside,

get up and follow the scent right through the wall of the room. Now I'm in a beautiful woods full of wisteria. I look back at the room that I was in and I can see my parents and husband clearly through the walls. My parents are unable to see me. My husband can see me but he doesn't know how to get out of the room to be with me.

The dreamer's awareness now includes the same limited space or perspective that her parents still inhabit. She shares their reality but they don't "see her" and cannot participate in her expanded consciousness of the world—know for themselves the depth and breadth of her expanded awareness. Unlike the parents of the dreamer, her husband is aware that her consciousness is more inclusive than his, but does not yet know how "to get out of the room to be with her"—how to embrace her more comprehensive perspective.

Here we have a visual illustration of the profound benefit of standing or "sitting" in the middle. To find the center is to move fully into the expanded consciousness of the Present Moment—to pause long enough to "smell the roses," or, in this case, to stand amidst the scent of wisteria. To do so is not to cut ourselves off from those we love, but rather to expand our consciousness of the reality in which we—and they—live.

For the dreamer, wisteria was an altogether fitting image. She always thought of that flower as one that people try to domesticate, but in her opinion one that should be allowed to grow according to its true nature as a wildflower. Indeed each of us has a natural need to step beyond the suffocating flower box of our conditioned consciousness and into the woods of our wildflower soul—here and now, centered and still in this Present Moment.

The importance of releasing our ego strategies is that these are strategies incompatible with experiencing the Present Moment. This is because the present is a domain that our ego and its favorite tools, thought and intellect, avoid, in fact cannot experience. Ego knows and thrives only on mental constructs, interpretations, judgment, memories, and predictions. In contrast, the now is the irreducible timeless living moment, free of abstractions—a place in which we feel fully alive and experience the unity of being.

The revered Zen monk Thich Nhat Hanh offers this illuminating example:

*Suppose I invite you to join me for a cup of tea. You receive your cup, taste the tea and then drink a little more.... Now suppose I ask you to describe the tea. You use your memory, your concepts, and your vocabulary to describe the sensations. You may say, "It is very good tea, the best...in Taipei. I can still taste it in my mouth. It is very refreshing."' You could express your sensation in many other ways. But these concepts and these words describe your direct experience of the tea; they are not the experience itself. Indeed, in the direct experience of the tea, you do not make the distinction that you are the subject of the experience and that the tea is its object. You do not think that the tea is the best or the worst.... There is no concept that can frame this pure sensation resulting from experience. And you yourself, when you are describing the experience, are already no longer in it. In the experience you were one with the tea. There was no distinction between subject and object, no evaluation and no discrimination. That pure sensation...introduces us to the heart of reality.*[9]

# The Crucible of Consciousness: Therein Lies the Fire

The Grail we seek on our Quest—the "heart of reality" or the "rapture of being alive"—lies just across the portal of the Present Moment, here and now. In other words, the Grail we seek on our Quest—the "heart of reality" or the "rapture of being alive"—lies just across the portal of the Present Moment, here and now. But it is in this same Present that we must experience what our ego fears most: compassionate self-caring, change, and the transcendence of ego itself. (Review Section II for a discussion of these three core fears.) For this reason the Quest has been long known by another name: the Dark Night of the Soul. Perhaps it's more accurate to say that it is the Dark Night of the Ego—a time when in waking life and dreams our ego must face over and over again its inability to spin gold from the straw of opposites—its powerlessness in providing us with anything but hazy, fleeting feelings of security, peace, and fulfillment—always followed by more angst and travail.

The Quest is a time when our ego's favorite strategies seem to generate more pain than pleasure—when distractions leave us feeling increasingly empty, efforts at control yield frustration and hopelessness, self-judgment creates the pain of unworthiness, and identification (attachment) with all that is impermanent results in continued feelings of insecurity and anxiety about loss. As poet and sage Bhartruhari has said:

*In enjoyment, there is fear of disease*
*With social position, the fear of being displaced*
*In wealth, the fear of hostile kings*
*In honor, the fear of humiliation*
*In power, the fear of foes*
*In beauty, the fear of old age*
*In...learning, fear of opposing views*
*In virtue, the fear of seducers*
*In body, the fear of death*
*All things of this world...are subject to fear....*[10]

Ironically, in our search for the answer to our suffering we cling to the same strategies that are responsible for that fear and suffering, and the longer we cling, the more frustrated and impatient we feel. Yet all is as it needs to be. An ancient Chinese proverb reminds us, "The gem cannot be polished without friction, nor the man perfected without adversity."[11]

Needless to say, learning to still the mind or ego through dreamwork, meditation, or any other spiritual practice requires time and the willingness to wait. This is not the waiting for new consciousness to develop, but for our ego to let go sufficiently into the consciousness that we already are. Indeed, our perennial spiritual leaders and visionaries have realized that the only way we can grow emotionally and spiritually is by persevering—that

> As we master the art of waiting, we begin to "experience" that the life energy we seek is not contained in one of the opposites, but in the larger ground from which they are both born.

is, waiting correctly through the ever-present and always-painful tension of "perceived" opposites in our life. Thus, this waiting process becomes the virtual crucible of consciousness—and the reason why Jung reminded us: "There is no birth of consciousness without pain."[12] In fact there is none at all without practicing mindfulness of our impatience both in our waking life and dreams. Indeed, in the time of our Quest, whether our Mentors are teaching us mindfulness of distraction, control, judgment, or attachment, the one underlying motif in most of our dreams is the growing impatience we feel and our wish to be done with our conflict and suffering—now.

Yet, as Jungian analyst Robert Johnson reminds us, "The ground between conflicting forces is a holy place"[13]—the sacred ground of the Present Moment for which we wait.

Until we arrive at this new ground though, we remain mired in what we experience as the worst kind of purgatory. "Therein lies the fire"—the almost unbearable heat of inner conflict we endure as we stand between the secular and sacred, distraction and stillness, controlling and following guidance, judgment and compassion, form and formlessness.

In World War II those survivors from sunken Navy ships who were left adrift in lifeboats for weeks would be more likely to die if they were initially younger and healthier than the others. Why? The older sailors tended to have had more experience with life-threatening situations and knew that even after a long period without rescue, it was still possible to be saved. So they sat in greater equanimity, internally more quiet and peaceful, accepting the Present Moment without taking sides for or against the possibility of living or dying in the future. Their younger counterparts with less experience in life-threatening situations did not know how to wait correctly and literally killed themselves by mentally fabricating a terrifying future in which they believed that they were sure to remain lost and eventually die. Remember Buddha's words: "All that we are arises through our thoughts. With our thoughts we create the world"[14]—for better or worse.

> In the furnace of these opposites we often feel that we won't be able to bear another moment if we don't choose one side or point of view, choose it now without delay, and choose correctly.

Practicing mindfulness of our impatience means learning how to wait for change rather than orchestrating it by yielding to our lifelong ego script.

Yet waiting is an anathema in our culture, which is so alienated from the cycle of nature in which we are full participants whether we believe it or not. Nature never doubts herself, but believing as our egos do that we are separate from nature, we live in doubt. If we have to wait it's almost proof to us that we must not be doing something right, perhaps we aren't taking sufficient control, or that others are being negligent and irresponsible. Sitting at a long stoplight sometimes feels intolerable.

Despite what seems implied in many self-help books, our emotional and spiritual journey is by necessity a slow one—one that may feel agonizingly slow at that. This is because intellectual understanding is usually helpful but never sufficient. The unstated premise of most self-help books is that we simply need to identify what is blocking our way and that understanding will allow us to proceed on. Growth is never based on intellectual understanding alone. Our task is to feel and experience the truth in our bones, and for this gift we must wait.

# Learning How to Hold the Tension

One of the best sources of guidance for learning how to wait is found in the ancient Chinese text, the *I Ching*, mentioned earlier in the book—a compilation of spiritual wisdom that has evolved over thousands of years. Its title, *I Ching*, means the "easy way" and refers to the philosophy that the easiest and most fruitful way to live life is to know when the time is right for action and when for non-action. The *I Ching* hexagrams reflect 64 archetypal times and situations, and provide advice about the correct and incorrect attitudes we may hold in each of these times. To act correctly for the time is to know the easy way—that there is a season for all things. In this respect, mindfulness about the time to act and the time to wait is a profound spiritual mandate. In brief, the only correct time to act is when our consciousness is grounded in the Present Moment. This is what Eckhart Tolle and others have called "Presence."

It is no coincidence that the central metaphors in two of our great spiritual traditions emphasize the prolonged agony of waiting that precedes redemption and illumination. Before enlightenment Buddha must wait under the Bo tree and relive 10,000 painful lifetimes, and Jesus must sweat blood in the Garden of Gethsemane, hang on a cross, and then wait another three days before rebirth. These are metaphors about persevering or waiting correctly through suffering that seems without end—and the great worth of such effort. When in pain, we too are sorely tempted, as they were, to yield to our confusion, give in to and act on every fear and desire that arises within us.

An old Zen story tells of a young student who comes to his master and complains: "Master, it is so hot in here, the heat is unbearable! How can I find relief? What can I do?" The Master responds, "If you seek relief then you must go to the bottom of the furnace." This means that we embrace the moment we are in without resistance. Yet embracing the moment, "holding the tension" and persevering "in the middle," is arguably the most frustrating, difficult, and painful task we are given in our lifetime. As my dream put it, when we try to hold the middle, we must withstand the heat of our (ego's) desire to "choose sides and get it over with." Yet as psychologist and holocaust survivor Victor Frankel reminds us: "What is to give light, must endure burning."[15]

Consider any stuck place in your life—often this will have occurred in the form of conflict or threatened loss of an important relationship with your husband, lover, boss, friend, or family member—and you will find a situation in which you are torn between opposite impulses. Remember just a little of the daily pain and agony—the anger and hurt you felt that seemed as if it would go on forever without resolution—impossible to live with, impossible to let go of—and getting worse. At such times we feel that we can no longer wait and we begin to take ineffective actions—first in one direction and then the opposite. Nothing is working and our pain is growing. This is what *I Ching* scholar Carol Anthony has called the "crescendo of awfulness."[16] We have not yet learned the spiritual imperative to "stand in the middle"—to not side with either of the opposing forces in our life—and wait.

> Waiting often seems most impossible of all and we begin to give up our vision that creative and healthy change is possible.

When you look more closely at these stuck places they always describe the conflict we feel between the legitimate need to protect and nurture our own growth and wholeness as well as that of others. Should I stay or leave? Assert myself or remain silent? Hurt him or hurt myself? Immediately, we begin to feel the stirrings of our ego's voice telling us we are ungrateful, selfish, and hurtful. If we persist in the path that serves our own growth, we begin to feel terrified of retaliation by the Collective ego—members of our family, friends, or unnamed "others"—who will brand us as bad, or ostracize or abandon us. Even if they don't, we project our self-hatred on to them and experience "their" judgment of us.

This power of the Collective Unconsciousness is felt as no less than a curse or spell capable of paralyzing our need to care for ourselves. We all face this dragon whether or not we consciously sign up for the Journey. The challenge is to approach our fear consciously and mindfully. In truth we can do nothing for others if we haven't healed ourselves first—or no more for them than we have learned to do for ourselves.

Where as my two pillar dream likened this process to standing in unbearable heat, another frequently recurring image is that of being torn apart or dismembered. The story of Jesus on the cross is so powerful because it speaks to this archetypal conflict so clearly. In this simple story we learn that we must bear the agony of being pulled apart in what seem to be opposite directions—ego consciousness versus the consciousness of Being—before we can release our resistance to the Present Moment and experience renewal or rebirth. Indeed, it is no coincidence that many spiritual traditions seem to expect some form of dismemberment before the sacred mystery is revealed. Across many cultures, the aspiring shaman reports having such an experience in a dream or vision prior to becoming a spiritual leader of the community. Within the Zen Buddhist tradition Zen students sometimes struggle for years with the Koan—a riddle without apparent solution. The struggle continues until their reliance on the ego's habits of perceiving the world sanctioned by the Collective is sufficiently dismembered. Only then can the student "awaken" to the unity of consciousness. (See Chapter 11 for more about Dreams of Apprenticeship.)

What is torn apart or dismembered is our ego's habitual mode of viewing reality as limited to a set of opposites from which it must choose one side. This Xollective habit of perceiving opposites seems more than reasonable. As mentioned previously, there appears to be nothing we can know or be conscious of without its opposite. What is good if we don't know bad? What is light without darkness? Kindness without cruelty? Hardness without softness? How can I be a doctor without patients, or a businesswoman without customers? The bedrock of our Collective (and personal) ego reality is the perception of opposites.

If we decide prematurely to attach, align, or identify with one side of our conflict, inevitably we doom ourselves to perpetual self-recrimination, guilt, or shame, and find ourselves retracing our path over and over again: "Why didn't I think about how she would feel?" Or, "Why didn't I consider my own needs for once in my life?" We even undo our decision and vacillate for long periods of time. For example, in marital separations we threaten to leave, then apologize and try harder. Or we leave and then return. Our original intention to minimize our pain, "decide and get it over with," has only led to an increasing crescendo of suffering and anguish—a different kind of pain and one more acutely painful than felt from the tension of standing in the middle.

In the *I Ching* hexagram of Waiting (notably also called Nourishment) there are three incorrect ways to wait: waiting in the sand, waiting in the mud, and waiting in blood.[17] These metaphors describe how in emotionally difficult times we must learn mindfulness of the way we wait incorrectly—in this case by "nourishing" ourselves with increasingly destructive thoughts about reasserting control, casting judgment, and resisting the loss we must face—thoughts that our Journey requires us to release if we are to change and grow.

We begin by waiting on the sinking sands of our doubt—creating catastrophic scenarios driven by our fear that we are losing control: "Why won't he listen to me? I don't know what I'll do if..." Alternatively, we make plans to regain control—imagining how great it will be "when he starts listening to me and finally changes, then I'll have everything I want."

As our doubts intensify we begin to "wait in mud." This is akin to slogging around endlessly in the act of judging by comparing ourselves to someone else. We become preoccupied with critical thoughts about the other person: "No matter how many times I'm there for her, she's never..." or "I'm so much more (thoughtful, giving, warm, kind) than him and he'll never..." We give up on their soul's innate potential, begin to judge those we love, and treat them as hopeless.

When our fears and panic grow and our desire to control and judge become more intense and bring no relief we now "wait in blood." At such times we begin to carry intractable resentment, or set up impossible criteria for others to regain our acceptance and heal our pain (which of course is our job, not theirs) and refuse to grieve. Whether we stay or leave the relationship, we may remain identified and attached to the form of the relationship we desired, resist grieving our loss, and stay for years or a lifetime immersed in intractable resentment.

Correct waiting, in contrast, does not require us to trust blindly in fate. We are challenged only to nourish an open and receptive attitude, and to give a benefit of the doubt to the third perspective—the beneficent healing ground of compassionate consciousness—the witness to our impatient agonizing about opposites that are not opposites and choices that don't need to be forced. We wait correctly when we are mindful that:

> We must release the thoughts that blind us to the creative energy of the Present Moment and hold us captive to past and future scenarios—thoughts about our right to be in control, to judge others for their past mistakes, and remain attached to our old identity and never let go.

- We cannot "take sides" for or against a particular solution. Instead we trust that when we "hold the tension" between the opposite solutions we will perceive a third, liberating perspective. A new quality of healing consciousness arises spontaneously in our awareness, one that does not require compromise of our values. This principle lies at the heart of the advice we give when we suggest to a friend that the answer will come if she'll just "sleep on it." Studies on the creative process show that our greatest insights come when we have almost given up finding a conscious solution or strategy. Then our ego is resting and we are better able to hear the quiet voice of the Creative.

- We must wait in the Present Moment without constant rumination about the past and future—this is waiting without resignation or hope, without expectation of failure or success, without planning the outcome.

- We give birth to this third perspective by recalling that there is a time and season for all things and that the learning process can not be rushed any more than a seed can be forced to flower when the ground is still cold.

- We can never change others—just ourselves. To think of how others need to change is to amplify our frustration and impatience exponentially.

- We change ourselves and heal our own pain only when we remember that our suffering results from the choices we make to live in any moment but the present.

In these ways, we gradually open to a new kind of waiting without the angst and mental torture—a waiting that is centered in the infinitely creative energies of the Present Moment. "Patience is bitter," said philosopher Jean-Jacques Rousseau, "but its fruit is sweet."[18] To wait with true mindfulness opens a quality of consciousness that deters our ego's readiness to act before the time is right. When we consistently act out of that consciousness we have entered the return phase of our Journey (about which you'll learn more in Section V).

Neither does correct waiting mean we should blindly trust that all will be as we desire. Rather, we are challenged only to give the benefit of the doubt and to return to "the center." Here is one concrete method we can practice found in the following tale:

> *A man visits a Native American village and speaks to an Elder there.*
> *The Elder tells him, "You know I have two dogs in my stomach?"*
> *"No! You do?"*
> *"Yes, one's a kind dog and one's a mean dog and they're always battling."*
> *"Well which one wins?"*
> *"The dog that I feed the most," says the Elder.*

Waiting correctly requires that we practice mindfulness of the experiences we are nourishing within us. We must ask ourselves on which thoughts we are placing our attention: "Which dog am I feeding? Which dog am I neglecting?" For example, often we find ourselves obsessing about some angry or painful scenario from the past and what may occur in the future. Think of how often we ruminate endlessly about something hurtful our spouse or boss has said, how wrong and unfair it was, what we're going to say back, and when he or she responds, what we're going to say or do then, and so on. Have you noticed how in one day you can engage 40 times in the same dialogue about some criticism or slight you received? We rationalize this process by telling ourselves that we are searching for the reasons that will prove the other person wrong and ourselves right, but in so doing we fan the searing flames of the furnace we have created with our own thoughts. The center between the opposites we perceive is a profoundly open, still, and peaceful space, but we heat it to extreme temperatures when we replay angry, critical, bitter, and resentful thoughts in our mind. Such thoughts cause us to re-experience the wounding, re-traumatize ourselves, and amplify the pain we feel.

The important thing is not to convince ourselves that we are right or wrong. If you think about it, you know that rarely ever works. We must simply say, "I won't feed that dog." This means we set the intention not to participate in that inner dialogue and on whatever fear about the future is driving it. I am not speaking here about engaging in denial or minimization of the problem. However, it is arrogant of us to think we know the future with certainty and that we alone (our ego) must find a way to control the outcome. Rather, we must consciously decide to re-enter the Present Moment and not feed the fear. Inwardly refuse to speak the lines of the neverending drama we have written for ourselves.

As it is said in the *Book of Changes*, the situation revealed in the hexagram of Waiting is one in which we are faced with danger and what is required of us is "restraint." While awaiting the proper time for action we must be "yielding and calm": "If one does not weigh the time conditions sufficiently and presses forward, restless and angry, he will certainly meet with defeat."[19]

By practicing this internal restraint we discover that the objective, all-encompassing, healing truth lies in the middle—not a muddled compromise of viewpoints, but a truth wholly new to our consciousness. Our work is to stop engaging altogether in position-making. Stop engaging in judgment about who is right. Stop engaging in fantasies of control. Stop identifying with a relationship that is by its nature impermanent. Stop panicking. Now. The redeeming third perspective may or may not come immediately, but it will never come when we focus on "our position"—on only one side of the conflict.

One primary feeling that makes it difficult to remain in the Present Moment is guilt. Instead of or in addition to nurturing our anger at another, we may begin by blaming ourselves. "How could I have let myself get so angry and hurt her? Why did I have to lose my temper? Why am I so selfish?" Then, in reaction to feeling guilty about having hurt someone, we salve our pain by telling ourselves stories that reinforce how we were right to have said or done what we did. "How could she be so mean? So unfair? So unconscious?" Indeed we may be right, but because we care about the other person we may also feel guilty for having hurt him or her in some way.

The remedy is mindfulness that all angry behavior and feelings arise from emotional hurt. We may have hurt someone else, but we too feel hurt and it was out of our own pain that we acted to defend ourselves—albeit too harshly or insensitively. When we remember that *both* of us are hurt, it is easier to feel sad, grieve, and let go, instead of indulging more angry rationalization. On the other hand, if I'm not conscious of the pain that generated my behavior, I can only conclude that I'm a selfish and bad person. After all, people who hurt others for no apparent reason are by definition selfish and mean.

When we are viewing the problem through our adversary's eyes and feeling guilty, we must acknowledge to ourselves the hurt that led to our anger. Then, foremost we stop generating the heat of conflict, and breathe into the witnessing Consciousness of compassion for ourselves. (You'll find more help with this in the Section Practices at the end of this section.)

In this way we stop feeding the dogs of guilt, self-hatred, or retribution—the dogs of judgment, control, and attachment to our own point of view.

Yet even when we set the intention to wait correctly, intellectual understanding carries us only so far. There is a world of difference between wanting and even "knowing" how to wait correctly—and resolutely holding to this knowing through the emotional storms that come at the time of the Calling and Quest in our lives. Because our growth is an organic process, we have our own personal seasons with which we must become intimate. The change we desire in our lives cannot be rushed or forced.

Until then we remain in the time of our Quest. Yet we do so knowing that this time in our life is a necessary and unavoidable one on our Journey. There is no way to embrace our Calling to change and grow without first learning how to let go of the familiar landmarks and guideposts, thoughts and beliefs we once trusted. To paraphrase St. John of the Cross, "If you want to find your way, first close your eyes and walk in the dark."[20]

> To know the time on your Journey is to know that there is no failure except from the perspective of our ego and its favorite habits.

We must be fully lost before we can be found. This is the meaning of the classic Grail story, "La Queste del Saint Graal," when it is said at the beginning of the tale: "Each entered the forest at a point that he, himself, had chosen, where it was darkest and there was no path."[21]

In our Quest in waking life and dreams we must walk in the dark and persist in searching everywhere for an answer to our suffering until we find it under our nose, where it rests in the still point between our breaths. Listen to Jesus in the Book of Thomas: "You examine the face of heaven and earth, but you have not come to know the one who is in your presence. You do not know how to examine the present moment."[22] Toward this end he advises us about how to wait: "Be like a servant waiting for the return of the master." He means that, as the servant must, we must stay attentive, receptive, and ever mindful of the Present Moment so as not to miss the gift of redemption—to remain open to its arrival in the only moment we have—the Present.

Indeed the Eternal Present is the experience of paradise—the Garden of Eden—imagined in virtually all of our world's spiritual literature. In fact, the dream of two pillars that you read at the start of this section is grounded in that same imagery of the Garden.

While still in the Garden, Adam and Eve initially eat from neither of the "two trees"—the tree of knowledge or the tree of life. The "tree of knowledge of good and evil" is the left-hand pillar—the consciousness of forms and their opposites—the knowledge of all "ethical systems," the perception of "good and evil." The tree of life is the right-hand pillar—consciousness of the formless. Not eating of either they are not aligned with either. They stand in the middle between them, so to speak, blissfully experiencing both in the Eternal Now of the Present Moment.

To eat of the tree of knowledge is to choose the world of forms as our primary source of sustenance—to judge one part of consciousness as more important than the other. And so, as Adam and Eve did, we too have chosen one of the trees and find ourselves in a barren place alienated from the consciousness of the Source—turned away from the Garden of the Present Moment.

Finally, Adam and Eve remain in suffering as their return to the Garden is blocked by a flaming sword—a fire. In the dream of two pillars this is the "fire" (sometimes interpreted in the Eden story as the "passions") that "lies in the middle" and whose opposing desires we must "wait through" without judging if we are to find our way back to the Garden.

This is also what the great Zen patriarch Sosan meant when he spoke beautifully of this idea 2,500 years ago:[23]

> *The Great Way is not difficult for those who have no preferences. When love and hate are both absent everything becomes clear and undisguised. Make the smallest distinction, however, and Heaven and Earth are set infinitely apart.*
>
> *If you wish to see the truth then hold no opinion for or against it. The struggle of what one likes and what one dislikes are the disease of the mind.*[24]

In David Wagoner's poem, "Lost," he captures the essence of what the Quest requires of us in his rendering of an old Native American story:

*Stand still.*
*The trees ahead and the bushes beside you*
*Are not lost.*
*Wherever you are is called Here,*
*And you must treat it as a powerful stranger,*
*Must ask permission to know it and be known.*
*The forest breathes. Listen. It answers,*
*I have made this place around you,*

*If you leave it you may come back again, saying Here.*
*No two trees are the same to Raven.*
*No two branches are the same to Wren.*
*If what a tree or a bush does is lost on you,*
*You are surely lost. Stand still. The forest knows*
*Where you are. You must let it find you.*[23]

When we step back from the confusing, frightened, distressing (experience of our ego in) dreams of the Quest, one sees a simple pattern emerge with three phases. These are the phases of our ego's resistance to crossing through the gate and across the threshold to the Present Moment—phases in which our ego slowly and painfully releases in increments its fear of being subordinated to the wiser intelligence of the Source.

In the next chapter, you'll read more about these three types of Quest dreams. In the meantime, review the following practices, which will help you to "hold the middle" and cool the heat of inner conflict.

> To know the time of our Journey is also to know that we do not have bad dreams, only dreams in which our ego resists assuming its rightful place in deference to the Source, not separated or superior to it.

# Section Practices

Reflect on a significant conflict in your life—internal or external.

⇝ Write down as many opposite feelings in this conflict as you can think of, such as:

- ❧ My fault vs. his fault.

- ❧ I am wrong vs. I am right.

- ❧ I am justifiably angry vs. I am guilty.

- ❧ I am being selfish vs. I am being self-caring.

⇝ Set the intention to stop analyzing either side—to stop thinking about it, to "stop feeding either dog."

Incubate dreams to assist you in waiting correctly and embracing the Present Moment without resistance. For example, seek the benefits of:

**Solitude and stillness:** Help me to still my thoughts about this conflict and to become quiet and peaceful within.

**Humility (accepting guidance):** Help me to accept and embrace the most healing perspective on this conflict (regardless of what my ego tells me).

**Compassion:** Help me to feel compassion for my own suffering in this conflict.

**Letting go and grieving:** Help me to release my attachment to whatever image of myself is at the source of my suffering in this conflict.

**Holding the tension and embracing the Present Moment without resistance:** Help me to wait without suffering in this Present Moment and to open to a new third perspective that will transcend this war of opposites within me.

# Chapter 10

# Dreams of the Quest

*There is a crack in everything. That's how the light gets in.*

—Leonard Cohen

*There came a time when the risk to remain tight in the bud, was more painful than the risk it took to blossom.*

—Anaïs Nin

There are three kinds of Quest dreams discernable by the degree of resistance our ego displays in releasing its old script. These can be described as Dreams of Chronic Resistance, Opposing the Collective, and Willing Sacrifice. What is most striking about Quest dreams is the frustration, the helplessness, and above all, the lack of resolution we feel in them.

However, as our ego becomes less resistant there are hints of increasing resolution and expanded consciousness.

# Dreams of Chronic Resistance: Refusing the Call

Early phase Quest dreams that we can call Dreams of Chronic Resistance appear and sound similar to the calling dreams or nightmares you read about. They reflect our ego's investment in the same four primary strategies, but these dreams do not end in mortal terror as do nightmares. This is because we (our ego) are no longer so completely identified with those strategies.

Quest dreams are the quintessential "lousy" dreams we've all come to know and hate. Though not quite as upsetting as nightmares, they are full of anxiety, fear, anger, frustration, and feelings of helplessness, guilt, and shame. Our ego remains stubborn and resistant in an increasingly restless and impatient search for relief—trying one avenue of relief and then another—just as in waking life. These dreams seem to offer little if any feeling of resolution as we stand beleaguered and embattled in the fire of inner opposites. We have not yet learned how to wait or to give the benefit of the doubt to the creative and healing energies of the Source. We are lost in the woods "where it is darkest and there is no path,"[1] as in the Grail story you read in Section III.

The grinding, repetitive nature of these dreams makes us want to follow a spiritual path other than dreamwork—to just give up, make a choice, and "settle on something." Yet the truth remains that a spiritual path without discomfort is by any other name a spiritual bypass. Though we will always find the light we seek in the darkness, we must learn to "walk in the dark" to reach our goal.

Very often these dreams may incorporate the entire spectrum of strategies as our ego fights for the status quo and struggles against change. For the sake of simplicity here are a few examples that correspond to each of the four primary ego scripts. As you read stay mindful of the lack of any apparent resolution in these dreams.

## Chronic Dreams of Distraction in the Quest: Practice Mindfulness of Solitude

> I'm attending some kind of spiritual retreat. I'm on my way to class and realize that I forgot to read the morning newspaper as I always love to do. I head back to my room where I'm staying but end up talking with the cook about the lunch menu. A young teenager walks by with a boom box and I can't hear what the cook's saying to me. I wake up incredibly irritated. I'm already stressed before I get out of bed and want to keep the day a low-key one.

## Chronic Dreams of Control in the Quest: Practice Mindfulness of Humility and Accepting Guidance

> I am in a car driving. My husband offers to drive for me. I tell him confidently that I will not be needing his help. Then we approach a sharp curve and I try to tighten my grip on the wheel, but my elbows are pulled back by some force so that I can't hold the steering wheel at all—and I'm scared. The car turns just as it's supposed to and we safely navigate the curve.
>
> I woke up still scared, but then realized that I need to trust that I am being guided and it's neither me nor my husband who is in charge.

## Chronic Dreams of Judgment in the Quest: Practice Mindfulness of Compassion and Self-Caring

> Just as in waking life, I attend a spiritual retreat in my dream where the guru recommends that I meditate three times a day. I return home and become upset as I watch my daughter shoot up heroin three times in a row, every day. Later I realized how much fear and resistance I feel to doing what would help me. I guess I saw the meditation as something addictive. I always seem to take the most critical view of things.

## Chronic Dreams of Attachment in the Quest: Practice Mindfulness of Grieving and Letting Go

> I'm with my friend Jim who is terribly ill, just as in real life. Only in the dream he is much closer to death and I'm feeling really a lot sadder, a lot worse than I've actually been feeling about him lately. I really don't like it. Then I think its just not right that this is happening and I start looking for a doctor to see if anything can be done to save him. I just can't let him die.

# Dreams of Opposing the Collective: Affirming the Source

Middle-phase Quest dreams reflect our ego's tentative and very ambivalent action on behalf of the Source and expanded consciousness. Notice that they remain remarkable for their lack of clear resolution. Yet in these dreams our ego's strategies are slowly weakening and we begin to express once-forbidden perspectives.

Our Journey in life starts with the necessity of being aligned with the Collective and the great security of containment that it offers. As adults we continue to suffer greatly for the price of that security. To conform with Collective expectations we reject life-enhancing experiences that would enrich our life and move us toward wholeness and the simple consciousness of Being.

Some readers may recall the *Star Trek: The Next Generation* story of the Borg. This was a tale of the immense suffering and pain felt by hapless humans caught in the soul-sucking technology of the Borg—a race of beings who would capture humans and plug them into a Collective mind-web. There they would merge and become one with the mind of the Borg. The only cost was their individual sense of self. Notably, unique to this process was the great fear those rescued from the web experienced in separating from the Collective—and the deep pain they felt in being subordinated to it. In this story the Collective is a name for the collective ego in which we are all immersed.

Similarly, the popular Hollywood tale *The Matrix* is a more modern version of the Borg. A great impersonal computer and its machines have taken over the world, and at birth humans are plugged into software that provides them with a simulated version of life—a virtual or "nearly real" experience. A savior, Neo, is born, whose expanded consciousness allows him to experience himself as part of something more than the Matrix mind-web—more than the limited perspective created by the Collective computer mind (ego).

> To release our lifelong ego script is a fearsome task for us all and one toward which we go only with the greatest reluctance.

A young woman in one of my dream groups shared a dream that speaks directly to this issue: As you'll see, this Dream of Opposing the Collective contains within it a motif of Judgment in which the dreamer fears attack, but it also speaks to our universal dilemma—our dread as well as desire to stand up to the Collective mind or ego (within us) on behalf of our own soul.

> I am Buffy the Vampire Slayer—the woman who slays all the demons—but I'm also a hostage. I'm with a group of men who are keeping me with them and pretending to be my captors, but they are afraid too and are secretly on my side. The problem is we're all afraid of the Dementors—you know, those characters from *Harry Potter* who have the power to make people think they are different people than they really are.

On our Journey we come to understand that the demonic powers are simply the compelling desires or strategies of our own ego and the collective ego—the Dementors—from which it has learned. Ironically, the role of heroine or hero we assume in our battle against the ego is just another ego role. To truly "oppose the collective" is not to destroy it or to deny its reality, but to stand up on behalf of the "the middle," the living, Witnessing Consciousness of the Present Moment in which reside the thought forms of the collective and personal ego as well as formless consciousness. To align only with ego consciousness is to believe that we "are different people than we really are." We think we have met the Collective enemy, but again, as Pogo says, "He is us."

For example, in *The Matrix* when Neo is proud of his new ability to dodge bullets, his mentor Morpheus tells him that someday "you'll see there are no bullets to dodge." That is to say, someday you will find that "you and the bullets"—you and your enemy—are part of your ego's more limited consciousness of opposites. You will know instead that they are part of a greater consciousness in which both the bullets and you are without real substance, as compared to the Source consciousness out of which all ego identities are born.

But the fear of opposing the Collective—that is, expanding our consciousness—runs deep within us all. Consider this dream told to me by Patricia, my client in Chapter 3 who felt that we "can't be in the zone all of the time."

Patricia had been denying her creative needs as a writer and letting her considerable talent lie fallow. Patricia dreamed:

> I have my journal—literally all of my thoughts and dreams—in the back trunk of my car. A policeman stops me and senses that I'm hiding something. He demands that I open the trunk. I do and the light shines in on my journal. I wake up frightened.

We are called by the Source to re-claim our vision, open to an expanded identity, and acknowledge our authentic self. In this dream it's as if the Source is prodding Patricia to face up to who she is—that there's no hiding—nor should there be. Here again we see that, though the policeman is perceived as a feared member of the Collective, he serves as Patricia's Mentor—prodding her to hold the tension of opposites and claim the values of the Creative Source as no more or less important than the values of the Collective ego.

Our psyche takes us step by step as it sheds light on the nature of the problem in which we are stuck and often does so most poignantly in small "snapshot" dreams such as Patricia's as well as this follow-up dream of hers.

> I wake up and find my clothes have all been shredded. I'm upset because only my husband's clothes fit me. At work everyone thinks I am my husband, Steve. I am crushed. A colleague of mine says: "Well the clothes make the man."

Patricia was choosing to appease the pragmatic values of her father and husband and to fit in with the masculine preferences of the Collective society around her, which offer little support for the creative soul. She awakened from this dream, aware of how she had succeeded so well at hiding her creative connection to the Source for the sake of acceptance by the Collective. In fact, she has become so expert at concealment—at clothing herself in masculine values—that no one knows the real Patricia. She feels a crushing sense of loss and now has more than just an abstract idea of what she has sacrificed by hiding her talents and the true self that gives them voice. (In Chapter 8 you read about such dreams of Imminent Loss in which we are warned about giving up something too precious to lose.)

Usually as each dream progresses through the night or over time, it shows us moving forward or backward on our path, depending on the degree to which we accept or resist the promptings of our psyche. In Patricia's case, her next dream that night showed her beginning to let go of her excessive alignment or attachment to Collective values. In the Quest, this letting go is of course always fraught with reluctance and anxiety. She dreamed:

> I have written something that the village finds offensive. I deny it but they say, "Well you did speak it though and then someone wrote it down." When I continue trying to deny that I did anything wrong, they punish me in the most hideous way by binding my hands so they will grow together. Entwined in the cords are strips of leather and red silk.

This dream begins by showing that Patricia has taken the risk of exposing her true self—her expanded consciousness from which the creative impulse is born. However, once again, her intense fear of being different than the Collective leads her to deny that she has even attempted to express herself creatively. Her Dream Mentors hold her feet to the fire, however, and say she can't deny what she thinks and feels and must own responsibility for having voiced these ideas.

Remember that Patricia's dream is not simply about conflict between herself and the "bad" or evil Collective powers that be. Recall Kahlil Gibran's words: "I have learnt silence from the talkative, toleration from the intolerant, and kindness from the unkind; yet strange, I am ungrateful to these teachers."[2] Patricia must learn to perceive those that seem to be punishing her as teachers or Dream Mentors showing her the "Way" to release.

The Collective world of forms and laws (for example, the police) is not against us if we do not oppose it. The attitude we must nurture is one of inclusiveness, not opposition. Gibran again puts this so eloquently:

> *All things in this creation exist within you, and all things in you exist in creation; there is no border between you and the closest things, and there is no distance between you and the farthest things, and all things, from the lowest to the loftiest, from the smallest to the greatest, are within you as equal things...in one aspect of you are found all the aspects of existence.*[3]

As I mentioned earlier, in all dreams, including nightmares, there is a healing medicine offered for our wound. In Patricia's dream of her journal being exposed, the medicine is to claim her thoughts and feelings as her own. In her "clothes make the man" dream, her Mentors' medicine is to provide a blunt snapshot of how well she has disguised herself and the precious creativity she will lose if she persists. Medicine often tastes bad going down!

In her third dream, as is so often the case in dreams, the perceived punishment by her Dream Mentors *is* the medicine. Patricia associates the position of her hands tied together with praying. The leather lanyard reminded her of her love of horses as a child and the freedom she felt to be herself while riding. Similarly, the strips of red silk reminded her of the ribbon she won for coming in third place with her horse and how much she once enjoyed the feeling of competence and mastery. Thus the dream medicine can be summed up as: "Keep your hands together in prayer. Do this until you recall the experience of how wonderful it feels to have the freedom to express yourself. This is an experience that you've already had and loved in life, but which you have come to shun, deny, and judge as 'hideous.'" Why hideous? Because due to past experience with family and Collective reprisals, the very thought of "being herself" was fraught with fear, and indeed a terrible punishment if enforced.

# Dreams of Willing Sacrifice: Seeking Guidance

Late phase Quest dreams or, as I call them, Dreams of Willing Sacrifice portray us (our ego) as so worn down that we find ourselves asking, demanding, praying, imploring, or begging for help—a sign that we have suffered enough, are prepared to sacrifice our most cherished defenses, give the benefit of the doubt to the Source, and accept guidance.

> Just as soldiers are said to find religion in foxholes, we may do the same in our Quest dreams of Willing Sacrifice.

Betsy had been in chronic severe pain for years due to a back injury. Neither medicine nor surgery could alleviate her pain. Raised in poverty by two physically and emotionally abusive parents, she was now in a deeply unhappy marriage. Concluding that every one of her efforts to improve her life and find relief had been unsuccessful, her depression and feelings of helplessness mounted until these two dreams—both within the same night—became a turning point for her: Notice the reference to the "middle" in both dreams:

I'm in the middle of a Coliseum and a boy around 8 or 9 years of age in tattered clothing and dirty is holding up a double-sided chalkboard to the crowd, turning around and around asking for help and answers about his health. I merge with him, then tell him what to say and how to say it.

Later that same night I dreamed that I am standing in the middle of the tallest skyscrapers I've ever seen—surrounded by them. I look up toward these powerful buildings and the sky is very blue, and at the peak of the skyscrapers is a beautiful, bright, almost blinding sun. The sky and the sun seem to go on and on forever. It's extremely beautiful and hard to describe. I realize that whoever owns this real estate is very powerful. Then I get a sense it is not a person who owns this land, but a powerful force. I feel calmer and deeply peaceful and I ask for help. I tell the "Source" that I hope I am understood because I am afraid and in pain and I speak a language that most people cannot understand.

The Coliseum—evocative for Betsy of life-threatening clashes between gladi-
ators and Christian martyrs willing to die for their faith—is the fitting setting
in which to surrender, pray for help, and open to guidance. The 8- or 9-year-
old child is the age in life until which she still held hope that there were others
who could love her. The language Betsy speaks that no one understands (except the Source ) is the expression of her suffering to which the Collective—
family and society—has been deaf. Until this set of dreams, Betsy's own ego,
had been deaf to her suffering—offering up constant self-blame for her condition and attached to an identity of helpless victim.

"Standing in the middle," Betsy is able to experience the "calm and deeply
peaceful," timeless quality of the Present Moment "as it seems to go on and on
forever." It is in this precious living moment residing in the center between all
opposites that Betsy finds her first strong glimmer of hope, but she remains
frightened and unsure whether the Source will care about her suffering.

These dreams mark a turning point in Betsy's life. Despite her continuing
physical pain, Betsy's depression lifts very slowly though steadily as she releases the old ego script of "deserving victim" that had sustained her feelings of
separateness and hopelessness.

In Chapter 6 you read about Janine, my client who shared a  Control
nightmare about the man who threw dirt in her car. She had sought therapy
due to her lifelong struggles with a highly dysfunctional family. She felt hope-
lessly alienated from her family and saw herself as their perennial scapegoat.
Having worked with a few dreams early in therapy, she came in one day tearful
and emotionally shaken. Here's her dream:

> I am in the midst of a war-torn city. Everywhere around me the build-
> ings are in ruins or on fire. It's very cold but the people are dressed in
> rags, myself included. A dirty old man stands over a barrel in which
> wood is burning and I see that people are circled around him and the
> barrel, warming their hands over the fire. I see that more than anyone
> else his own clothing is the most torn and ragged, he has a straggly
> long beard and looks as though he hasn't washed in months. I'm afraid
> but something in me pulls me to him. He ignores me but then I ask
> him for help. He turns and smiles. I look deep into his eyes and see
> that it is God and for the first time in my life feel unconditional love.

Janine awoke from this dream feeling compassion for her own suffering—an experience never felt from her own family—and turned a corner in her life, opened to guidance from her dreams, and embarked on a life-changing Journey. You'll learn about another one of her Dreams of Apprenticeship in Chapter 11.

Keep in mind that any dream in which you find yourself pleading or screaming for help is probably one of Willing Sacrifice—and that the willingness to do so signals a time in your dreams and waking life when you have grieved, have found compassion for your suffering, and are preparing to release control, open to guidance, and enter the time of Illumination.

Read on to familiarize yourself with the hallmarks of the Illumination in your waking life and dreams.

# Practicing Mindfulness of Quest Dreams and their Lessons in Everyday Life

To work with any Quest Dream, return now to Chapter 4 and choose one or more of the mindfulness practices described there.

Journal about or recall events in your near or distant past in which you have felt frightened to "strike out on your own," be different than family or friends, or simply "be yourself."

- Have you transcended that fear yet? Are you still concealing your true identity in some ways?

- Incubate a dream and ask to embrace compassion for the suffering in which you have remained so long.

- Alternatively, ask for guidance about how to explore your potential without the disabling fear you've been experiencing.

# Section IV

## The Time of Your Illumination:
### Finding the Divine Mirror

*When your chest is free of your limiting ego*
*Then you will see the ageless Beloved*
*You can not see yourself without a mirror;*
*Look at the Beloved. He is the brightest mirror.*

—Rumi

It is never up to our ego to decide when we have waited long enough or whether we have done enough work on our Journey. Though it's true that the turning point often occurs when we've released the conviction that logical solutions to our suffering—ego strategies—can be devised to end our suffering. As Thoreau suggested, "It is only when we forget all our learning that we begin to know."[1]

In Zen circles there is a well-known story about a university professor who went to visit a famous Zen Master. While the master prepared to serve tea, the professor chatted on and on about the philosophy of Zen. The master poured the professor's cup to the brim and kept pouring. The professor watched the overflowing cup until he couldn't hold back his distress: "It's overfull! No more will go in!"

"You are like this cup," the master replied. "How can I show you Zen unless you empty your cup?"[2]

It was sometime after I had given up thinking I knew much at all, that I dreamed:

> I am on a sidewalk in the city on a warm and pleasant afternoon. I find myself with friends I know in waking life. Suddenly we are Zen monks on our knees and we are chanting the mantra OM. With each repetition of the word my body is rocked with ecstatic waves of energy that I experience as holy and deeply sacred. This powerful energy dissolves my sense of separateness from the world. I am filled with, and then realize that I am one with, this energy that can only be described as Divine Compassion. As we continue to chant I see and then become waves of compassion that ripple out around us in all directions and transmute the city, its buildings and people. Everything, even the bricks, are alive and conscious and I know this is the true unchanging nature of the universe—a living, loving, divine consciousness as it has always been, and is now, eternally—and I am conscious and one with it.

Compassionate or awakened consciousness is often experienced as a sublime awareness known and celebrated by all the great spiritual traditions of the world. Compassion is not simply great empathy or a deeply loving feeling, not really an emotion at all, but rather a quality of consciousness that knows no boundaries between I and Thou. Mother Teresa is often quoted as having said of her work with impoverished orphans that she was ministering to the crucified Christ in each of them—as we too must attend with compassion to our own suffering.

> If the work of the Journey is any one thing, it is the work of the heart. It is in the place of heart-consciousness or compassion where human meets divine and where our work is consecrated.

All life is sacred, and it is our work to redeem its shattered parts in the crucible of compassionate consciousness. The Jewish mystical text, Kabbala, calls this process "Repairing the Face of God."

Compassion is also a quality of consciousness in which we experience our mistakes in life as a necessary part of our growth and not a reason to condemn ourselves. Whether awakened initially in us through our suffering, or received in meditation, prayer, or dreams, this is a profoundly healing energy that calls us to see our ego's perspective as the source of our suffering.

A central lesson of the Illumination is that the world of form is the "nearly real" illusion of ego consciousness. Our ego identifies with forms. Then we suffer when those forms—our bodies, the "things that are ours" and our "concept" of who we are— inevitably die, are lost, or change. It is this same endless suffering in the time of our Quest that prompts us to find another way—the way of compassion in the time of our Illumination.

Refusing to judge any part of ourselves as unworthy, compassion for our suffering prompts us to let go of our deadening attachments to things we have gained or lost in the past and thoughts of gain or loss in the future. We are opened instead to the Present Moment of living experience in which lies a new expanded consciousness of Being that that is beyond name and form. As Eckhart Tolle explains, this is a consciousness that redeems us from suffering because once you "are aware that you are identified with a thing, the identification is no longer total. I am the awareness that is aware that there is attachment. That's the beginning of the transformation of consciousness."[3]

> In the Illumination we discover that our Dream Mentors embody this same compassionate witnessing consciousness and so we open our heart increasingly to the many shapes and forms they assume in our dreams.

Prior to this time on our Journey we were so identified with form that the very presence of our Mentors was experienced as deeply threatening to our "identity"—our ego's attachments. Now in Mindful Dreaming we practice "I am that!" In so doing we increasingly release our attachment to the narrow identity, limiting thoughts, and prejudices conditioned by our family and society.

I read once the dream of a woman shared by the Jungian analyst Edward Edinger. In her dream she saw:[4]

> [A]n old man sitting on a bench...ragged and encrusted with filth. He was like the dregs of humanity...the disreputable poor, beyond the pale of society, the outsider, the "least among you."
>
> The man says, "They ought to do something about the small animals." (Then) I see strewn on his lap are three dead rats, and one dead grey rabbit. A cloud of gnats veils the man's head. At first it looks to me like a halo, but rather than being horrified and running, I feel great compassion for him. I hear that this is Christ. We decide to call someone to help him.[4]

Of course, it was Jesus himself who said, "[A]s you did it to one of the least of these My brethren, you did it to Me."[5] The perennial spiritual lesson is that the entire world—all of creation, every last gnat and filthy beggar are an expression of divine consciousness. Indeed, Witnessing Consciousness is the ground and Source of the world of forms. Quantum physicist David Bohm calls this consciousness the Implicate Order out of which the world of form arises.[6]

Perennial philosophy calls this eternal ground of pure awareness or Being, the Unmanifested.

# The Mirror of Shame

We (our egos) are so lacking in compassion for our pain. Over time I have realized that feelings of shame are the main obstacle to the experience of compassion for ourselves. It is shame—the most powerfully negative human thought—that alienates us from awareness of our true nature.

Many of us lump shame and guilt together, though they are very different. When we feel guilty we can think of ways to undo that guilty feeling and to make amends. If we apologize and our apology is accepted, then we feel relieved of our emotional burden. However, when we feel shame we hold the thought that what we have done is unpardonable and that our whole self is bad and unredeemable: "I am a bad person. No one can or should forgive me. I feel worthless, insignificant, and unlovable. I want to hide and disappear."

What triggers such profound self-abandonment and rejection?

I recall some years ago reading a fascinating little research study on the nature of the shame response in humans—what were called "still face" experiments. Researchers found that full-blown bodily shame reactions occur in infants and toddlers if the child reaches out happily to a mother who responds neutrally without expression on her face.[7]

In other words, we are born requiring a positive mirror for our growth and development. In fact, scientists learned many years ago, in now-famous studies, that infants in an orphanage had a remarkably high rate of illness and death when they were well-cared-for physically, but treated by their nurses in an emotionally detached way—that is, without positive emotional mirroring.

Actually, what once happened to infants in orphanages happens to us all in varying degrees throughout life. As adults we often experience this painful lack of mirroring. Think of a time when a friend, teacher, or family member simply wasn't attentive to what you were saying, or simply appeared uninterested. Even a minor slight over a relatively unimportant topic can sting badly. This is all the more painful for us as children, when we are so vulnerable, undefended, and ready to believe whatever messages our parents—often deeply wounded themselves—communicate to us. In truth there are so few times in life that we feel compassionately and unconditionally mirrored, that we stand constantly in apprehension of being hurt, if not shamed.

Scottish poet Robert Burns wrote: "Oh wad a pow'r the gifted g'ie us, to see oursels as others see us!"[8]

This belief that others around us are the objective mirror we seek, prompts us to expect family, friends, lovers, and authority figures from politicians to therapists to act as our mirror of reality. Yet therapists are human beings as well, with biases and blind spots. Even our parents can positively mirror for us only those experiences that they can accept in themselves. For the remainder they provide at best a "still face," leaving so many of our feelings unacknowledged. Early in life we conclude that these unmirrored experiences must be unworthy of attention, and therefore shameful.

> We may indeed meet a lover and lifetime mate, but after the first blush of love we find the mirror they hold blemished and, if we are honest, so is the one we hold up for them.

Allowing our self-image to rest upon the shifting sands of others' opinions, we suffer constantly. What others think of us and how they mirror and judge us becomes the flawed and torturous measure of our self-esteem. Recall the Dalai Lama's observation that he knew of no other culture whose people feel so badly about themselves, and so unworthy.[9]

Even when we can't find that mirror in our family and friends, we cling to the hope that we will find "the one" who will be that perfect mirror for us—who will reflect back all that is special about us and respond with compassionate acceptance to those parts of us still underdeveloped, scared, and ashamed.

This yearning for a mirror is so great that we may go for years or a lifetime trying to heal and "fix" those whom we love, in part out of compassion for their suffering, but also in the hope that "if I can fix my parents or spouse then they will love and validate—mirror back—all of me as well."

Fortunately, not even shame can destroy our capacity to experience. Rather, our Dream Mentors return to us each night, embodying those same unmirrored experiences we have rejected—experiences that would return us to wholeness—if we didn't initially fear the shame of feeling that way. So during the first half of our Journey, our Dream Mentors continue to appear to us as "enemies" until we embrace compassion for the unmirrored parts of us that suffer. Recall Rilke's words: "Perhaps all the dragons in our lives are only princesses waiting for us to act, just once, with beauty and courage. Perhaps everything that frightens us is, in its deepest essence, something helpless that wants our love."[10] When we risk embracing the experience our Dream Mentors embody, they reveal to us both our wholeness and the wound we have suffered—a suffering that will heal only with the balm of our own compassion.

# Losing and Finding Our Mirror: Betrayal, Forgiveness, and Absolution

Our universal desire for a mirror lies behind the devastation of betrayal. Consider what happens when we feel betrayed. In betrayal we experience acute pain and resentment because a loved one has lied about our worth to him or her, or simply stopped feeling that way. At that moment what is actually betrayed is our dependency on that person as a mirror of our worth. The "gift" of betrayal, however, is that it forces us back on our own resources to see for ourselves what the other seemed to see—to acknowledge and claim as our own the experience that we hoped another would provide us.

When we are able to find our own mirror and directly experience our worth, we can let go of resentment for not being mirrored.

Most of those whom we label our enemy in daily life are those whom we feel have betrayed us—that is, those who have failed or refused to mirror our innate worth. For example, I spoke with a woman, Cassie, who years after her divorce still felt betrayed and resentful because her ex-husband rejected her sexually. Her sexuality unmirrored and unaffirmed, she became inhibited in subsequent relationships, feeling ashamed of her own sexual energy. In our work together, she attended eagerly to her dreams, and soon thereafter, experienced this graphic and vivid dream:

> Herein lies the nature of true forgiveness: We forgive the loss of mirroring only when we have found our own compassionate mirror— that is, when we have reclaimed our own worth.

I am with this man and I'm telling him how since my marriage I'll never be able to feel sexual or attractive again. He says, "You know that's bull!" Then he takes me in his arms and we make love in a way that that I can't ever recall. But what I felt was more than sexual fulfillment. It was on all planes—mind, body, and spirit. It was as spiritual as it was physical. Though I've never made love quite like that before, I remember these feelings in me before my marriage. Now they're back to stay. I won't let them go again.

Cassie awoke without need of her ex-husband's empty mirror. She had reclaimed her sexuality in the healing mirror of compassionate consciousness held by her Dream Mentor. Her resentment dissolved and she was able to grieve for the loss of what she had hoped for from her marriage. Only then was she able to forgive him. We cannot truly forgive others until we reclaim for ourselves the experience they failed or refused to mirror. Then, fully healed, all we feel is sadness for the limitations of those who could not be the mirror we desired.

This kind of true forgiveness is actually what we call absolution. Absolution returns us to a condition of innocence without need of forgiveness because in the larger compassionate perspective no wrong was ever done.

In truth Cassie absolved her "ex." He had been innocent all along because her sexuality was never something he could steal from her. Indeed, the pain she felt came from her dependency on a man whose own limited experiences made him a less-than-adequate mirror for her. Nor did Cassie need forgiveness for wanting him to be her mirror. Every one of us wants a mirror. We usually just don't know where to look.

When we honor the compassionate mirror of the Source embodied in our Mentors, we transcend forgiveness and discover absolution for ourselves and those around us. Original sin becomes original innocence and we move toward redemption and wholeness.

# The Divine Mirror

How do we see ourselves as we really are?

Clearly, mirroring is the alchemical catalyst for our experience of healing, growth, and wholeness. Therefore it's no surprise that the mirror has always been seen as an archetypal image of the Divine—a bridge between human-kind and the Source—and as a sacred tool with which to reflect objective truth. In the Buddhist tradition there is a ritual celebration of Buddha's first bath, in which a mirror is washed while the image of Buddha remains reflected in it.[11] By participating in this ritual one is reminded that the Self or Source is an objective mirror of our true Buddha nature that can become clouded by the thoughts and concerns of our ego.

So too, we look to gurus and spiritual leaders to be the objective mirror of our true nature. The exalted Aztec leader Montezuma was described as "the mirror in which we are able to see ourselves and in which we are all reflected."[12] Then of course it is Christ who said, "A mirror am I to thee that perceivest me."[13]

Here is a dream of a young woman, Sarah, a member of one of my dream groups, that is a particularly fitting illustration of how our dreams are both the mirror and gateway to the awakened consciousness we seek. (In her dream, "government" refers not to the center of Collective authority, but to the center of Divine authority. Also notice again the reference to the "third," which recurs again and again in our experiences of epiphany.)

> I am on the third floor of a government building, alone, and I'm browsing through a mirror shop. I wonder why someone would want to sell mirrors on a floor so high because people will have to carry them down so far. I walk down the stairs and out into a huge parking lot to find my husband. As I approach him in the parking lot, I can't get his attention no matter what I do. Then I realize that I have inhabited someone else's body and he doesn't recognize me. Realizing the miracle of what has happened, instantly I

become aware that I am conscious of my complete interconnectedness with all things in the universe and with the Source of all energy. Being one with this energy, being the Source, allows me to experience life in whatever body I want. I decide that I'd like to communicate with my husband and set the intention to shift back into the body that he will recognize.

In the Upanishads it is said of the Source: "Not female, nor yet male is it, neither is it neuter. Whatever body it assumes, through that body it is served."[14]

In Sarah's dream she wonders at the difficulty of having to "carry the mirror down" from such a high place. This is a difficult task for us all. But this is our challenge: to find the Divine mirror, see ourselves in its light for the pure consciousness that we are, and "carry" that experience down with us into the mundane "parking lot" depths of everyday life. Sarah's dream calls her as it does us all to move beyond the intellectual abstractions about the gifts of the Journey. In the time of our Illumination we open to the experience the Divine in every shape and form it assumes on this Earth—including our own.

Though we all hear most about the sudden flashes of illumination referred to in Zen as Satori, true awakening is an ongoing process that extends into the time of the Return that you will read about in Section V.

In the next chapters I'll provide you with examples of how in the Illumination, we assume the role of Apprentice to our Dream Mentors. You'll see how Mentors provide the healing mirror that prompts us to more fully embrace solitude, humility, compassion, and a Witnessing Consciousness that transcends our ego's attachment to the world of opposites, good and bad, right and wrong, past and future.

You'll also read of dreams in which we become our own Mentors. In these Dreams of Embrace and Mastery we practice successfully what we've been taught on our Journey without the direct intervention of our Mentors. Then you'll learn about Dreams of Embodiment that serve as a gateway to the blissful experience of the Present Moment in which we feel the joy of awakened consciousness directly in our body. You'll also

> It seems that as a species we are ever in search of the perfect mirror in whose reflection we can find the objective truth of our wholeness.

be introduced to Dreams of Being in which the formless Witnessing Consciousness is experienced as both eternal and independent of our body and other material forms. This is the Grail consciousness that offers redemption for our suffering in the eternal here and now of the Present Moment.

These dreams also can be seen as moving us from the consciousness of form to formless consciousness—that is, from intellectual instruction through the experience of embodiment—the marriage of head and heart—and on to an awakened consciousness without reference to the intellectual or physical forms of knowing. And in the end, we can hear the words of author Albert Camus with new ears and say as he did: "In the depth of winter, I finally learned that within me there lay an invincible summer."[15]

# Section Practices

## Reflections on Betrayal

- ➣ Recall a time when you felt betrayed by a friend or loved one. What did the betrayer do or fail to do? What part of you felt negated, unmirrored?

- ➣ Do you still feel resentful? Shameful?

- ➣ Do you feel that your betrayer took a precious part of you with him or her when the relationship ended?

- ➣ Have you felt disconnected from that part ever since that time?

- ➣ Incubate a dream and request assistance in reclaiming that energy, perspective, or experience that has been unmirrored since the betrayal.

- ➣ Ask for a dream that will assist you in embracing compassion for your suffering.

## Reflections on the Time of Illumination in Your Life

The Illumination is a time when we surrender in devotion to the inner mirror and the redemption from suffering it offers. Incubate a dream in which you ask for help in embracing its truth and light more consistently and wholeheartedly.

# Chapter 11

# Dreams of Apprenticeship

*All the arts we practice are apprenticeship. The big art is our life.*

—M. C. Richards

After the long and arduous struggle through the Quest, our dreams reflect a growing trust and willingness to follow the guidance of our Dream Mentors. As you read in Chapter 9, after a period of continued resistance, in our dreams we begin to pray for help and even fearfully stand up somewhat to the Collective mind (within us) on behalf of our Self.

Little fear is present in Illumination dreams and what is present quickly wanes as the dream progresses. We move into the role of apprentice to our Mentors who no longer appear threatening. Instead, we experience them as helpful friends and sages offering us timeless guidance and wisdom on our Journey.

> Now in the time of our Illumination our dreams feel fulfilling and there is an experience of resolution rather than frustration.

Let's look at some dreams shared with me by friends and clients that reflect their own experience of apprenticeship as they learn to embrace the values that foster expanded consciousness. Take note that these are Dreams of Apprenticeship because in each we are just beginning to learn. We do not act on our own as in the Dreams of Embrace and Mastery that you'll read about next. We merely receive instruction in a heartfelt manner from caring Mentors. The deepening of the lesson—our true initiation—comes in later Illumination dreams.

# Mindfulness of Solitude and Stillness

Evie had been a member of my Mindful Dreaming group for some months and had been taking very seriously the guidance she received from her Dream Mentors about releasing ego strategies, especially self-judgment. Then she shared this dream in which her Mentors, members of the dream group, were teaching her about the benefits of solitude and how to become quiet within:

> Each of you was trying to teach me a game that involved pebbles and stones that were being buffeted by the strong current of a stream. I was supposed to keep the stones still by using my mind. I was not very good at it but each of you spent time giving me tips. It seemed that the game was part of an ancient ritual.

Here Evie is an apprentice to her Mentors who are "giving her tips" about an "ancient," perennial lesson: the importance of stilling her thoughts. The dream likens her thoughts to pebbles and stones buffeted by the heavy current of a stream. Her task is the same as ours—that is, to quiet her thoughts and keep them still despite the strong current of energy generated by her ego's plans and fears. As Eckhart Tolle reminds us, "The stream of thinking has enormous momentum that can easily drag you along with it. Every thought pretends that it matters so much. It wants to draw your attention in completely. Here is a new spiritual practice for you: Don't take your thoughts too seriously."[1]

Indeed it is no coincidence that in Evie's dream the work of stilling her thoughts is not serious but rather a "game," and the mood of the dream is one of playfulness. Why play? Because what other activity better suits the Present Moment? In play, as in the stillness of the Present Moment, we don't nurture thoughts about the past or future, no worries or concerns. We simply smell the roses.

In the dream Evie must "use her mind" to still her thoughts. This "mind" is the mind of Witnessing Consciousness in which we experience that we are not our thoughts. Again, Tolle says it so well: "The realm of consciousness is much vaster than thought can grasp. When you no longer believe everything you think, you step out of thought and see clearly that the thinker is not who you are."[2] An "ancient ritual" indeed!

My client Gale set the intention to fulfill her own needs for the first time in her life and to be less exclusively centered on caretaking her husband and family. She frequently told me that she wanted a "sign from God" that this new path in life was a correct one and not simply a "selfish wish." Praying for an answer to this question, she dreamed:

> A friend of mine is leading me into a churchyard, whereupon the hand of God—it's gigantic—appears right in front of me. On God's finger stands the most beautiful angel dressed in white and with white light radiating out of her and all around her. She's almost too brilliant to see. I'm in awe but we keep walking and now I'm alone in the church, which is one of those Spanish-looking adobe buildings, like the old traditional Catholic churches where I had some of my most moving experiences. Someone says that the service can't start until I put on a veil.

After describing the dream in detail, Gale lamented, "If only I could have a sign from God that I'm doing the right thing." I laughed out loud, but she was quite serious. Then I realized what she intuitively understood. We'll discuss her intuition in Chapter 13, but first let's return to Gale's very important experience of apprenticeship in the current dream.

It's interesting that Gale doesn't even pause as she walks by the brilliant angel on God's finger—she just "keeps walking." What could be more important than a radiant image of God and an angel right before her eyes? The answer lies in the second scene of the dream.

The church service—the ritual for accessing the Divine—cannot start until Gale wears a veil. This is the veil with which we create the solitude and stillness needed to experience the Witnessing God-Consciousness within. In her dream it's as if the external image of God and angel, despite its extraordinary beauty, is just that: an image, not the opportunity for true communion. Gale's Dream Mentor is the anonymous voice that treats her as an apprentice, instructing her to put on a veil and find stillness before she can experience the answer to her prayers. When we discuss her Mentor's advice Gale resolves that she will make more time to be alone, reflect, and look within. It was only about a week or two later that she returned with the dream she was seeking. You can read that dream in Chapter 13 about dreams of embodiment.

# Mindfulness of Humility and Receiving Guidance

Remember the dream I shared with you in Chapter 3 when algae-like plants grew up through the floor in the shape of letters and words that formed messages from the Divine? Soon the growth became so profuse that I couldn't read a single word or letter. I had to release control and assume an attitude of reverence and humility toward the Source as a respectful apprentice needing to learn. *Then* I was given the tool—huge hedge clippers—with which to do the work of pruning so I could continue to understand and follow the guidance offered.

You read another Dream of Apprenticeship about following guidance in Section I. Remember Lenny? He followed his Mentor, complaining all the way about the roughness of their path and worrying constantly that they were lost. But when push came to shove, so to speak, Lenny committed to remaining his Mentor's apprentice and took the proverbial "leap" right off the cliff. The lesson of his apprenticeship was the importance of finding the humility to surrender control, to give the benefit of the doubt to the Source and accept guidance.

I'll share with you a lesson I received from a Dream of Apprenticeship in an earlier period of my life when I was intent on being kind at all costs, overly concerned about not hurting anyone and wanting to protect loved ones from feeling loss, rejection, or pain.

> I dreamed that I was driving down a country lane, across which cute little ducklings were being herded. I turned my car around to drive the other way, but it simply ran backwards, even though I stomped on the brakes many times. When the car did stop many ducklings had been run over. Aghast and horrified, I apologized to the duck herder, who then admonished me with great kindness, saying, "Many of these ducklings would have died if left on their own in nature. There's pain and death in life, David, and you must face that in the end you have no control over that."

As my Dream Mentor's apprentice I learned about my own limitations. I realized that pain is a great teacher and there was no way I could or should protect others from the lessons to be learned from their own suffering.

# Mindfulness of Compassion

Perennial wisdom teaches that the rational mind, our ego, focuses on issues of fear and survival, whereas the thoughts of our heart are concerned with all that sustains and nourishes life. The great Indian sage and yogi Patanjali has said, "Peace can be reached through meditation on the knowledge which dreams give. Peace can also be reached through concentration upon that which is dearest to the heart."[3]

Our egos thrive on future plans and goals, creating a purpose with which to rationalize our worth or existence, whereas when we release the need to prove our worth—empty our ego's purpose—we clear a space in the Present Moment to experience the sheer joy of life for its own sake, and our heart is filled. Dreams, too, work to clear a quiet space for the voice of our heart to be heard behind the incessant drumbeat of our ego's thoughts. In Mindful Dreaming we serve as apprentices to our Dream Mentors and set the intention to witness with compassion the limitations and suffering caused by our ego's demands.

A Dream of Apprenticeship shared by my friend Martin illustrates beautifully the importance of compassion:

I am feeling despair that I will never grasp all the complex rules of the board game in front of me. Then, a beautiful woman begins to seduce me. At the same time, she pulls her heart out of her chest, placing it on the game board. When she does so, the board seems to glow and I immediately grasp the rules and the nature of the game. I awaken realizing she came to show me that only the values of my heart, not my head, will provide the experience I seek in life—my heart's path.

Speaking of awakened consciousness as the Philosopher's Stone, alchemist Petrus Bonus simply said, "To find the Philosopher's Stone, we need to look with our eyes but see with our heart."[4]

Here's another poignant dream tale told by my cousin Tricia. Her Dream Mentor would stop at nothing to get her attention about this central issue in our lives:

My dear old friend I've known since I was a child takes me into my bathroom. Bending down, she says, "You've got to see this!" She reaches deep into the toilet and pulls out my own beating heart.

I wake up in sorrow for the years I've wasted trying to please everyone but myself, doing what I thought they wanted—and hating my self for "failing." But I knew things would be different from that moment on.

# Mindfulness of the Formless (Transcending our Attachment to Form)

These dreams help us understand more fully why we've been learning to grieve and release our attachments. We are being prepared to experience formless consciousness. Dreams of the Formless teach us that the material forms of the world are a creation of pure consciousness. Put another way, Dream Mentors show us that physical or material forms are impermanent and more or less interchangeable. Instead, consciousness itself is primary, existing independently of our bodies. This is the meaning of the old Chinese proverb: "I am only interested in what remains after the pot has been broken."[5]

The phenomenon of shape shifting in dreams is an excellent example of the secondary importance of form in the world of consciousness. In waking life we may think something such as this: "My father Irv is my father Irv and his favorite chair is just his favorite chair." In the world of our dreams, however, all bets are off. Consider the following dream I had about my father:

> I am sitting in my father's favorite chair and expressing my gratitude to him for all that he has done. In waking life he recently passed on, and in fact, is not anywhere to be seen in the dream.

My dream (a type of Return dream that you'll read about in Section V) reminds me that through my lifetime part of the core experience of my dad is embodied in his chair. To this day when I sit in his chair, I feel his vigilant energy, lighten in the aura of his humorous pontifications, feel the warmth of his affection for the entire family, and see the virtual glow his love cast upon the entire house from that one place. The image of his chair is not simply a metaphor, but literally carries for me the energy—the consciousness or *experience* of "my dad" that a mere image of him does not evoke. What we love about people and what I loved about my father is the quality of their energy—the experience of life and quality of consciousness they evoke in us. In my dream, the chair is an embodiment and gateway for that experience no less important than my father himself. To dream of sitting in that chair is to embrace that experience of life as my own—one that has not passed away with the material form of my father's consciousness.

In waking life we use mementos of a cherished relationship in the same fashion to access not only the memory of that experience, but also the experience itself. In indigenous cultures the shaman may take an additional step. For example, she may lead a mourner through a ritual experience of healing and then use a feather or stone from that ritual as an amulet for the mourner to carry with him—now infused with the memory and experience of that healing process. The core idea here is that conscious experience makes the world go 'round—not the form it takes.

Another example: A client of mine, Patricia (whose dreams of conforming to and hiding from the Collective you read in Section III), worried that she was sometimes too harsh with friends and loved ones. She dreamed she was a beautiful rosebush. A boy reached out and was pricked by one of her thorns. In her dream she understood through the *experience,* or the consciousness of being a rosebush, that her nature was both beautiful and sharp-edged, neither good nor bad, and that she was not herself to blame for the careless attitude with which people approached her. As the saying goes: "There is no gathering the rose without being pricked by the thorns."

So is it more accurate for Patricia to identify with her image in a photo or the image of the rosebush in her dream? Which better clarifies the nature of her true self? Which provides the direct *experience* or consciousness of redemption from self-doubt and blame?

Every dream image embodies a quality of consciousness—no matter how much we want to label and categorize its symbolic meaning. To consider the rosebush or my father's chair as mere metaphor and to intellectually understand its "meaning" is to shortchange the conscious experience their image carries and produces in us.

Even more problematic is the waking life attitude in which we see ourselves distinct and separate from the chairs, rosebushes, and material world around us—even from other people. As it is said in the Hindu Upanishads, "Who sees all beings in his own Self, and his own Self in all beings, loses all fear."[6] This is why it is so important to meditate on every Mentor and object in your dreams, because the consciousness or experience they embody when embraced is an aspect of our true self. Listen to the great poet Rumi in "The Sufi Path of Love":

> *If you are born of Adam, sit like him and*
> *Behold his progeny within yourself.*
> *What does the vat contain that is not in the river?*
> *What does the room encompass that is not in the city?*
> *This world is the vat, and the heart the running stream,*
> *This world the room, and the heart the city of wonders.*[7]

When we speak about forms we are referring not only to material objects and our physical bodies, but to the forms we create with our thoughts such as our self-image (how we view ourselves) and our social image or persona (how we want to appear to others). All are forms with which our ego is identified and to which it's attached.

My friend Stan shared with me that he had been feeling "stuck" for a long time in his life—stuck in a job that he didn't really like and in a marriage that he knew had lost its vision long ago. But Stan was afraid: "I'm 55 years old and I think that's just too old to do any real changing. Don't you?" I answered Stan as I'm prone to do when anyone asks me a question that I think is too important to rest on my own limited perspective: "Why don't you try incubating a dream about it and see what you're told?" I explained how that process works (You can read about it again in Chapter 2).

The next day Stan shared this Dream of the Formless with me:

> It was really weird. There was what I'd call a quietly powerful woman. That's the only way I can describe her because her shape and appearance changed every time I encountered her—yet each time within the dream I knew she was the same person.
>
> In my dream she has been trying to teach me something I don't understand by repeatedly killing herself in various ways—an approach I think is very odd. Then I watch again as she places herself in a crematorium. I see her burning up in the raging blue fire, her clothes are melting to her skin, and her body turning to ashes. I walk by feeling disturbed by the sight, but now absolutely certain that she won't return. I enter an adjoining room shocked to see her standing there, fully alive and well, brushing off the ashes from her arms and legs.
>
> When I woke up I understood right away what she was trying to say: Life is about being creative. Age has nothing to do with it. I can reinvent my self as many times as I want. I shouldn't take who I think I am so seriously!

Stan's Dream Mentor shows him that the very nature of life is ever changing, ever dying, and ever being born again. The material world, our bodies, and the images of ourselves with which we are so identified, all change and dissolve, but our true nature—consciousness—remains eternal. This is why even though Stan's Mentor returns every time in a different body, he can still recognize her. We are the formless essence of consciousness itself and we know its face when we see it. I am that!

Through Mindful Dreaming we stand with our Mentors as apprentices in the common ground of witnessing consciousness, embracing with humility and compassion the infinite array of shapes and faces—the suffering and the wise within and around us. Only then can we release our iron grip of attachment to "one shape of reality" and awaken to the guiding presence of the Creative Source in our lives—here and now.

Stan continued on as an apprentice to his Dream Mentor in many subsequent dreams. When you understand the dream's message you know that there really is just one Mentor and that is the Source whose many manifestations appear nightly clothed in different bodies. No different are we than waves of the ocean that arise and return to our Source.

Here's a dream of my own that demonstrated with humor how I needed to release my attachment about how a dreamworker should appear to others— the appropriate "form" or "look" of a dreamworker. You'll recall my Calling nightmare of Section II in which I was surrounded by the broken bricks of a devastated city. In that dream, the last remaining brick I was about to break became a contract for a program that a radio producer asked me to sign. One reason I didn't want to sign that contract was my belief that a serious dreamworker wouldn't stoop to the crassness of sound bites on a radio call-in program when teaching others about the profound nature of dreams. Here's my simple and to-the-point dream:

> I'm watching Thich Nhat Hanh on stage spreading his message to thousands of cheering people—as a world-renowned rapper.
>
> I listened for a while and he was actually quite good! More important, of course, was the relief as well as chagrin I felt at being reminded that it's not the image, stupid! It's the message! Not the form, but the truth that's spoken—the quality of consciousness that's conveyed.

Let's conclude with a dream reported by my friend and master dreamworker Rev. Jeremy Taylor that demonstrates the profound reward of learning to let go and release our attachments. A friend of Jeremy's shared this dream, which she had the night after the September 11, 2001, attack. She was visiting New York

City at the time, not knowing if her childhood friend, who worked on the 32nd floor of Tower 2, had escaped or not. Here's the dream:

> In my dream, I find myself in the midst of a forest that has been clear cut—nothing but great, big stumps in all directions as far as I can see. I am devastated. I am weeping. I walk through the destroyed landscape asking myself, "Who could do such a thing?" Then I am drawn to stop and look at the spiral pattern in one of the stumps. I realize how very old this forest was, and it makes me even more filled with anger at the loss of this beautiful old forest. Then I begin to be drawn into the spiral. As I sink down into the spiral and into myself, I realize that this is a part of the tree that I almost never got to see. I am drawn more and more deeply into the spiral—down into a place of myself that is so wise, calm, and deep that it is simply greater than my intense grief and the horror.

She awakened from the dream with a sense of calmness and clarity that allowed her to get through the next day, even with all of her friends "freaking out."

"It is such a startling dream," said Jeremy, "because the spiral of the growth rings that serves as the pathway to the deepest truth and beauty would not be visible if the tree had not been cut down. At one level, [the dream] is a metaphor of doing the psycho-spiritual work necessary to be a person in whom such a metaphor of healing can rise to consciousness." On the other hand, he says, the dream demonstrates that "it is often through our worst wounds and injuries, both individual and collective, that we are opened to healing and more direct communication with the Divine."[8]

I would add that in this case the dream does not provide a literal Mentor for the dreamer. Indeed, there is no one in the dream but the dreamer. Such dreams are quite common and are still apprenticeship dreams, as the dream is the teacher. Her Dream Mentor is the ancient, formless Source itself that draws her into the forest and teaches her that there is a quality of consciousness that transcends the world of form—one that to be *experienced* requires us to embrace the inevitability of change, grieve, and let go.

Before moving on to the next chapter, take a few moments to explore some of the practices at the end of this chapter. In the meantime remember that at any time on our Journey we are capable of receiving such uplifting dreams of guidance as well as other profound dream experiences in the chapters that follow. Our ego is always happy to tell us that we haven't earned something we want and it will have to wait for some time in the future when we've worked hard enough, suffered sufficiently or have more time for it. Yet, all that really matters to our Dream Mentors is our attitude of openness and humility when asking for guidance. When you are consistently at one with that attitude you enter the time of Illumination—and receive its gifts.

Though these dreams of Apprenticeship touch us deeply and shift our conscious perspective, later Dreams of Embrace and Mastery, Embodiment, and Being actually transmute our awareness as full-fledged initiates in a radically new consciousness. Until then, Dreams of the Formless simply point us toward our destination and we may take solace from the words of poet Robert Browning: "Ah, but a man's grasp should exceed his reach, Or what's a heaven for?"[9]

# Chapter Practices

## Remember the Experience of Apprenticeship in Your Waking Life

Many of us have had the experience of being mentored by a parent, teacher, or friend in some important area of our life. This is always a landmark event in our lives.

If you've had such an experience, take a few moments to write about it in your journal. Breathe back into the experience for the joy of it or for the feeling of gratitude that it evokes in you.

It's true as well that most of us have a remaining hunger or unspoken yearning for a guru, teacher, or Mentor in some aspect of our lives. In your Journal explore what you long for or yearn to be taught and why this is important.

Incubate a dream to receive that specific help from a Dream Mentor.

## A Simple Way to Work with Your Dreams and Dream Mentors

Here's an elegant and simple approach you can use with any dream as well as an easy way to receive the guidance offered by your Dream Mentor. I've adapted the core method from a gestalt technique created by my friend and fellow dreamworker Bob Hoss.

Remember that every dream character is a Mentor who has a gift of wisdom waiting for you if you take the time to get to know more about that Mentor and if your attitude is an accepting or positive one. First, get to know your Mentor.

- Step 1: Imagine yourself as the Dream Mentor that you are interested in learning more about and let that Mentor speak in the first person:

  - a) Describe who/what you are and your key characteristics: "I am _____." ( You can write this in your journal if you prefer not to speak aloud.)
    **Note:** If the Mentor is a known person from waking life, then become that person and state (or write) : "My main similarities with the dreamer are_____; my main differences with the dreamer are: _____."

  - b) "As (this Mentor) my purpose or function is to _____."

  - c) "As (this Mentor) I like _____."

  - d) "As (this Mentor) I dislike _____."

  - e) "As (this Mentor) what I desire most is _____."

- Step 2: Now that you have come to understand more, consider your attitude toward that Mentor: Are you angry? Avoiding? Running away? Loving? Embracing? Deceiving?

- Step 3: If your attitude is hostile or negative, consider the advantages of giving him or her the benefit of the doubt. Ask yourself how incorporating his or her perspective—if only in moderation—would be helpful in improving the quality of your daily life in some way. If your attitude is positive, ask yourself how you can embody his or her energy or perspective in the coming week.

# Chapter 12

# Dreams of Embrace and Mastery

*If people knew how hard I worked to get my mastery, it wouldn't seem so wonderful at all.*

—Michelangelo

*If thou canst walk on water, thou art no better than a straw. If thou canst fly in the air, thou art no better than a fly. Conquer thy heart that thou mayest become somebody.*

—Ansari

Dreams of Embrace and Mastery reflect an important shift in us as dreamers.

More fully embracing the lessons once viewed as a threat to our ego's existence, we try our own hand at mastering or embracing what we've learned without direct help from Mentors. Although Dream Mentors continue to provide support and guidance in many of our Illumination dreams, we feel a growing confidence and competence and stand up successfully and more often for our new perspectives.

Not surprisingly, some of these dreams are initially fraught with anxiety, or emotional or physical pain, before we experience resolution. Such suffering is a reflection of our ego's continuing resistance. As a result, the narrative or story lines of these dreams often reflect the presence of old ego strategies alongside initial feelings of fear and avoidance. However, consciousness of the new values learned from our Mentors always prevails, and we find ourselves in the end feeling competent and successful.

> Braced by the guidance of our Dream Mentors we act out of a new expanded consciousness and actively practice mindfulness of values that our ego once viewed as a threat to its existence.

Following are some examples of the suffering that finally yields to embrace and mastery in our dreams.

# Embracing Solitude

Joe is an old friend of mine who has struggled to achieve what he refers to as the much-needed self-discipline to follow his spiritual path. Prior to this dream he had tried for many years to achieve some consistency in his efforts at meditation, only to feel seduced time and again by the distractions of family and responsibilities at work. Here is his self-explanatory dream that marked a turning point in Joe's efforts:

> I am at a party and everyone is having a great time, except me. The longer it goes on the more irritated and bored I get. I tell people that they have to leave and no one listens. Now I'm really upset. I mean really angry. I shout at them that the party's over! Slowly, they start to file out and I feel kind of good that for a change I've followed through without feeling too guilty. The whole room has cleared out and I'm just sitting there and listening to how quiet it's become. I can hear my breathing. I start to meditate and feel like the outside quiet is inside me now. I wake up feeling really good.

Joe told me this dream of standing up to the distractions in his life some months after having it. Since that time, he said, he had been able to meditate much more consistently than before—but just as importantly, he felt that he was "quieter inside" when he was going about the everyday responsibilities of his life.

# Embracing Humility

As mentioned earlier, our culture views humility with a subtle disdain, and one who is humble is often seen as ineffectual, self-effacing, and lacking self-esteem. Jessica, a friend of mine, shared a simple but beautiful dream that speaks to the power of humility:

> I am standing at the end of a pier at the ocean on a bright, sunny day. I see that nearby many dolphins are playing and having a grand time frolicking around. They seem to be having so much fun that it's like they're almost dancing in the waves. This thought moves me to imagine the music they're dancing to. Feeling playful now myself, I move one finger around, keeping time to the music. When I do this, voila! They swim in much closer to the pier and actually begin to dance! I'm in awe. The whole scene is so beautiful. I'm so amazed and excited that instead of my finger I begin to swing my entire arm around as if it's a conductor's wand and I'm the conductor of the whole symphony they're dancing to. But the more I wave my arm the less they dance and the farther they recede from the pier. I realize what's happening—that its me that's caused this—and I return to keeping time with my finger. When I do they swim back and dance some more.

In this beautiful tale of humility embraced, Jessica finds that, even to imagine herself as the conductor in charge of the dance and in control of nature's rhythms, alienates her from the energies of life. In these dreams, unlike dreams of the Quest, we release resistance and embrace our calling to humility. When we simply "keep time" with life's rhythms, and return to harmony with the Source—the dance begins again. Perhaps though, better to say we rejoin the dance—already in progress!

Remember Janine's Control nightmare (in Chapter 6) in which she was horrified when a man threw dirt in her new car? As many of us have, Janine had spent a lifetime caring primarily about others' needs to the exclusion of her own. Now she found that she had drawn into her life a severely alcoholic and hostile woman. The woman would call her at all hours, even in the middle of the night, insistent on talking about her many problems and asking for advice, which, of course, she would never take. She would even admonish and bully Janine when she did not call her back immediately. Janine knew she needed to put an end to the relationship, but could not quite face the anger and hurt she knew her rejection would create in the woman. She dreamed:

> I am ironing clothes and reach over the iron to move the cord. Somehow my left index finger brushes the iron and sticks to it. It's really stuck, and the longer I am leaving it on, the more pain I feel and the more damage I know is being done. The pain is almost unbearable. Finally, I have to use all my strength and I'm able to jerk my finger off the iron. Once I've done it I see that my finger is completely healed.

The dream message was very clear to Janine. She had a choice: She could use her strength to successfully extract herself from a very painful and self-destructive situation—or not. She also understood that she had a broader choice in front of her: continue to bear responsibility for ironing every wrinkle out of other people's lives and do permanent damage to herself, or release control, find compassion for her own suffering, and allow herself to be "completely healed."

Note that in this Dream of Embrace there is no Mentor present. However, in the end, whether it is control, distraction, judgment, attachment, or impatience that is the cause of our suffering, in truth it is the divine and healing energy of Witnessing Consciousness that is the source of the compassionate perspective needed to end our suffering. Later in Dreams of Being we realize our true identity as the Compassionate Witness, but in Embrace dreams we simply draw on its guiding energy.

# Embracing Compassion

Consider the following dream of my client Lila, a woman in her 50s who also drew on this same source of healing. Lila was struggling to stand up to an aggressive and cruel brother who had always intimidated her, as well as to her mother who had often sided, out of fear, with her brother. Lila was feeling for the first time that the emotional cost of remaining loyal and engaged with her family was a price not worth paying. She dreamed:

> I am at a grocery store and I see my brother's head severed and sitting in a clear acrylic box full of acid. I watch as the features of his face dissolve and melt away. I feel grossed out and sad, but relieved. Then I hear a friend calling me to come to the frozen foods area of the store, where I see a woman lying frozen in an open food cabinet. The woman looks like my grandmother who raised me—a very loving woman with great strength and character.

As I stare at her frozen body, the store butcher comes out—his apron full of blood from the work he has been doing—and begins to give the frozen woman CPR. However, now I'm feeling that it is really up to me to save her and I start to panic. I know I'm a nurse and I work in the mental health field, but I have no confidence with the physical side of nursing. I call out for my boss, who's an M.D., but he doesn't come. Then I find myself looking into the eyes of this woman and feeling compassion for her condition. Suddenly she starts to breathe and comes back to life.

Notice how Lila initially resorts in her dream to an old ego script in which she views herself as helpless and incompetent, but then realizes that "it is really up to me to save her." That's the beginning of embrace. On our Journey we must become our own heroine or hero and the sacrifice required is always no less than the release of our ego's favorite way of viewing ourselves—the self-defeating habits of thought that we have taken so much for granted.

In Lila's dream she is the master of the sword. Her firm intention to embrace compassion for her own suffering is the "butcher's knife" that has severed the head of her cold and unloving brother. Recall the words of Jesus and Krishna that we must take the sword to (the ego values of) family and friends with which we have identified. (See Section II.)

The result of Lila's resolve—similar to the outcome in the story of Medusa—is that her brother's "head" (his ego) is severed and the features of his face that once turned Lila stone cold with fear now dissolve and melt away. She has succeeded in severing her attachment to the abusive relationship with her brother, *as well as her ego's attachment to being his powerless victim.* Indeed, in Dreams of Embrace and Mastery we empower ourselves.

However, we must remain mindful that, though mastering the sword comes first on our Journey, it's not the masculine energy of the butcher with his axe that can renew life nor the rational thinking of her boss "who's an MD." Indeed, in the dream her boss "won't come" because, as you'll recall, when we seek out solutions in our dreams that are not in our best interest, either our wish is not granted or our attention is called to the painful loss entailed by having our wish come true.

Rather, when the time is right, we must, as Lila did, put down the sword and, from the heart of compassion, look squarely into the mirror of our own suffering. In so doing we bring back to life within us the strength of character and resolve that Lila's grandmother embodied for her—the healing medicine she most needs at this time in her Journey.

# Embracing Non-Attachment

My client Rosy had struggled to release much guilt about her divorce and to give up her image of herself as someone who would never hurt somebody she loved. She was feeling lighter and less depressed, but she worried that her guilt would return and that there was probably more to work on. She dreamed:

> I am standing in front of my house where my husband and I lived for all those years—and feeling bad. Now it's kind of crumbling and some bricks are falling out of the foundation as I watch. I start to worry that maybe there's someone still inside and that I better warn them to get out before it all caves in. Then I realize it's not inhabited and, besides, it's not my house anymore, and it's really not my job to rescue anyone anyway. I just keep walking.

Rosy awoke from her dream knowing that she had released attachment to her past identity as the guilty one once and for all.

Dreams of Embrace and Mastery are both uplifting affirmations of our progress and continuing lessons about how to deepen and embrace our learning more fully.

# Chapter Practices

## Identifying What We Need to Grow and Heal

Our egos are notorious for their self-serving interpretations of what it is we need in our lives. We may tell ourselves that we are rarely judgmental, and yet our dreams may be replete with feelings of mistrust and suspiciousness, which we—our ego—project routinely on to our Dream Mentors. Or we may view ourselves as introverted and not needing any more time alone, though our dreams speak reams about our love of distraction.

Consider incubating a dream in which you ask for an objective assessment of your (ego's) progress on your path. You may ask, "What ego strategy do I most need to release at this time in my Journey?" Or request an affirmation about how you are doing in your efforts to embrace and master the Source's values.

# Chapter 13

# Dreams of Embodiment

*I swear to you there are divine things more beautiful than words can tell.*
—Walt Whitman

*Life is a pure flame and we live by an invisible sun within us.*
—Thomas Browne

A story is told of a well-known guru whose young student left her work with him in India to return to the States. Some time later he received a letter describing her difficult adjustment when she came home to a family that didn't understand or accept her spiritual practice. In her letter she explained how this painful experience eventually led her to an epiphany: When I'm a Buddhist they hate me. But when I'm the Buddha they love me.

The importance of her insight, of course, is that any system of "belief" we hold may be experienced by others as implying that those who disagree are "wrong" and at worst, bad or evil. J. Krishnamurti said it well: "When you call yourself an Indian or a Muslim or a Christian or a European, or anything else, you are being violent. Do you see why it is violent? Because you are separating yourself from the rest of mankind. When you separate yourself by belief, by nationality, by tradition, it breeds violence. So a man who is seeking to understand violence does not belong to any country, to any religion, to any political party or partial system; he is concerned with the total understanding of mankind."[1]

Even Buddhism with its precepts of non-violence and tolerance of other religions can sound to the ego of a Muslim or Christian as to a threat to *their* beliefs.

The ego always has to have a position and always has to be right. In contrast, the spiritual experience is in its essence one with no rules or precepts, nor one that requires adherents or believers. It is an experience of Being, not a collection of thoughts, judgments, rules, or regulations.

Dreams of Embodiment as well as the Dreams of Being that you'll read about in Chapter 14 illustrate this truth simply and beautifully. Such dreams reflect the essence of spirituality—as an experience that one *is*, a quality of consciousness, of Beingness in the Present Moment. To read, hear, or directly experience such dreams is to move further from the realm of ego—to "be the Buddha" rather than to be a Buddhist—or Christian or Jew or Muslim.

> We awaken feeling blessed with a profound peace and above all a deepened experience of the joyful nature of life, the vibrancy of merely being alive, right here and now.

These dreams open us as dreamers to an experience that profoundly affirms the importance and reality of the path we've been seeking in life—but have doubted was possible.

As have those who have shared their near-death experiences, in these dreams we have known the Divine Presence and return to waking life with a major shift in our values—a deepened selflessness and compassion and less attachment to material goals.

There are still elements of old waking life drama as well as newer feelings of mastery and empowerment present in these dreams, but now there enters an experience that opens us to the existence of a more inclusive divine Consciousness that is none other than I, We, Us.

Just as in Patricia's dream, when she walked right through the wall of a room without windows or doors directly into Nature, these dreams allow us to step into an experience of spaciousness that is the living, breathing moment of the here and now. The experience is akin—though far more encompassing—to that of astronauts when they find themselves peering down from the moon toward an Earth that is now just one of many twinkling lights in the Universe.

Both Dreams of Embodiment and Being frequently serve in many of us as the seed for dramatic change and growth. Even if we have not experienced such dreams of our own they have surely had an influence on us because they have served as the stimulus for virtually all the world's mainstream religions—and continue to inform the life of indigenous peoples throughout the world.

The difference between Dreams of Embodiment and Dreams of Being lies in the realm of form and formlessness. Embodiment dreams are ecstatic, vibrant, joyful experiences in our body, in the world of form. That's not to say that they are merely felt on a physical level. Rather, what we have been learning ever more deeply in our head and heart is now a full bodied experience as none we've ever had before.

Recall Cassie's dream (from Section IV) in which she made love "on all planes, mind, body, and spirit." Also, you read in Chapter 1 the Embodiment dream of a man who had completed a sad and painful divorce just as in waking life. He is exhausted and feels doubt about the decision he has made:

> Then I hear the bells of a church tolling in the distance and as the chimes get louder an ecstasy builds in my chest until I'm going to explode with joy. I realize in the dream that this is the joy of liberation. I've liberated my soul. But it's not liberation from my marriage, just the prison of deadening rules I had made for myself throughout my life. I feel no more of that agonizing doubt and now know in my heart that I have done the right thing.

In contrast, Dreams of Being initially may include the body, but by the end of the dream are no longer primarily centered in the body or concerned with the importance of form. You'll read more about them in Chapter 14.

Some more vivid examples of Dreams of Embodiment follow.

A reader of a magazine column in which I wrote about dreamwork kindly shared the following dream, which illustrates beautifully the profound shift in consciousness and infusion of joyful energy that are the hallmark of Embodiment dreams. She wrote to me that before her dream she had been particularly depressed in the realization that she would have to leave her marriage and face an ugly custody battle and divorce. At the time of the dream she was working two jobs and was experiencing extreme stress and physical exhaustion. In her dream the sun's light is veiled by a depressing gloom that shrouds the entire landscape. She says it is as if her neighborhood has been bombed, the walls of the homes and the grass around them blackened and burnt. Nowhere can be seen any children or adults. Suddenly, her cousin appears from within one of the houses and points to a nearby tree, charred, twisted, and blackened as its surroundings are. The following are her own words:

> I looked and saw the tiniest sign of color at the base of the tree. I bent over and moved some burnt leaves aside. Beneath the leaves was a tiny, fresh, pink rosebud. I picked it up and placed it in my palm to admire it. As I did so, it suddenly bloomed into a beautiful rose. As it bloomed, something truly miraculous happened!
>
> The blackness disappeared, replaced by a blazing blue sky and a bright sun, warm against my skin. The houses became whole and bright white again, children were laughing and playing everywhere, adults stood around laughing and talking, the grass turned green, and the trees sprouted green leaves and became whole again.
>
> But the most incredible thing was the way I felt when the rose blossomed. My soul blossomed along with it and there were rays of bright, golden light spilling out of my chest, and warmth from the sun radiating into me and lighting me up. I was glowing, feeling unbearably happy and blessed. As I have faced adversity since then, friends have often commented on how positive I am.

When she wrote to me it had been more than a year since the dream and she was indeed still transformed. She told me, "I can trace my permanent change in attitude to that single dream."

Remember Gale, who wanted a sign from God that her desire for a fulfilling life of her own wasn't just a selfish wish? When she dreamed she was in a churchyard walking by the Hand of God with an radiant angel sitting on his gigantic finger, she awoke deeply disappointed that she hadn't yet received her sign!

However, Gale had received instruction from a Dream Mentor in which she was told to put on her veil before the church service could start. Understanding the veil to be a call to solitude, she spent the next two weeks in greater solitude and inner reflection. On her next visit to my office she came in beaming. Here is her Dream of Embodiment:

> I'm alone in my house playing my favorite music. I get up and start to dance even though I'm alone.
>
> Suddenly my body is filled with joyful, ecstatic energy from head to toe. I can't really tell you in words what an unearthly joy it was!
>
> Then I hear a powerful voice calling me by name, saying, "Gale, continue what you are doing and you will heal yourself."

Beaming with resolve, she told me, "Now I have my neon sign!" However, she told me that more powerful than the spoken words of God in her dream was the direct experience of joyful knowing and divine energy felt throughout her body as she danced—the knowing that transcends words—and the "sign" that was missing in her first dream, despite its powerful encouragement.

Gale shared with me how she now understood that behind the veil she was asked to wear lay the healing that would come from reclaiming her passion in life. Her fears of selfishness dissolved immediately, and I've rarely seen a healing as powerful as Gale's. Her chronic depression lifted, she regained her self-esteem, and her very deeply alienated marriage of many decades has become the light of her life. Gale views the turning point in her life as her sign from God—her Dream of Embodiment.

Here is another example of that spiritually healing energy at work in our body.

Nick, a friend of mine, was known by all as one of the friendliest people around, always ready to say hello with a big booming voice and something kind to say that made you feel special in his eyes. However, Nick had spent the last five years in his own kind of hell, in intense conflict with his wife and in trouble financially. As he began to face the certain end of his marriage and pending separation, he felt dread about his future and agonizing guilt as he knew the large share of responsibility he carried for its demise. Nick shared with me a feeling of doom that he would never find peace. He worried, too, that his wish to leave the marriage reflected a "neurotic" tendency in him to escape and avoid responsibility. Perhaps, he thought, he could release some of his intense guilt and shame by staying in that deeply unhappy relationship and do what he could to make amends. He didn't know if he could succeed but that was his intention. Then he dreamed:

> I am walking alone on a beautiful, quiet beach. There is no one in sight. I'm watching my feet as I take each step. The waves are rolling over my toes as I walk, the sun is warming my face—you know, in that perfect kind of way it does sometimes on the beach. Then I feel a strange compelling urge to turn around and look over my shoulder. When I do I see that my footprints are gradually being washed away by the waves. I look again and they have vanished.
>
> I was filled with such immense relief and joy. In that moment my whole body was absolutely cleansed, as if it had been carrying all of the shame I'd been feeling and now—all in that one moment as I was standing there, I was a new man. Everything is okay now.

That "one moment " is the eternal Present Moment in which we awaken to the grace and joy of the simple consciousness of Being—absolved—without shame or guilt. In the next few days after the dream Nick became aware of a new energy of resolve in his body, having experienced within the dream his own healing. Whether he decided to leave his marriage or stay, he could live now without the anxiety and disabling guilt he had been feeling. He could feel forgiveness for himself, release the past, and move on with his life. Not surprisingly, he felt that he was more likely to stay in his marriage and to feel more wholehearted about the commitment.

Our dreams often care little for our conscious point of view, and in this case Nick's perspective about his past had been quite negative. Yet the dream showed his "footprints"—the effects of his past actions in life—as having no further impact on the world around him. Indeed, by the very end of his dream his footprints were entirely washed away.

As you read in Section IV, Nick's dream experience is better described as one in which his past is "absolved" rather than forgiven. By absolved I mean the realization that his mistakes in life had been a necessary part of his growth and not a reason to condemn or punish himself—not a basis on which to judge himself as "bad." Absolution never results from an intellectual belief in our innocence, but rather from an experience at our physical core of being loved unconditionally without judgment.

When we are fully open and surrendered to the Present Moment we are absolved through Dreams of Embodiment, meditation, or Divine Grace—and never through the work of our ego and rational mind. This is the healing power of the compassionate Witnessing Consciousness.

In the eyes of the Compassionate Witness—our own pure consciousness of Being—we are already innocent and always will be.

Such dreams again and again remind us that we are okay. Our mistakes are not who we are, any more than the body we inhabit. A more beautiful dream of absolution I've never encountered. "Every day, God gives us the sun," said author Paulo Coelho, "and also one moment in which we have the ability to change everything."[2]

You read about Laura in Chapter 3. Her oppressive sense of responsibility for others and belief that she needed to be in control of her feelings and behavior at all times led to a Dream of Imminent Loss. In that dream she looked in the mirror and saw her balding uncle who had committed suicide—a portent of a bleak future if she didn't relinquish her love of control. Practicing mindfulness about releasing control and the importance of finding the humility to be led, some months later Laura shared this Dream of Embodiment with me:

> I am lying on the bow of a sailboat and my friend Carol, who is a confident and very trusting person, steers the boat. I've chosen to stand in a canvas enclosure that surrounds me completely so that I have no aids to see where we're going. It's as if I'm completely blindfolded. I'm even unphased by the huge waves that hit the boat. Amazingly I'm not feeling panicked the way I always would have felt in the past. I'm just immersed in the joy of the wind and water, not caring where we're headed. It's the most glorious experience to feel such peace in my body.

Amazing indeed, as this image in one of Laura's earlier dreams would have been a remarkably frightening nightmare—one that might have sounded this way:

> Knowing how much I like things to be in control, my best friend has for some reason decided to betray me in the most cruel way. She has subjected me to a horrible form of torture in which I am made to stand blindfolded in a small boat as the waves from a terrible storm at sea are slamming into us. Why would she do something like that to me, her best friend?

Of course, the answer to that question would have been that in all dreams our Mentors offer us precious gifts if only we had the eyes to see them.

An explanatory note: In Laura's dream, she has a Mentor, a "very trusting" friend. But having a Mentor doesn't constitute a Dream of Apprenticeship. In these dreams the central experience is not what is being taught or learned, but what is felt in the body. Also in her dream, she has taken the initiative to engage or embrace the experience. The Mentor is there as if to lend a helping hand and facilitate the dreamer's intentions.

Let's look now at the profound experience and gift that Dreams of Being bring to our lives.

# Chapter Practices

## Practicing Embodiment

Embodiment Dreams provide powerful healing medicine in our lives. Review the methods learned in Chapter 4 to step back into an embodied dream you may have had. Through the process of deepening these experiences we become increasingly mindful of the habitual thoughts that compete with or negate the direct "knowing" such dreams make available to us. To work with your Embodiment Dream return now to Chapter 4 and choose one or more of the mindfulness practices described there.

Additionally, as you deepen and more fully experience this new energy, you may want to check in with the areas of your body that are in need of physical healing. Note how these areas experience this new energy.

> Be mindful of what interferes with this meditation experience and note if the body sensations change as thoughts arise.

> Bring yourself back to your embodied experience if distracted, noting how much ease or difficulty you are experiencing with this. Practice coming back to this experience when distracted.

## Help With Embodying the Consciousness and Energy of Your Dream Mentors

In working with any dream on your Journey it is central to remember, as you learned in Chapter 2, that the power of dreamwork lies in our readiness to experience dream imagery directly rather than to reduce it to "meaningful symbolism" or intellectualize about it. The *aha* of a dream when experienced is an epiphany we feel in our body, and only later one we think about in our head. Our Dream Mentors embody experiences we are meant to incorporate and integrate in our life—not just think about. For this reason, an experience that unfolds from our work with *any* dream—not just Dreams of Embodiment—requires honoring or enacting in waking life. To honor our dream means that we hold the new bodily experience in consciousness throughout the week and for as long as possible thereafter. When you feel that *aha* make a special effort to be mindful of how that experience feels in your body and how the experience is different than you were feeling before you unfolded the dream.

## Practice Embodiment in Waking Life

During the coming week be mindful of how your body feels. Notice more than what you are thinking. Make a bridge to your body and take special note of whether you are "in your body" when you are interacting with others. Also note your body language as you interact. Are your arms folded in self-protection? If you are seated, is your body facing one way and your face another? When you think you are happy or angry or frustrated, make a conscious effort to feel what those emotions are like in your body.

# Chapter 14

# Dreams of Being
## (Witnessing Consciousness)

*The Atman is the witness-consciousness that experiences the action, the actor, and the world of separate things. It is like a light that illuminates everything in a theater, revealing the master of ceremonies, the guests, and the dancers with complete impartiality. Even when they all depart, the light shines to reveal their absence.*

—Panchadashi

*A person is neither a thing nor a process, but an opening or clearing through which the Absolute can manifest.*

—Martin Heidegger

Author Henry Miller once wrote, "If there is to be any peace it will come through being, not having."[1] Dreams of Being open us to the experience of the "middle" or "third" perspective—pure Witnessing Consciousness. This is not a consciousness that separates us in any way from our bodies or diminishes the physical as anything less than the sacred expression of life that it is.

Those of you who have experienced lucid dreams—dreams in which we are conscious that we're dreaming—can relate to that often ecstatic sense of being

> In Dreams of Being, the Witnessing Consciousness lifts the clouded veil of our ego's thoughts and fears in such a complete way that we feel more alive and present in our body than ever.

"more alive" than in waking life. This is because in lucid dreams we are drawing upon the Witnessing Consciousness. The paradox of this Consciousness is that within it we feel profoundly present and rapturously alive, even as we are aware that the people and forms we encounter are only "nearly real," temporary phenomena arising at our behest out of pure consciousness. Put another way, the joyful liberation of this lucid experience is the awareness—the witnessing—that our consciousness defines the forms, bodies, and events we perceive, and not the other way around.

We are not dependent on forms that we thought defined our world—we continue to exist. As my Zen monk dream that began this section suggests, our body, thoughts, and things are manifestations of the Compassionate Witnessing Consciousness itself.

So let us look at the way these Dreams of Being help us on our Journey to "wash the dust off the Buddha's birthday mirror." You have already read Sarah's dream at the start of this section. In that dream, having browsed in the "government's mirror shop," she was able to experience herself as interconnected with everything in the universe. Now one with the energy of the Source, she was able to inhabit any body she chose.

Let's look at some other Dreams of Being. In each case I have titled the experience of the dream from the perspective of our ego. For example, the following dream is one in which the dreamer's ego initially experiences the Witnessing Consciousness as being a Redeemer, and subsequent dreams in this chapter reflect the ego's perception of the Witness as Destroyer or Healer. Yet in the end the common experience of each dreamer is the realization that they *are* the Witness and that their consciousness is one and the same as Divine Consciousness.

# The Witness as the Redeemer

Larry is a middle-aged man who in his therapy was successfully working through severe depression. His emotional state had resulted from a lifetime of traumatic beatings by his nearly homicidal father and considerable abuse as well from his extended family—all of whom attended a very stern fundamentalist church. He slowly realized the degree to which he had learned to view himself through the distorted mirror of his father's eyes. Ironically his worst enemy had become his own self-hating ego whose values and defenses he knew had to be dismantled and released. He was making remarkable progress and one day came beaming with excitement to share this Dream of Being:

> I dreamed that I am the star in my own salvation. To honor this fact in my dream I had to come up on stage in front of an audience. The crowd is cheering wildly for me. I have two associates with me—Red and Blue—and I stand in the middle between them as we face the infinite and eternal crowd. Red throws something down hard on the stage and says, "It's a bomb that will destroy the universe" and the crowd laughs and claps with joy. Then "Blue" says, "The universe is a tortoise," and I know intuitively that means "the cosmos is in perfect harmony." I also know in the dream that my salvation lies in having conquered the extremes of the universe by standing in the middle and not surrendering to either side. As I stand there in the middle, the joy I feel is so exquisite there are no words for it. Just utter joy and peace.

This beautiful dream shows Larry having transcended the seemingly irreconcilable opposites of chaos and harmony, death and life, evil and good that coexist in our ego consciousness as we view the world around us. The key lies in the embrace of Witnessing Consciousness that "stands in the middle" and sees all opposites as part of a larger whole.

We usually think of chaos as bad and harmony as good. We hate chaos and we love harmony, don't we? But the crowd in Larry's dream laughs and claps when Red drops the universe-destroying bomb. Why?

A central lesson—and illusion—of the Journey is that, in the material world of opposites as our ego perceives it, there is an unavoidable cycle of life and death in which we all participate. Yet in Larry's dream he and "the eternal crowd" have found "salvation" or redemption from this cycle of suffering. Salvation simply means that in his dream Larry has experienced the transcendent third perspective, a perspective in which there is no identification with or resistance to either life or death—to the harmony of life or to the chaos of disintegration and death—no resistance at all to the eternal consciousness that resides in the Present Moment.

How is this possible? We unconditionally accept the cycle of life and death in this moment when we experience that we *are* the Witnessing Consciousness of itself.

This is the experience of Awakening even if it lasts just a few moments, as in Larry's dream or the others you'll read in this chapter. When we know our identity *as* the Witness we easily accept the death of our body in the cycle of life, because we "know" our nature to be pure consciousness, undying, unchanging, and formless. There is nothing to lose or gain. As the Buddha said, "I gained nothing at all from Supreme Enlightenment and for that very reason it is called Supreme Enlightenment."[2]

What greater, more compassionate liberation can there be for our egos than to be released from the ever-present fear, worry, or apprehension in which we live throughout our lives? To be the Compassionate Witness is to step off the cross of opposites on which we suffer—to become part of the "eternal crowd." "Awake! Be the witness of your thoughts," said the Buddha. "You are what observes, not what you observe."[3]

Marie von Franz, the famed Jungian analyst, reported this dream of a woman who was terminally ill, and extremely agitated and frightened about her impending death. Shortly before she died, she shared her dream of the Witness as Redeemer. In that dream she "sees a candle lit on the window sill of the hospital room and finds that the candle suddenly goes out. Fear and anxiety ensue as the darkness envelops her. Suddenly, the candle lights on the other side of the window and she awakens."[4]

> Witnessing Consciousness is described as compassionate because in that awareness we no longer identify with the form of our body as "what we are," and so no longer worry or suffer the fear of death.

Here again we see through the eyes of Witnessing Consciousness that our body and all forms come and go, but the pure consciousness of Being remains. As it is said in the Yoga Vasishtha Maharamayana, "The same undivided and indivisible space is outside and inside of a thousand pots. Likewise the Self pervades all beings."[5]

Immediately after her dream, the dreamer experienced a deep peacefulness, and (her body) died.

# The Witness as the Eternal One

Here's another similar dream of transcendent awareness that Irv, an author and client of mine, experienced some years ago.

> I find myself walking out of an unfamiliar house in the middle of the night. I look up into a pitch-black sky. The blackness of the sky begins to fade as if a veil is being drawn back. At the same time an immense, gargantuan sun slowly appears. Its colors have an unearthly and indescribable beauty. I call to a friend in the house to come and witness this cosmic event but he doesn't respond. As I continue to stare, transfixed by the radiant and beautiful light of this sun, I notice that the sky has remained dark. Now next to the sun rests a moon almost as large.
>
> I awaken in awe, aware that I have witnessed the unveiling of day and night—and have seen behind the screen of clouds the eternal unending moment of creation going on right now.

Joseph Campbell speaks of this experience as he describes the traditional image of Shiva, the Hindu god that is not only the destroyer but the "creator of life, its generator, as well as illuminator."[6] In Shiva's hair, says Campbell:

> *...Is a skull and a new moon, death and rebirth at the same moment. In one hand he has a little drum that goes tick-tick-tick. That is the drum of time which shuts out the knowledge of eternity. We are enclosed in time. But in Shiva's opposite hand there is a flame which burns away the veil of time and opens our minds to eternity.*[7]

Irv's dream then speaks to another aspect of Witnessing Consciousness, as an experience of the eternal present. This is why the god Shiva is both an "illuminator" and destroyer. To *be* the Witness of the eternal moment of creation is to die to the identity that our ego has so carefully crafted and to "lose" all we (our ego) are attached to that we call "myself." In exchange we experience our oneness with consciousness in the eternal now—we are illuminated. To further quote Campbell:

> *The concept of time shuts out eternity. It is over the ground of that deep experience of eternity that all of (our) temporal pains and troubles go. There is a Buddhist ideal of participating willingly and joyfully in the passing sorrows of the world. Wherever there is time there is sorrow. But this experience of sorrow moves over a sense of enduring being, which is our own true life.*[8]

An old friend, Benjamin, once shared a dream that is similar to mine in its theme of the continuity of consciousness and its eternal nature. He received this dream many years ago at a time when he knew only that it might be a good idea to write it down:

> I'm outside and it's nighttime, though there is much ambient light with which to see. I'm about to walk down some stairs and suddenly without warning of any kind I experience that the entire universe is conscious and alive and when my body dies pure consciousness remains. I even tried to imagine in my mind that I'm an old man and that I'm dying—a thought that would normally feel like a nightmare for me. Yet I feel no fear—just the seamless oneness of being conscious. There were buildings and landscape in the dream but they were products of consciousness, as was my own body in the dream. I awaken in a feeling of profound awe.

# The Witness as Destroyer

There is an old wives' tale that if you die in your dream, you will die in waking life as well. Old wives' tales, just as fables and fairytales do, usually contain some kernel of psychological truth. In this case the truth is that the experience of death in dreams is the experience of a radical and final ending to some part of our waking life identity to which we've been attached. In Dreams of Being we may even experience our own annihilation—a kind of death that heralds the monumental shift in consciousness that perennial traditions view as spiritual rebirth—being "born again." But this birth is into the world of Being or pure consciousness. Typically these are the dreams of shamans, healers, and those called to become spiritual teachers.

The central power behind dreams of annihilation is that, though there are myriad things in life to which we attach ourselves, there is no stronger attachment than to our body. Until we experience the spiritual truth that there is an undying continuity of consciousness we maintain a profound fear that when our body dies, so do we.

The notion that consciousness is created by our body or brain and dies with it is nowhere more prevalent than in the West. Our Western culture retains many religions, but most of them long ago stopped teaching methods for contemplative awareness or for direct communion with Witnessing Consciousness. Thus those who have had such experiences are most often those who have been near death and resuscitated.

On the other hand, in indigenous cultures the future shaman is either spontaneously drawn or formally led through an initiation process. What such initiations have in common is that they dispense with our last core attachment or identification with form (our body) and usher us into a new world in which consciousness is the primary ground of the material world. Dreams of Being offer such initiations as well.

For example, I'll share with you one I experienced when I was 21 years old. The life context of the dream was the late 1960s hippie era. I'd been floundering without direction for some time and had been feeling an increasing sense that there was more to life and "reality" than met the eye. I had read some of what Jung had to say about our core spiritual nature by the time I was 17 and had become interested in the *I Ching*, of which I've spoken in previous chapters. However, never would I have imagined this experience:

> I am observing an ancient, black, and chaotic sea, a raging storm at the time of this planet's birth. I am feeling in awe of the primal energy that moves these storming waters. Suddenly, I'm bobbing in that dark cauldron, the waves towering above my puny head. To my horror I find that my body is breaking down, coming apart, dissolving into its constituent molecules—my atoms flowing back into the timeless churning abyss in which I'm floating. I feel stark, raw terror as I see my body has now washed away. Then I am one with the formless energy of creation. I know I am dead—or my body is—but I am also still conscious, part of something infinitely large, holy, eternal—and alive.

✤

# The Witness as Compassionate Healer

We've looked at the Witnessing function of consciousness as a gateway to transcendent reality. However, it is also a healing consciousness. A beautiful example of this is a moving dream that Larry (whose Redeemer dream you read) shared with me as he successfully worked through his severe depression.

His dream points to a different aspect of the Witnessing Consciousness that is a loving, compassionate witness to the suffering of our own ego: It will help to know that in many of his previous dreams he found himself "looking for the one that loves me," a phrase with which he referred to his unceasing search for the unconditional love that he had never experienced as a child. Though he sometimes thought of "one who would love him" as a kind of soul mate, he assumed that the source of this love was the Divine itself.

This is Larry's amazing dream of being a very unconditionally loving Witness to his own healing. Keep in mind that the "I" of which Larry first speaks is the I of the Witnessing Consciousness:

> My dream was wonderful. Somehow I knew that now I was the "one" that loved me in the other dreams that I had always searched for. I was whole and well and totally conscious. I had before me the three stages of the development of Larry—the one I love, but who in the dream I am more than.
>
> All three of the Larrys are egg-shaped, actively living forms of him inside a very thick cellophane seal I know is time in the material plane. I pick up each, one at a time, starting with the past, and hold him lovingly in my hands, knowing what a wonderful treasure I have in him. In the past I know he went through complete hell and sorrow, and I sense pride in myself that he made it through, and place him back. Next I pick up his form in the future and hold him lovingly also and am proud of the transformation he produced to become exactly what I wanted for him and that he needed. I place him back and go to the center Larry and pick him up, where I know he is confused, anxious, depressed, unhappy, and feeling lost. He is struggling to get out of the confinement he is in and is approaching panic and crisis. This is the only one of the three that looks through the cellophane at me. He is conscious of me and is protected from the eternal in a shell of life—and I love him the most of the three.
>
> He is poised and balanced between the two halves of his existence and this is a thrilling time for me as I bring him to my breast and we become one. I sense him stirring in his sleep and hear him say yes, that he is aware of me, and I reach out with a projection of love and see him reach out to it and we are drawn into each other internally. Now we can both go to our rest, his in the consciousness of me within him awake, and me in the consciousness of him asleep. I let go completely and he/I wake up.

Perhaps there is nothing further to say except to recall the words of Sufi Mystic al-Hallaj who speaks of the same eternal ground of identity:

> *I am he whom I love, and He whom I love is I.*
> *We are two spirits dwelling in one body,*
> *If thou seest me, thou seest Him;*
> *And if thou seest Him, thou seest us both.*[9]

Pure consciousness—what we are—is the eternally present ground of awareness out of which the body we identify with is born, and into which it returns— always, here, now in the eternally Present Moment. "What is there to fear?" said novelist Michael Murphy. "Life and death are simultaneous. We are living flames, burning at the edge...of this incredible joy."[10]

# Chapter Practices

## Practice Mindfulness of Witnessing

The experience of Witnessing Consciousness is not a phenomenon limited to the dream state or to mystical experiences. Even in our everyday waking lives we can practice mindfulness of this consciousness, but to increase our awareness of it, dream incubation and meditation are extremely helpful.

We can see the presence of the Witness in many of our seemingly mundane dreams whenever we dream that we are both the actor in our dream and the observer. From the "dream observer's" point of view we frequently understand the nature of what is occurring better than does the "dreamer," whose ego is more entangled in the drama that is unfolding.

Also, when we are mindful enough in waking life to step back and observe dispassionately what is occurring we are relying on a degree of Witnessing Consciousness—an awareness that is not tied—or less tied—to our ego's concerns—and therefore wiser.

Indeed, the goal of meditation can be said to be the refinement of our Witnessing Consciousness in which we set the intention to observe our thoughts rather than to identify ourselves with them—to remain mindful that "we are not our thoughts" but rather the observing Consciousness that is aware of them.

We can set the intention to develop this awareness in our dreams as well. As I mentioned, lucid dreaming is a direct pathway to this experience. I would recommend Steven Laberge's seminal book on how to dream lucidly, *Lucid Dreaming*, for assistance with that method.

You may also set the intention to experience the Witness through dream incubation. You can simply say, "Help me to experience the Witnessing Consciousness." It will help to engage in meditation before sleep as this experience is strongly correlated with our ability to quiet our thoughts.

# Section V

# The Time of Your Return:
## Becoming Your Own Mentor

*The secret of health for both mind and body is not to mourn for the past, not to worry about the future, or not to anticipate troubles, but to live in the present moment wisely and earnestly.*

—Buddha

*The highest destiny of the individual is not to rule but to serve.*

—Albert Einstein

In our own personal lives the Return is a time when we integrate the lessons we have learned throughout our Journey and "walk the walk"—fully embody and live out these new values in our everyday life. Yet this is not a time to rest on our laurels, but rather to redouble our practice of mindfulness about all we have learned.

> Just as one can see in the trials of the Quest the long and arduous season of Winter, and in the Illumination the bloom of life in Spring, the Return is the time of Summer in which nature's work now fully blossoms and matures.

Even when we find ourselves walking "in the center" the Return is never a time—nor is there ever any time—in which we can afford to relax our practice of mindfulness and indulge even a little in our old ego strategies without losing our balance.

In the last chapter you read of Larry's dream that so beautifully describes one aspect of Witnessing Consciousness. Subsequently Larry shared with me another dream that addresses the importance of learning the resolve to remain mindful in the time of our Return:

When my dream starts, I am Jesus on the cross and everywhere around me is devastation. However, when I look at myself I see that while my arms are still outstretched, I'm actually no longer on the cross at all and there are no more nails in my hands. In fact, I'm feeling incredibly healthy and whole. I know now that I can simply walk away from this scene of devastation and live the life I've always wanted—but I'm aware that I'm possessed by an energy that keeps my arms outstretched and staring at the devastation.

A central message of Larry's dream is that even when our greatest suffering has ended and we feel the profound wholeness of redemption, we must hold an attitude or position of willing sacrifice—arms outstretched—about remaining unattached to our old ego values. Similarly, "to stare at the devastation" means remaining mindful of the fragmented and alienated experience of life created by our ego. In this way we remember the importance of what we accomplished and avoid slipping back complacently into the old ego script that devastated our life in the past. We ensure that we stay in the joyful flow of life energy that is the living Present. Dreams of the Return reflect our growing capacity to act out of the stillness and wisdom of the Present Moment, one now increasingly clear of "old baggage"—the resentment about our past and concerns about our future.

We are grounded far more now in the middle—the once-formidable furnace of opposites in which we burned with conflict, guilt, and fear—now a place of joy and fulfillment.

Few writers have described the time of the Return as well as Eckhart Tolle, who speaks in part about what occurs when we release the fears that create our resistance to living in the simplicity of the Present Moment:

> To offer no resistance to life is to be in a state of grace, ease, and lightness. This state is then no longer dependent upon things being in a certain way, good or bad. It seems almost paradoxical, yet when your inner dependency on form is gone, the general conditions of your life, the outer forms, tend to improve greatly. Things, people, or conditions that you thought you needed for your happiness now come to you with no struggle or effort on your part, and you are free to enjoy and appreciate them—while they last. All those things, of course, will still pass away, cycles will come and go, but with dependency gone there is no fear of loss anymore. Life flows with ease.[1]

We act now from our heart, remembering as in Larry's dream that, having experienced redemption, we are resolved to remain mindful of the devastation and suffering we have endured on our ego's cross of opposites.

Having reached that place of resolve to act on behalf of our own healing, we find that we are spontaneously more giving and loving to those around us—not less—and we do so with joy—not exhaustion and resentment. Having found compassion for our own suffering our heart spills over.

On the other hand, in our relationships we no longer expect our significant other or family members to make us happy or to save us from our suffering. In the time of our Return, we accept that our relationship is here, as Eckhart Tolle has said, to make us "conscious instead of happy."[2] Relationships are a superb container or vehicle for becoming more conscious. Yet remaining mindful in the midst of conflict has been very difficult. In the past we reacted to judgmental words and looks with hurt, guilt, or shame that almost instantly turned to anger—or we projected our own unwanted qualities on to those around us. We responded with righteous indignation to their perceived judgment and the downward spiral began as we returned judgment with more judgment. Now in the Return, we don't confuse others' unconscious behavior with who they are and respond increasingly from the Witnessing Consciousness that compassionately observes rather than reacts.

In the following chapter, you'll find that Dreams of the Return reflect the resolve to remain a mindful and compassionate witness of the Present Moment as well as the natural impulse to "return" or give back to others still suffering.

# Section Practices

Recall and journal about one or more times in your life when you felt in a place of conscious resolve, when previous fears no longer haunted you and you acted without reservation.

- Incubate a dream and request a better understanding of the obstacles to that experience of resolve in some important part of your life. Or ask, "How can I live more wholeheartedly in the Present Moment?"

- Also consider requesting a dream in which you experience or learn more about embracing or remaining the Witness even in the midst of painful conflict.

Don't forget that the goal of Mindful Dreaming is to live out the answers we receive from our Dream Mentors and to integrate what we learn in our daily existence. How ironic if you were to request assistance in living more wholeheartedly and with resolve, but didn't make an authentic effort to incorporate that wisdom in your life. Remember to honor your dreams by making concrete efforts to enact their message in your daily life.

# Chapter 15

## Dreams of Resolve and Dreams of Charity

*We have not even to risk the adventure alone; for the heroes of all time have gone before us; the labyrinth is thoroughly known; we have only to follow the thread of the hero-path. And where we had thought to find an abomination, we shall find a god; ...where we had thought to travel outward, we shall come to the center of our own existence; where we had thought to be alone, we shall be with all the world.*

—Joseph Campbell

*Anybody can observe the Sabbath, but making it holy surely takes the rest of the week.*

—Alice Walker

In these Dreams of Return we have already experienced the insights we were seeking for a new vision of life and now, having "returned home" from our Journey, it is our task to remain mindful of those epiphanies—to embody and live them out in daily life. This is what author Alice Walker means when she says that it's not enough to observe the Sabbath. Rather, we must honor what is holy every day of our lives.[1]

To return home is to return to the old issues that have always been there, yet they no longer feel threatening. Just as the student learned to "be the Buddha" rather than a Buddhist with her disapproving family, we approach conflicts now in dreams and waking life from a place of deep presence without the demands of our ego "to take a stand." Simply put, we are increasingly present without resistance to the moment that is, and we act from within that presence.

> In Return dreams we stand with resolve and presence in the face of what once most frightened us.

These dreams are unlike Dreams of Embrace and Mastery in that they do not begin with fear, anger, conflict, or anxiety. We don't feel as if we are fearfully trying our hand at something new.

To respond with presence means that we respond with what is truly needed in the moment rather than out of our ego's old habits of thought. We feel deeply empowered.

In contrast to Calling and Quest dreams, Dreams of the Return present us with Mentors who often embody our ego's old attitudes and we are prompted to become the Mentor *for them.*

Where once we were obliged to give our Mentors the benefit of the doubt, now we assume, in fact know, the correctness of our own perspective. It's quite easy: None of the angst, dread, anxiety, insecurity, guilt, or shame arises within us when we act in these dreams.

There are two discernible types of Return Dreams: Dreams of Resolve and Dreams of Charity.

# Dreams of Resolve

Notice that in these dreams resolve arises out of a great compassion we embody for our own suffering. This compassion virtually releases us from any further attachment to the relationships that are the source of that suffering. Yet compassion for others in these dreams is not the central focus as it is in Dreams of Charity. It is implied though in the dreamer's thoughts or in the lack of anger and judgment toward those who have wounded us in the past.

Margie, in her mid-40s, had a fundamentalist Christian mother who pressured her for years to attend church with her. She had worked diligently on that relationship and all of its attendant problems for the past few years and then dreamed:

> Mother asked me in her usual snide manner why I didn't want to go to church and I told her I didn't agree with what she believed intellectually, but that I was with her emotionally. I told her that it was how I felt about her that was most important. I gave her a long, warm hug and said I just couldn't respect myself intellectually if I went to church. There was a feeling of reconciliation between us. But most important to me in the dream was that "how she felt" wasn't the issue. I knew that I loved her (limitations and all) and had told her so. I was at peace within myself. It's so good to be in this place finally after all these years.

In earlier chapters you will recall Janine's nightmare of dirt thrown in her car and her Dream of Embrace and Mastery in which she successfully extricated her finger that was stuck to a hot iron. As she continued to work consistently on embracing compassion and self-caring she felt more empowered to face the trauma of rape that she experienced in her adolescence. Here is her Dream of Return that reflects the depth of her own efforts at healing:

> I'm in a crowd of people and an absolutely hideous man abducts me with the intention of raping and murdering me. I tell him that he may well succeed at raping me, but never will he kill me. I warn him with a complete, unhesitating confidence that I feel throughout my whole body. I am without fear. He immediately backs off, intimidated, and leaves, and I know he'll never return.

"When I woke up from this dream," said Janine, "I wasn't afraid anymore and I could think back to my rape without any anxiety." Notice that in her dream Janine knows and acknowledges that she has no control over whether someone can physically overpower and rape her. But she also knows that she cannot be killed. She means that, unlike her earlier experience of rape, she can no longer lose the inner mirror of her own worth. Her body may be wounded, but she is now grounded in the fierce resolve of compassion for her own suffering that no physical event or trauma can steal. When we are squarely in this con-sciousness of resolve then what threatens us loses its power and simply "leaves," never to return.

Over time as we become more proficient at waiting in the middle without "taking charge," wandering off in distractions, or judging either side of the conflict, we embrace the center—the Present Moment—more fully and feel the liberation and peace that arises naturally within us.

For example, recall Patricia, the woman who dreamed in Chapter 10 that she was being punished by the Collective for writing down her feelings. Patricia slowly realized that honoring her own creative process was a path for affirming her own needs and that this self-affirmation did not mean that she was rebel-ling against or disrespecting the values that others held. It simply wasn't a matter of right versus wrong—whether others might think so or not.

Politically liberal, a moderate feminist in principle, and a firm supporter of abortion, she now dreamed:

> I am being asked to speak on behalf of a pro-choice group against the pro-life group. I'm aware that in waking life I'm an absolute believer in the pro-choice cause, but in the dream, I won't take sides or affirm one perspective as better—so I simply refuse the offer. It's then that a child suddenly appears and dumps a bucket of ice over my head the way they do with coaches who have won a football game and they're celebrating.

Here we see that when Patricia refuses to negate or affirm either side, she is treated as victorious and the celebration begins. Notice that she is not con-flicted, anxious, or defensive—simply firm in her resolve.

One might also think about the ice as the final cooling down of the heat or fire that rages in us unabated while we wait for the experience of a new third perspective. It seems the only choice necessary is to choose to hold the tension and to wait for that perspective—the compassionate acceptance of both sides—that transcends what initially seemed to be an impossible conflict—and leaves us celebrating life grounded in the Present Moment.

As you read in Section II, foremost among the Collective values that armor and harden our heart with secret resentment are those who teach us we are good to care for others and selfish to attend to our own pain and hurt. Yet on the Journey we learn that compassion for ourselves and our own suffering leads to compassion for others. If we cannot redeem our own pain and suffering, then how can we help to heal or be truly open to theirs? We can offer solace and empathy but we can not model release. In the end we discover there is no choice to make as to whether oneself or others are more deserving. Compassionate consciousness knows that all life is sacred—every last gnat and beggar, "the dregs of humanity." To embrace this consciousness we need only wait without resistance or judgment in the middle—in surrender to the Present Moment.

Grace, an erudite woman in her 60s, was a devoted Irish Catholic and scholar of her religion. She once joked with me that earlier in her life, when she was needing support during her divorce, she sought counseling from a Jesuit priest and received down-to-earth, practical advice. Now she was seeking spiritual direction from a psychologist who wanted her to believe in the spiritual nature of her dreams. In truth she had originally started counseling out of concern for her adult alcoholic daughter and the stress in their relationship. However, when she dreamed that she was leading her daughter across a bridge that her daughter could not cross, she became aware that her goals had changed and her inner work was now her spiritual path.

Many months later, Grace shared with me a dream similar to Patricia's prolife tale, but with an additional element present that was only implied in Patricia's dream.

> I am walking with my dog Sy, who is the most unconditionally loving being I know. Someone comes up to me and asks if I will attend a political meeting. I refuse because at this time in my life I'm no longer into supporting political groups. I keep going and another person who is a leader of an anarchist group wants me to come to their meeting and join with them against the political establishment. I refuse again because I'm not opposed to people setting up laws and rules for themselves. I just don't want to be a part of these groups—or for that matter against them. I keep walking with my old dog Sy.

Clearly, Grace now walks with an attitude of unconditional love—her dog, Sy—that allows her to transcend the painful pull of opposites and live at peace in the Present Moment. Living in the Present means standing in the place of Witnessing Compassion for all the warring and alienated parts of our own ego and the ego of others—the Collective mind—that demands we take sides in everything we do in life.

As we embrace the Compassionate Witness we know that the opposing viewpoints are part of our consciousness, but that we are infinitely more than that. This is a perennial theme echoed in all of our spiritual literature. As Lord Krishna said to his student Arjuna in the *Bhagavad Gita*, "All beings are in me but I am not in them."[2] And Yahweh reminded the Israelites, "[M]y thoughts are not your thoughts."[3]

# Dreams of Charity

In Dreams of Charity we experience the same feelings of resolve, but compassion for others is now increasingly the focus of our consciousness. This is a dream of a young client, Bill, in his mid-20s, who had worked with great motivation on his chronically dysfunctional relationship with his father:

> My dad and I are facing off again, but this time I'm not afraid. My father says, "You need to listen to me." And I say, "Dad, I have my own life to lead." I'm not even angry. I just walk my father to the door and say goodbye. He leaves without any resistance. Actually I feel sad for him.
>
> When he leaves I look out the front door and see my little garden— only it's in the front of my house now and it's much larger. I go outside and drop fresh seeds on the ground. The wind blows some of them into other people's yards.

In this dream we see, in part, the classic hallmarks of a Dream of Resolve: The dreamer feels no fear or defensiveness. In fact, in the place of that fear and anger now there are elements of compassion ("Actually I feel sad for him," for his father's own limitations and the suffering it creates in his own life). Finally, *when* he asks his father to leave *then* he sees his garden that has "grown much larger." It's out front now, not in the back (of his awareness), and the seeds he plants are blown into the yards of others.

In the language of the Return this means that the beauty he creates in his life expands when he acts with resolve and compassion on behalf of his own needs. In Tolle's words, now "life flows with ease" and the outcome is that the seeds of compassion for ourselves drift naturally into the lives of those around us. We become the Compassionate Mentor and model for others what we have learned from in our previous dreams.

Here is a remarkable Charity dream shared by Lawrence. Recall in Chapter 8 that you read of Lawrence's nightmare of Imminent Loss. In that dream, over-identified with or attached to his mother's values, he was faced with the threat of being buried in his mother's grave. Having never lived his own life, her name—Maria—would be carved on his own tombstone.

After that dream Lawrence saw the writing on the wall—or tombstone, as it were—and worked hard to remain mindful of compassion for the suffering in his life he had created by identifying with his mother's values. He now understood the urgent need to reclaim a life of his own.

The following dream came some months later at a time when he considering stepping out of the suffocating box of his past life with creative professional projects that he wouldn't have risked or even thought of prior to that dream. Evoked by his earlier nightmare of Imminent Loss, here is his dream of releasing attachment, mastering grief, clearing a space for a new life, and helping others to move on as well:

> I am in a crowd of mourners in a country similar to India. They are all sitting in passive ritual around the decaying body of a woman that floats in the water. I see them as self-defeating in their passivity. I work my way through the crowd and pick up the body and carry it across a very busy, dangerous intersection without any fear that I will be hurt or that the mourners will be angry with me. I walk right up to an old sage and place the body in front of him. I communicate with him telepathically in an otherworldly experience of communion. He accepts my offering and I return to the group excitedly to tell them that the mourning is complete and we can move on with our lives.

What else is there to say? Well, perhaps just a few interesting details to consider. We can see in Lawrence's dream a clear consciousness that the mourning is over and a resolve that "passivity" is no longer appropriate. The feeling of true resolve always arises out of a wholehearted conscious embrace of the Present Moment in which our ego's concerns about the past or future are understood as simply not relevant. Lawrence has fully and completely grieved. His identification with what his mother valued has come to an end. The past is the past. Nor is he concerned with whether in the future others "will be angry" and hurt that he is ready to move on. Lawrence is fully resolved in the Present Moment and for this reason even the crossing of the dangerous intersection is something he takes in stride "without any fear that I will be hurt." It has been said that Zen can be defined as "doing one thing at a time." So too this is the meaning of resolve: doing one thing at a time with complete attention to what is in that moment.

To give the body to the old sage is as if to say "I have no more claim on this identity, and being no longer attached to it, I return it to the Source from which it came." Finally, notice that the body is not identified as that of his mother specifically. In this respect, Lawrence is not simply finished grieving for a superficial attachment, the loss of a persona, or a mere dependency on his mother. Rather, he is releasing or returning to the Source a broader identity and way of being that no longer serves him, or others, in life. The Journey is not complete without the Return.

Lawrence is "excited" to return to the group and tell them that they can move on now with their lives. The attitude of charity and compassion for others, typical in these dreams, is not to be confused with the compulsive giving of co-dependency. Codependent giving is done to appease others in hope that they will in turn love and give back to us, whereas the giving of those in the time of their Return has no ego motive and comes from the selflessness of compassion.

You read another Dream of Charity in Chapter 1 in which a woman driving in a disastrous snowstorm continues on unafraid even when her own car is stopped in the snow. She goes on to help others dig out their buried cars, realizing that the danger and hardship we perceive are a matter of our own conditioned perspective: "Everyone is stuck in wet, heavy snow only because that is how they've learned to perceive it."

This is the wisdom arising from Witnessing Consciousness that holds no judgments or prejudices from the past about the nature of the work one does in the Present Moment. To provide help to others with the joyful energy of the Present Moment is the most compassionate attitude of charity and gift one can offer.

A friend that was serving as an apprentice to a shaman dreamed:

> I am climbing a mountain to find the source of an eternal stream that now seems to have dried up at the foot of the mountain. As I climb I find beautiful artifacts left by travelers who have not made it all the way to the top. I don't know if I can make it either. I place the artifacts in my pockets. They are all polished and worn smooth over eons of time. When I get to the top of the mountain I find that they are spread everywhere. Then I realize to my embarrassment that they are not there to be taken away, but to be offered and shared. I empty my pockets and make an altar with them to express my gratitude.

This dream speaks to the sacred nature of our actions in the time of our Return. The purpose of the Journey is to learn compassion for oneself and all sentient beings.

Some dreams just leave us feeling sincere gratitude for their moving insight and inspiration. This final dream of Larry's addresses each stage of the Journey and the lessons in mindfulness they teach. Notice that in his previous dream of merging with the healing Witness, that Larry—his ego—was the object of compassion and healing by the Witnessing Consciousness. At the start of this next dream, he—his ego—is telling the story, but eventually merges again with the Witness and goes on from there to complete the Journey. Read through it now without stopping. Then we'll examine it more closely.

I am jolted into reality as I see the picture that my doctor has painted on the wall in front of me.

As I step toward it I once again know I have to go down into death having everything stripped away to emerge closer to my true reality. It is similar to many things I have had to do in my life all combined into one. I crawl down under a wall and emerge as a hunchback-deformed beggar.

Now I have gathered all the information that is necessary to do what I came to do. I see a sparkle and turn to look at my left hand holding onto a diamond the size of a baseball, cut perfectly and set on the top of a walking stick. I am still looking for that one that is looking for me.

I sigh as I head toward the garden that I have hidden in the center of the city I am in. The garden is in the center of the most disgusting area and is the home of every rejected people and person in the world and throughout all eternity.

At the center of all this, I step into the idyllic setting of blue birds, squirrels, rabbits, and fawns. The perfume of the flowers and scent of the forest uncover my true form that is one with all.

I gather all my servants to me and release the knowledge I have just gleaned. This gives them what they need to know—and to do what each requires to slowly penetrate the darkness of red hate and violence that surrounds us all in the world.

In the dream I know that I am slowly but surely changing the outcome of everything at once through all space and time so that the best will be brought forth. It requires so much self-searching and compassion that most cannot endure the suffering of the truth they have to face about themselves. I know it is the only way because it was the only way I could find the hidden gardens where innocence is the reward and no barriers exist between any. All are one here and conscious of all around them in an infinite realm of possibility where joy is discovered in every aspect of encounter. I have found the one I have needed all my life and it was, as always, I.

I see the bed in the center of the garden and as I go toward it for rest I feel so happy that I can remember so much now…and I pass the cycle of life to death to life again and again. Each time expanding my consciousness with every trip. The joy seems to be multiplying with each drumbeat of my heart as I slowly emerge foggy headed into my bed where I tiredly wake up.

I look to see if it is Monday and time to go to work. I feel totally relieved as I remember it is Saturday and is a day to be enjoyed.

Let's briefly review now each phase of the Journey and its lessons in mind.

## The Calling

I am jolted into reality as I see the picture that my doctor has painted on the wall in front of me.

From the Doctor's point of view—the Source—our one and only Calling is to transcend the suffering in our life and "to find our bliss." Yet our Calling often comes as a jolt or shock from the universe as we have fallen into distraction.

## The Quest

As I step toward it I once again know I have to go down into death having everything stripped away to emerge closer to my true reality. It is similar to many things I have had to do in my life all combined into one. I crawl down under a wall and emerge as a hunchback-deformed beggar.

As I mentioned, Larry is still in search "for the one" that will love him and has not yet merged with that greater Witnessing Consciousness.

To release ourselves from suffering we "go down into death." Simply put, this means we go down from the place of our head where our ego thrives to the place of our heart where lies the Grail of the Present Moment—the compassionate Witnessing Consciousness. This is the place of death to our ego, as in this place, "everything is stripped away" that our ego holds dear. From the viewpoint of our wounded, dying ego, what is left (of our ego) can be likened to a hunchback-deformed beggar—a disgusting untouchable—"the least of us." We have released our ego's control and embraced the true humility that will allow us to receive guidance.

## The Illumination

> Now I have gathered all the information that is necessary to do what I came to do. I see a sparkle and turn to look at my left hand holding onto a diamond the size of a baseball, cut perfectly and set on the top of a walking stick. I am still looking for that one that is looking for me.

Once we have "gathered all the information that is necessary," and thus, "stripped away" the ego, we are open to receiving the gift of the Illumination which is the precious gem—the diamond-like indestructible, unchanging, brilliant clarity of Witnessing Consciousness. We already have the Staff of this Supreme Authority, but initially do not recognize that we are the Witness. We "still look for the one that is looking for me"—the one that loves me, what Sufis call the Beloved.

> I sigh as I head toward the garden that I have hidden in the center of the city I am in. The garden is in the center of the most disgusting area and is the home of every rejected people and person in the world and throughout all eternity.

Already holding the diamond staff of Consciousness, the "I" that has placed the garden in the center is the eternal I and not the ego. What seems "hidden" is always from the ego's limited perspective.

We continue to move toward the Garden in the Center. But the true Center is the eternal present that is home to all sentient beings, including "every rejected people and person in the world and throughout all eternity"—those "most disgusting" to our judging ego. To embrace the Center is to embrace all and so it is that we must find the compassion as Larry has done in this dream to "kiss the beast" before our consciousness is transformed.

> At the center of all this, I step into the idyllic setting of blue birds, squirrels, rabbits, and fawns. The perfume of the flowers and scent of the forest uncover my true form that is one with all.

The only "true form that is one with all" is the formless Witnessing Consciousness that is in all forms and one with them. In the center between all the warring opposites of ego consciousness is the eternal peace of the Garden we seek: the experience of Paradise—the pure consciousness that is found in the unresisting embrace of the Present Moment.

## The Return

> I gather all my servants to me and release the knowledge I have just gleaned. This gives them what they need to know—and to do what each requires to slowly penetrate the darkness of red hate and violence that surrounds us all in the world.
>
> In the dream I know that I am slowly but surely changing the outcome of everything at once through all space and time so that the best will be brought forth. It requires so much self-searching and compassion that most cannot endure the suffering of the truth they have to face about themselves. I know it is the only way because it was the only way I could find the hidden gardens where innocence is the reward and no barriers exist between any. All are one and conscious of all around them in an infinite realm of possibility where joy is discovered in every aspect of the encounter. I have found the one I have needed all my life and it was, as always, I.

Here again "I" means not the ego "I," but the Self or Source or diamond Witness that I am. I am the I that is one with all. In this knowing the compassion we have found for ourselves now spills over for others. True charity means unconditional compassion for those who still suffer, and so we "release the knowledge" and wisdom of the Witness and share what we have learned. In this way we penetrate the "red hate and violence" of ego consciousness "that surrounds the world."

To embrace Awakened Consciousness is indeed to "change the outcome of everything through all space and time"—to embrace our timeless, eternal Self. This is the profound task referred to in the Kabbala as "Repairing the Face of God." To look into the face of God "in this hidden garden" (hidden only to the ego) is to know our own true face as the Eternal Witness. In that knowing we find the peace of absolution where "innocence is the reward." To discover "joy in every encounter" means that we have embraced without resistance the "middle" or "center"—the Eternal Present where joy reigns.

And here in the Eternal Now we find the "I" we've always searched for and always were: "If you go on working with the light available," said the great sage Ramana Maharshi, "you will meet your guru, as he himself will be seeking you."[4]

> I see the bed in the center of the garden and as I go toward it for rest I feel so happy that I can remember so much now…and I pass the cycle of life to death to life again and again. Each time expanding my consciousness with every trip. The joy seems to be multiplying with each drumbeat of my heart as I slowly emerge foggy headed into my bed where I tiredly wake up.

On our Journey as we let go our ego little by little, we each "pass the cycle of life to death to life again and again." Over time the quality of our life improves and the best is indeed "brought forth." We embrace a stillness and peace at the center of our Being that is ever more enduring and "the joy multiplies with each drumbeat" of our heart.

> I look to see if it is Monday and time to go to work. I feel totally relieved as I remember it is Saturday and is a day to be enjoyed.

At the end of our Journey—that is, in the consciousness of the Eternal Present—we have crossed the threshold once again and returned to the same world from which we started—though now we are in the world, but not of it. Rather we are grounded in an unwavering mindfulness that the Sufi Teacher Llewellyn Vaughan-Lee reminds us is the practice of "solitude in the crowd: whatever one's outward activity, the inner attention remains in the heart."[5] 11th-century Sufi and Teacher Abu Sa'id ibn Abi-l-Khayr described this quality of Awakened Consciousness quite simply:

*The perfect mystic is not an ecstatic devotee lost in contemplation of Oneness, nor a saintly recluse shunning all commerce with mankind, but "the true saint" goes in and out amongst the people and eats and sleeps with them and buys and sells in the market and marries and takes part in social intercourse, and never forgets God for a single moment.*[6]

As it is said in Zen, "When an ordinary man attains knowledge he is a sage; when a sage attains understanding he is an ordinary man."[7]

Yet the work of the Journey always goes more slowly than we desire—and more rapidly than is comfortable for us. We so easily fall prey to old habits, ignore our dreams, forget to practice mindfulness, and lose ourselves in the world. It seems that our ego must journey to the perennial source hundreds of times to become mindful that we are in service of the Divine and not in charge of it. Slowly, we come to see that our waking identity is transforming. This repeated crossing of the threshold gradually transmutes our sense of self, deepening our awareness of the ancient ground we tread and of its profound energies. As we continue to journey mindfully and honor our dreams, we accept increasing responsibility for the quality of our life, learn to let go of thoughts that keep us stuck, and become a conduit vessel for healing energy—for ourselves, for our communities, and for the Earth.

*May your dreams guide you swiftly along your path.*

# Appendix

For more information regarding all aspects of dreams and dreaming, please contact the International Association for the Study of Dreams (IASD):

IASD Central Office
1672 University Avenue
Berkeley, California 94703

Phone/Fax: (209) 724-0889
E-mail: *office@asdreams.org*
Website: www.asdreams.org

# Notes

## Introduction

1. Young, *Dreaming*, p. 25.
2. Ibid., p. 7.
3. Ibid., p. 7.
4. *New King James Bible*, Genesis 28:1–14.
5. Young, *Dreaming*, p. 76.
6. Ewen, *Introduction*, p. 62.
7. Matt, *Zohar*, p. 109.
8. Shelburne, *Mythos*, p. 29.
9. Campbell, *Hero*, pp. 19-20.
10. Campbell with Moyers, *Power*, pp. 120–21.

## Section 1

1. Seligman, "Building."
2. Brown, *Nietzsche*, p. 14.
3. "Emerging," *www.beliefnet.com/story/137/story_13726_1.html*.
4. "Wondrous," *www.thebuddhadharma.com/issues/2005/winter/ wondrous_path.html*.

5.  *ONE.*
6.  Russell, *"Happiness" www.peterussell.com/WUIT Happiness.html.*
7.  Eliot, *Waste*, p. 55.
8.  Edinger, *Ego*, p. 101.
9.  Frager, *Essential*, p. 23.
10. Jaworski, *Synchronicity*, p. 137.
11. Curtiss, Depression, p. 38.
12. Hanh, *Miracle*, p. 14.
13. Andreas-Salome, *Nietzsche*, p. 22.
14. Gookin, *Nols*, p. 44.
15. Prechtel, *Secrets*, p. 170.
16. Boa, *Business.*
17. Snyder, *Prospects*, p. 104.
18. Campbell with Moyers, *The Power*, p. 56.

## Chapter 1

1.  Gookin, *Nols*, p. 92.
2.  Dayton, Journey, p. 156
3.  Barks, *Essential*, Mathnawi IV 3654-67, 3628-52, p. 112.

## Chapter 2

1.  Freedman, *Life*, p. 5.
2.  Herzog and Kaufman, *How Shall*, p. 267.
3.  Campbell with Moyers, *Power*, p. 60.
4.  Campbell, *This Business.*
5.  Bratnick, *Awakening*, p. 231.
6.  Marshall, Nature's, p. 105
7.  Taylor, *Where People*, pp. 31–2.
8.  Prechtel, *Secrets*, p. 151.
9.  Miller, *Plexus*, p. 53.
10. Some, *Healing*, p. 107.
11. Ibid., p. 50.
12. Ibid., p. 50.
13. Brunton and Venkataramiah, *Conscious*, p. 153.
14. Rilke, "Little," *www.cise.ufl.edu/~ddd/zen.html.*
15. Lautermilch, *Grass*, p. 142.

## Chapter 3

1. Selby, *Seven*, p. 75.
2. Matt, *Zohar*, p. 109.
3. Hannah, *Encounters*, p. 6.
4. Vaughan-Lee, *Catching*, p. 216.
5. Christian, *Philosophy*, p. 221.
6. Sri, "Twenty," *www.dlshq.org/download/sivananda_dls.htm*.
7. Barks, *Essential*, p. 36.
8. Bartok, *Daily*, p. 190.

## Chapter 4

1. Anthony, *Other*, p. 13.
2. Gendlin, *Focusing-Oriented*, p. 1.

## Section II

1. Deonaraine, *Book*, p. 86.
2. Scott, *Easy-To-Use*, p. 10.
3. *New King James Bible*, Matthew: 10:34-39.
4. Hughes, *Voice*, p. 18.
5. Hanh, *Miracle*, p. 64.
6. Whyte, National Institute, 1998.
7. Bronte, Wuthering, p. 85
8. Gautama Buddha, *www.opendharma.org/ instructions_webpages/lovingkindnessmeditation.htm*.
9. Wisdom Quotes, *www.wisdomquotes.com/001040.html*.
10. Trafford, *My Time*, p. 23.
11. Freidman, *Heart*, p. 112.
12. Ewen, An Introduction, p. 62.
13. Edinger, *Ego*, p. 101.
14. Wilhelm, *The I Ching*, p. 197.
15. Ibid., p. 198.
16. Ibid., p. 197.
17. Ibid., p. 198.
18. Schiraldi, *Post-Traumatic*, p. 222.

19. Hassumani, *Salman*, p. 104.
20. Nin, Winter, p. 56.
21. Vaughan-Lee, *Catching*, p. 11.
22. Hannah, *Encounters*, p. 6.
23. Coleridge, Aids, p. xvi.

# Chapter 5

1. Tsu, Lao, *Tao*, p. 91.
2. Whyte, *Crossing*, p. 130.
3. Miller, *Visions*, p. 18.
4. Grayson, *Mindful*, pp. 57–8.
5. Tolle, *Power*, p. 14.
6. Bartol, *Daily*, p. 89.
7. Campbell, The Power, p. 92.
8. Fishel, *Journey*, p. 73.
9. Edinger, *Ego*, p. 172.
10. Brunton and Venkataramiah, *Conscious*, p. 176.
11. Solitude Quotes, *twotrees.www.50megs.attic.com/quotes solitude.html.*
12. Selig, Thinking, p. 50..
13. Ingram, *Passionate*, p. 26.
14. Hudson, *Text-book*, p. 591.
15. Ingram, *Passionate*, p. 24.
16. Wyatt, *Upanishads*, p. 25.
17. Lao Tsu, *Tao*, p. 91.
18. Rilke, *Letters*, p. 35.
19. Emerson, *Self-Reliance*, p. 48.

# Chapter 6

1. Bolen, *Tao*, p. 98.
2. Hawkins, *Eye*, p. 69.
3. Gore, *Earth*, p. 14.
4. Wilhelm, *I Ching*, p. 66.
5. Ibid.

6. Ibid.
7. Dean, *Night*, p. 5.
8. Goldman, *Healing*, p. 102.
9. Whyte, *What*, p. 26.
10. Schaeffer, *Love's*, p. 127.
11. Harvey, *Perspectives*, p. 255.
12. *21ˢᵗ Century King James Bible*, Ecclesiastes 3.
13. Campbell, *The Hero*, p. 55.
14. Van De Castle, *Our Dreaming*, p. 23.

## Chapter 7

1. Harvey and Weber, *Odyssey*, p. 233.
2. Paul, *Becoming*, p. 46.
3. Krishan, *Radiant*, p. 125.
4. Caruso, *Power*, p. 23.
5. Woodward, *Teachings*, p. 119.
6. *New King James Bible*, Matthew 25:40.
7. Walker and Walker, *Healing*, p. 406.
8. Teasdale, *Mystic*, p. 31.
9. John-Roger, Loving, p. xiii.
10. Gautama Buddha, *www.opendharma.org/ instructions_webpages/lovingkindnessmeditation.htm*.
11. Rilke and Kappus, *Letters*, pp. 79–80.
12. Jackson, *Moments*, p. 172.
13. Peake, *Healthy*, p. 62.
14. Ingram, *Passionate*, p. 54.
15. Campbell, *Power*, p. 123.

## Chapter 8

1. Tart, *Living*, p. 59.
2. Buddhist Quotes, *Buddhism.kalachakranet.org/resources/ buddhist_quotes.html*.
3. Compassionate Ocean Dharma Center, *www.oceandharma.org/ dtfall01.htm*.
4. Van De Castle, *Our Dreaming*, p. 315.
5. Gibran, *The Prophet*, p. 4.

6. Tzu, *Tao*, p. 108.
7. Hesse, p. 158.

## Chapter 9

1. Taylor, *Where People*, pp. 31–2.

## Section III

1. Leshan, *Medium*, p. 71.
2. Ibid.
3. Selig, *Thinking*, p. 9.
4. Jeans, *Mysterious*, p. 148.
5. Godwin, *Lucid*, p. 205
6. Nikhilananda, *Gospel*, p. 150.
7. Campbell with Moyers, *Power*, p. 3.
8. Prechtel, *Secrets*, p. 158.
9. Hanh, *Zen*, pp. 43–4.
10. Kaji, *Common,* p. 27.
11. Haines and Yaggy, *Royal,* p. 533.
12. Beath, *Consciousness*, p. 46.
13. Levoy, *Callings*, p. 55.
14. Beversluis, *Sourcebook*, p. 255.
15. Millman, *Sacred,* p. 28
16. Anthony, *Guide,* p. 121.
17. Wilhelm, *The I Ching,* p. 26.
18. Rousseau, *Julie*, p. 104.
19. Wilhelm, *I Ching*, p. 415
20. St. John of the Cross, *Dark*, pp. 85–6.
21. Campbell, *Hero,* p. vii.
22. Meyer, *The Gnostic*, p. 22.
23. Godwin, *Lucid*, p. 205.
24. Wagoner, Lost, p. 10.

## Chapter 10

1. Campbell, *Hero*, p. vii.
2. Seaward, *Stand*, p. 55.
3. Oman, *Prayers*, p. 52.

## Section IV

1. Thoreau, *Uncommon*, p. 4.
2. Senzaki and Reps, *Zen*, p. 19.
3. Tolle, *New*, p. 46.
4. Edinger, *Ego*, pp. 153–54.
5. *New King James Bible*, Matthew 25:40.
6. Bohm and Nichol, *Essential*, p. 148.
7. Cohn and Tronick, "Three," pp. 185–93.
8. Burns, To a Louse, p. 278.
9. Brown, *Nietzsche*, p. 14.
10. Rilke, *Letters*, pp. 91–2.
11. Goldberg, *Mirror*, p. 63.
12. Ibid., pp. 84–5.
13. Ibid.
14. Christian, *Philosophy*, p. 558.
15. Camus, *Lyrical*, p. 169.

## Chapter 11

1. Tolle, *Stillness*, p. 14.
2. Ibid., p. 18.
3. Hamilton-Parker, *Psychic*, p. 67.
4. "As We Transform," *www.jungcircle.com/muse/ lettersclarissa.html*.
5. Brehony, *After*, p. 237.
6. Wyatt, *Upanishads*, p. 25.
7. Chittick, *Sufi*, Ode 55.
8. Permission granted from Rev. Jeremy Taylor through personal communication with the author.
9. Browning, *Pocket*, p. 33.

## Chapter 13

1. Krishnamurti, *Freedom*, pp. 51–2.
2. Coelho, *By the River*, p. 7.

## Chapter 14

1. McLaughlin, *Tramping*, p. 115.
2. "The Nondual Highlights," *www.nonduality.com/h11029.htm.*
3. "Consciousness," *www.gurdjieff-ouspensky-centers.org/English/ quotations/consciousness.shtml.*
4. Franz, *On Dreams*, p. 64.
5. Freke, *Wisdom*, p. 52.
6. Campbell with Moyers, *The Power*, p. 224.
7. Ibid.
8. Ibid., p. 223.
9. Vaughan-Lee, *Catching*, p. 179.
10. Murphy, *Jacob*, p. 87.

## Section V

1. Tolle, *Practicing*, p. 105.
2. Ibid., p. 95.

## Chapter 15

1. Walker, *In Search*, p. 351.
2. Kripananda, *Jnaneshwar's*, p. 115.
3. *New King James Bible*, Isaiah 55:8.
4. Brunton and Venkataramiah, *Conscious*, p. 231.
5. Vaughan-Lee, *Catching*, p. 36.
6. Ibid., p. 37.
7. Dayton, *Quiet*, p. xi.

# Bibliography

Andreas-Salome, Lou. Mandel, Siegfried, trans. And ed. *Nietzsche.*
Champaign Ill.: University of Illinois Press, 2001.

Anthony, Carol. *The Other Way: Meditation Experiences Based on the I Ching.*
Stow, Mass.: Anthony Publishing Company, 1990.

——————. *A Guide to the I Ching.* Stow, Mass.: Anthony Publishing Company, 1988.

Ashlag, Rav Yehuda. *Introduction to the Book of Zohar: The Science of
Kabbalah (Pticha).* Toronto: Laitman Publishers, 2005.

"As We Transform Our Own Darkness." Jungcircle.com. *www.jungcircle.com/
muse/lettersclarissa.html.*

Barasch, Marc Ian. *Healing Dreams: Exploring the Dreams that Can Transform
Your Life.* New York: Penguin Putman, 2000.

Barks, Coleman, trans. *The Essential Rumi.* San Francisco: Harper San Francisco, 1995.

Bartok, Josh, ed. *Daily Wisdom: 365 Daily Daily Buddhist Inspirations.*
Somerville, Mass.: Wisdom Publications, 2001.

Beath, Andrew. *Consciousness in Action: The Power of Beauty, Love and Courage
in a Violent Time.* New York: Lantern Books, 2005.

Beradt, Charlotte. *The Third Reich of Dreams.* Translated by Adriane Gottwald.
Chicago: Quadrangle Books, 1968.

Beversluis, Joel D. *Sourcebook of the World's Religions: An Interfaith Guide to Religion and Spirituality.* Novato, Calif.: New World Library, 2000.

Bischoff, Erich. *The Kabbala: An Introduction to Jewish Mysticism and Its Secret Doctrine.* Boston: Red Wheel/Weiser, 1985.

Boa, Frazer. *This Business of the Gods: Joseph Campbell in Conversation with Frazer Boa.* Ontario: Windrose Films, Ltd., 1989.

Bohm, David, and Lee Nichol. *The Essential David Bohm.* New York: Routledge, 2003.

Bolen, Jean Shinoda. *The Tao of Psychology.* New York: Harper and Row, 2004.

Bratnick, Raechel. *Awakening the Dreamer.* Philadelphia: Xlibris Press, 2003.

Brehony, Kathleen. *After the Darkest Hour: How Suffering Begins the Journey to Wisdom.* New York: Owl Books, 2001.

Bronte, Emily. *Wuthering Heights.* New York, NY: E.P. Dutton & Co., 1907

Brown, Kristen. *Nietzsche and Embodiment.* Albany, N.Y.: SUNY Press, 2006.

Browning, Robert. *Pocket Volume of Selections from the Poetical Works of Robert Browning.* London: Smith, Elder, 1890.

Brunton, Paul and Venkataramiah, Munagala. *Conscious Immortality.* Tiruvannamalai, South India: Sri Ramanasramam, 1996.

Buddhist Quotes. *Buddhism.kalachakranet.org/resources/buddhist_quotes.html.*

Burns, Robert. "To a Louse: On Seeing One in a Lady's Bonnet in Church," in Allan Cunningham, *The Works of Robert Burns; with His Life.* London: James Cochrane and Co., 1834.

Campbell, Jean. *Group Dreaming: Dreams to the Tenth Power.* Norfolk, Va.: Wordminder Press, 2006.

Campbell, Joseph with Bill Moyers. *The Power of Myth.* New York: Doubleday, 1988.

Campbell, Joseph, ed. *Myths, Dreams, and Religion: Eleven Visions of Connection: Alan Watts, Rollo May, Norman O. Brown, Ira Progoff, and Others.* New York: MJF Books, 1970.

————. *The Hero With a Thousand Faces.* Princeton, N.J.: Princeton University Press, 1973.

————. *This Business of the Gods.* Caledon East, Ontario: Windrose Films, LTD. 1989.

Campbell, Joseph. *Creative Mythology: The Masks of God.* New York: Penguin, 1991.

————. *Myths to Live By.* New York: Penguin, 1993.

Camus, Albert. Phillip Thody, ed. *Lyrical and Critical Essays,* New York: Vintage, 1970.

Caruso, Joe. *The Power of Losing Control: Finding Strength, Meaning, and Happiness in an Out-Of-Control World.* New York: Gotham, 2004.

Chittick, William C. *Sufi Path of Love: The Spiritual Teachings of Rumi.* Albany, N.Y.: State University of New York Press, 1983.

Christian, James L. *Philosophy: An Introduction to the Art of Wondering.* Belmont, Calif.: Thomson Wadsworth, 2005.

Coelho, Paulo. Alan R. Clarke, trans. *By the River Piedra I Sat Down and Wept.* New York: Harper Perennial, 1997

Cohn, J. F., and E. Z. Tronick. "Three month old infants' reactions to simulated maternal depression," *Child Development: 54*, 185-93. New York: Harper Perennial, 1997.

Coleridge, Samuel Taylor. *Aids to Reflection of a Manly CHaracter on the Several Grounds of Provence, Morality, and Religion.* Liverpool, England: Edward Howell, 1873.

Compassionate Ocean Dharma Center. Dharma Talks: Newsletter. *www.oceandharma.org/dtfall01.htm.*

"Consciousness." Gurdjieff-Ouspenski Centers. *www.gurdjieff-ouspensky-centers.org/english/quotations/consciousness.shtml.*

Curtiss, Arline B. *Depression is a Choice: Winning the Battle Without Drugs.* New York: Hyperion, 2001.

The Dalai Lama with Varela, Francisco, ed. *Sleeping, Dreaming, and Dying: An Exploration of Consciousness with The Dalai Lama.* Boston: Wisdom Publications, 1997.

Dayton, Tian. *Journey Through Womanhood: Meditations from our Collective Soul.* Center City, Minnesota: Hazelden Press, 2002.

————. *The Quiet Voice of Soul: How to Find Meaning in Ordinary Life.* Deerfield Beach, Fla.: Health Communications Inc, 1995.

Dean, Amy E. *Night Light: A Book of Nighttime Meditations.* Center City, Minn.: Hazelden Publishing and Educational Services, 1986.

Deonaraine, Ramesh. *The Book of Wisdom for Students: How to Get the Most Success Out of Your Student Years.* Lincoln, Neb.: Writers Club Press, 2002.

Edinger, Edward F. *Ego and Archetype: Individuation and the Religious Function of the Psyche.* Boston: Shambhala Publications,1972.

Eliot , T. S. *"Little Gidding" in Four Quartets.* New York: Harcourt Brace & Company, 1971.

————. *The Waste Land and Other Poems.* New York: Penguin Putnam Inc., Penguin Classics, 2003.

"The Emerging Feminine Face of Buddhism, Peay, Pythia." *www.beliefnet.com/story/137/story_13726_1.html.*

Emerson, Ralph Waldo. *Self-Reliance and Other Essays.* Minneola: Courier Dover Publications, 1993.

Ewen, Robert B. *An Introduction to Theories of Personality*. Mahwah, N.J.: Lawrence Erlbaum Associates, 2003.

Fishel, Ruth. *The Journey Within: A Spiritual Path to Recovery*. Deerfield Beach, Fla.: Health Communications Inc. 1987.

Frager, Robert, ed. *Essential Sufism*. San Francisco: Harper San Francisco, 1997.

Franz, Marie-Louise. *On Dreams and Death: A Jungian Interpretation*. Boston: Shambhala Publications, 1986.

Freedman, Ralph. *The Life of a Poet: Rainer Maria Rilke*. Evanston, Ill.: Northwestern University Press, 1996.

Freke, Timothy, ed. *The Wisdom of the Hindu Gurus (The Wisdom of the World)*. London: Godsfield Press, 1999.

Friedman, Maurice S. *A Heart of Wisdom: Religion and Human Wholeness*. Albany, N.Y.: SUNY Press, 1992.

Gautama Buddha. Loving Kindness Meditation. Loving Oneself. *www.opendharma.org/instructions_webpages/lovingkindnessmeditation.htm*.

Gendlin, Eugene T. *Focusing-Oriented Psychotherapy: A Manual of the Experiential Method*. New York: The Guilford Press, 1998.

Gibran, Kahlil. *The Prophet*. Ware, Hertfordshire: Wordworth Editions, Ltd., 1999.

Godwin, Malcolm. *The Lucid Dreamer: A Waking Guide for the Traveler Between Worlds*. New York: Simon and Schuster, 1981.

Goldberg, Benjamin. *Mirror and Man*. Charlottesville, Va.: University Press of Virginia, 1985.

Goldman, Caren. *Healing Words for the Body, Mind and Spirit: 101 Words to Inspire and Affirm*. New York: Marlowe & Company, 2001.

Gookin, John, ed. *Nols Wilderness Wisdom*. Mechanicsburg, Penna.: Stackpole Books, 2003.

Gore, Albert. *Earth in the Balance: Ecology and the Human Spirit*. Boston–New York: Houghton Mifflin Books, 2000.

Grayson, Henry, Ph.D. *Mindful Loving: Ten Practices for Creating Deeper Connection*. New York: Gotham Press, 2004.

Hanh, Thich Nhat. *The Miracle of Mindfulness*. Boston: Beacon Press, 1987.

————. *Zen Keys: A Guide to Zen Practice*. New York: Doubleday, 1995.

Haines, T. L. and L. W. Yaggy. *Royal Path of Life Or Aims And AIDS to Success And Happiness*. Chicago: Western Publishing House, 1877.

Hamilton-Parker, Craig. *Psychic Dreaming*. New York: Sterling Publishing, 2004.

Hannah, Barbara. *Encounters With the Soul: Active Imaginations as Developed by C. G. Jung.* Boston: Sigo Press, 2001.

Harvey, John H. and Ann L. *Perspectives on Loss and Trauma: Assaults on the Self.* Thousand Oaks, Calif.: Sage Publications Inc. 2002.

Harvey, John H. and Ann L. Weber. *Odyssey of the Heart: Close Relationships in the 21st Century.* Mahwah, N.J.: Lawrence Erlbaum Associates, 2002.

Hassumani, Sabrina Rutherford. *Salman Rushdie: A Postmodern Reading of His Major Works.* Madison, N.J.: Fairleigh Dickinson University Press, 2002.

Hawkins, David, M.D., Ph.D. *The Eye of the I: From Which Nothing Is Hidden.* West Sedona, Ariz.: Veritas Publishing Company, 2001.

Herzog, Anne F., and Janet E. Kaufman. *How Shall We Tell Each Other of the Poet? The Life and Writing of Muriel Rukeyser.* New York: Palgrave, 2001.

Hillman, James. *The Dreams and the Underworld.* New York: Harper & Row, 1979.

Hoss, Robert, J. *Dream Language: Self-Understanding Through Imagery and Color.* Ashland, Oreg.: Innersource, 2005.

Hudson, Henry Norman. *Text-book of Prose: From Burke, Webster, and Bacon.* Boston: Ginn Brothers, 1891.

Hughes, Marilynn. *The Voice of the Prophets: Wisdom of the Ages, Volume 1 of 12.* Morrisville, N.C.: LuLu Press Inc, 2005.

Ingram, Catherine. *Passionate Presence: Experiencing the Seven Qualities of Awakened Awareness.* New York: Gotham Books, 2003.

Jackson, Thomas L. *Moments Of Clarity.* Philadelphia: Xlibris Corporation, 2004.

Jaworski, Joseph. *Synchronicity: The Inner Path of Leadership.* San Francisco: Berrett-Koehler Publishers, 1996.

Jeans, Sir James. *The Mysterious Universe.* Cambridge, Mass.: Cambridge University Press, 1930.

John-Roger, Loving Each Day for Peacemakers: Choosing Peace Every Day. Los Angeles, Calif.: Mandeville Press, 2002.

"Joseph Campbell in Conversation with Fraser Boa: This Business of the Gods." Center for Psychotherapy and Emotional Bodywork. Festival of Dreams. *spiritcentral.com/dreams/2002-2.htm.*

Jung, C.G., Aniela Jaffe, ed., Clara Winston and Richard Winston, trans. *Memories, Dreams Reflections.* New York: Vintage Books, 1989.

Kaji, Dhruv S. *Common Sense About Uncommon Wisdom: Ancient Teachings of Vedanta.* Honesdale, Penn.: The Himalayan Institute Press, 2001.

Kripananda, Swami. *Jnaneshwar's Gita: A Rendering of the Jnaneshwari.* Albany, N.Y.: SUNY, 1989.

Krippner, Stanley, ed., and Mark Robert Waldman, ed. *Dreamscaping: New Techniques for Understanding Yourself and Others.* Boston: Lowell House, 1999.

Krishan, Shubhra. *Radiant Body, Restful Mind: A Woman's Book of Comfort.* Novato, Calif.: New World Library, 2004.

Krishnamurti, Jiddu. *Freedom from the Known.* New York: HarperCollins, 1975.

LaBerge, Stephen. *Exploring the World of Lucid Dreaming.* New York: Ballantine Books, 1990.

Lao Tsu, trans. by Gia-Fu Feng and Jane English. *Tao Te Ching.* New York: Vintage Books, 1997.

Lautermilch, Steve. *Grass Script.* Stony Point, N.Y.: Alms House Press, 1991.

Leshan, Lawrence. *The Medium, the Mystic and the Physicist: Toward a General Theory of the Paranormal.* New York: Ballantine Books, 1974.

Levoy, Gregg. *Callings: Finding and Following an Authentic Life.* New York: Three Rivers Press, 1998.

Lichtmann, Maria R. *The Teacher's Way: Teaching and the Contemplative Life.* Mahwah, N.J.: Paulist Press, 2005.

Literature Classics.com, Classics Network. *www.literatureclassics.com/ browselitquotes.asp?subcategory=AC&author=Coleridge.*

*A Little Zen.* Excerpted from *The Little Zen Companion,* David Schiller, Workman Publishing Company, 1994. *www.cise.ufl.edu/~ddd/zen.html.*

Mack, Joshua. *101: What Goes Around Comes Around...and What You Can Do about It.* Gloucester, Mass.: Fair Winds Press, 2002.

Marshall, Peter. *Nature's Web: Rethinking Our Place on Earth.* Armonk, NY: M.E. Sharpe, 1996.

Matt, Daniel Chanan. *Zohar: The Book of Enlightenment (Classics of Western Spirituality.* Mahwah, N.J.: Paulist Press, 1983.

Maulana Jalal al-Din Rumi, trans. Jonathan Star with Shahram Shiva. *A Garden Beyond Paradise: The Mystical Poetry of Rumi.* New York: Bantam Books, 1992.

McLaughlin, Bill. *Tramping Through Mexico and Other Adventures.* Philadelphia: Xlibris Corporation, 2003.

Meyer, Marvin W. *The Gnostic Gospels of Jesus: The Definitive Collection of Mystical Gospels and Secret Books about Jesus of Nazareth.* New York: HarperCollins, 2005.

Miller, Henry. *Plexus.* New York: Grove Press, 1965.

Miller, James. *Visions from Earth.* Victoria, British Columbia: Trafford Publishing, 2004.

Millman, Dan. *Sacred Journey of the Peaceful Warrior.* Novato, Calif.: HJ Kramer, 2004.

Murphy, Michael. *Jacob Atabet: A Speculative Fiction*. Berkeley, Calif.: Celestial Arts, 1977.

*New King James Bible*. Nashville, Tenn.: Thomas Nelson Inc. 2006.

Nikhilananda, Swami, trans. *The Gospel of Sri Ramakrishna*. New York: Ramakrishna Vivekananda Center, 1978.

Nin, Anaïs. *Winter of Artifice*. Denver, Colo.: Alan Swallow, 1948.

"The Nondual Highlights." Nonduality.com. *www.nonduality.com/h1029.htm*.

Oman, Maggie, ed. *Prayers for Healing: 365 Blessings, Poems and Meditations from Around the World*. York Beach, Maine: Conari Press, 2000.

"ONE: The Movie" Documentary produced and directed by Ward M. Powers and Scott Carter. Interview with Robert Thurman.

Power of Myth Excerpts. *www.whidbey.com/parrott/moyers.htm*.

Paul, Jordan. *Becoming Your Own Hero*. Seattle, Wash.: Paul & Freshman Partnership, 2003.

Peake, Thomas H. *Healthy Aging, Healthy Treatment: The Impact of Telling Stories*. Westport, Conn.: Praeger/Greenwood, 1998.

Prechtel, Martin. *Secrets of the Talking Jaguar Memoirs from the Living Heart of a Mayan Village*. New York: Tarcher, 1999.

Rilke, Maria. "A Little Zen." University of Florida. *www.cise.ufl.edu/~ddd/zen.html*.

Rilke Maria, and Franz Xaver Kappus. Stephen Mitchell, trans. *Letters to a Young Poet*. Novato, Calif.: New World Library, 2000.

Rilke, Rainer Maria and Franz Xaver. *Letters to a Young Poet*. Novato, Calif.: New World Library, 2000.

Rinpoche, Sogyal, Patrick Gaffney, and Andrew Harvey, ed. *The Tibetan Book of Living and Dying*. San Francisco: Harper San Francisco, 1993.

Rinpoche, Tenzin Wangyal. *The Tibetan Yogas of Dreams and Sleep*. Ithaca, N.Y.: Snow Lion Publications, 1998.

Rousseau, Jean Jacques. *Julie, Or the New Heloise: Letters of Two Lovers Who Live in a Small Town at the Foot of the Alps*. Hanover: UPNE, 1997.

Russell, Peter. "Happiness: The Mind's Bottom Line." *www.peterrussell.com/WUIT/Happiness.html*.

Schaeffer, Brenda. *Love's Way: The Union of Body, Ego, Soul & Spirit*. Center City, Minn.: Hazelden PES, 2001.

Schiraldi, Glenn R. *Post-Traumatic Stress Disorder Sourcebook*. New York: McGraw-Hill, 2000.

Scott, David. *Easy-To-Use Zen: Refresh and Calm Your Mind, Body and Spirit with the Wisdom of Zen*. Great Britain: Vega Limited, 2002.

Seaward, Brian Luke. *Stand Like Mountain Flow Like Water*. Deerfield Beach, Fla.: Health Communications Inc.,1997.

Selby, John. *Seven Masters, One Path*. New York: HarperCollins 2003.

Selig, Jennifer Leigh. *Thinking Outside the Church: 110 Ways to Connect with Your Spiritual Nature*. Kansas City, Mo.: Andrews McMeel Publishing, 2004.

Seligman, Martin E. P., Ph.D. "Building Human Strength: Psychology's Forgotten Mission." *APA Monitor, January 1998, Volume 29, Number 1*

Senzaki, Nyogen, and Paul Reps, comp. *Zen Flesh, Zen Bones: A Collection of Zen and Pre-Zen Writings*. North Clarendon, Vt.: Charles E. Tuttle Co.,1957.

Shelburne, Walter A. *Mythos and Logos in the Thought of Carl Jung: The Theory of the Collective Unconscious in Scientific Perspective*. Albany, N.Y.: SUNY, 1988.

Smith, C. Michael. *Jung and Shamanism in Dialogue: Retrieving the Soul/ Retrieving the Sacred*. Mahwah, N.J.: Paulist Press, 1997.

Snyder, John. *Prospects of Power: Tragedy, Satire, the Essay, and the Theory of Genre*. Lexington, Ky.: The University Press of Kentucky, 1991.

Solitude Quotes. *twotrees.www.50megs.com/attic/quotes/solitude.html*.

Some, Malidoma. *The Healing Wisdom of Africa: Finding Life Purpose Through Nature, Ritual, and Community*. New York: Tarcher, 1998.

Sri Sivananda and the Divine Life Society. "Twenty Hints on Meditation." *www.dlshq.org/download/sivananda_dls.htm*.

St. John of the Cross. *Dark Night of the Soul*. Mineola, N.Y.: Courier Dover Publications, 2003.

Strauss, William, and Neil Howe. *The Fourth Turning: An American Prophecy*. New York: Broadway Books, 1997.

"Tao Te Ching: Lao Tsu and Taoism." Nonduality Salon. Contributed by Bob Crowder, *www.nonduality.com/laotsu.htm*.

Tart, Charles. *Living the Mindful Life: A Handbook for Living in the Present Moment*. Boston: Shambhala Publications, 1994.

Taylor, Jeremy. *The Living Labyrinth*. Mahwah, N.J.: Paulist Press, 1998.

———.*Where People Fly and Water Runs Uphill: Using Dreams to Tap the Wisdom of the Unconscious*. New York: Warner Books, 1992.

Teasdale, Wayne. *The Mystic Heart: Discovering a Universal Spirituality in the World's Religions*. Novato, Calif.: New World Library, 1999.

Thinkexist.com. Inspirational Words. *www.thinkholistic.co com.cfm?nid=793*.

Thoreau, Henry David. *Uncommon Learning: Thoreau on Education*. Boston: Houghton Mifflin Books, 1999.

Tolle, Eckhart. *A New Earth: Awakening to your Life's Purpose.* New York: Dutton Adult, 2005.

—————. *Practicing the Power of Now: Essential Teachings, Meditations, and Exercises from the Power of Now.* Novato, Calif.: New World Library, 1999.

—————. *The Power of Now: A Guide to Spiritual Enlightenment.* Novato, Calif.: New World Library, 2004.

—————. *Stillness Speaks.* Novato, Calif.: New World Library, 2003.

Trafford, Abigail. *My Time: Making the Most of the Rest of Your Life.* New York: Basic Books, 2004.

*21st Century King James Bible.* Gary, S.D.: Deuel Enterprises, 1994.

Tzu, Lao. *Tao Te Ching: 25th Anniversary Addition.* New York: Vintage, 1997.

Van De Castle, Robert. *Our Dreaming Mind.* New York: Ballentine Books, 1994.

Vaughan-Lee, Llewellyn. *Catching the Thread: Sufism, Dreamwork and Jungian Psychology.* Inverness, Calif.: The Golden Sufi Center, 2003.

Wagoner, David. Lost in Traveling Light: Collected and New Poems (Illinois Poetry Series. Champaign, Ill.: University of Illinois Press, 1999.

Walker, Alice. *In Search of Our Mothers' Gardens: Womanist Prose.* NY: Harvest Books, 2003.

Walker, Marsha Jelonek, and Jonathan D. Walker. *Healing Massage: A Simple Approach.* Clifton Park, N.Y.: Thomson Delmar Learning, 2003.

Whyte, David. *Crossing the Unknown Sea.* New York: Riverhead Trade, 2002.

—————. *The House of Belonging.* Langley, Wash.: Many Rivers Press, 1996.

—————. Presentation at National Institute for the Clinical Application of Behavioral Medicine, 1998.

—————. *What to Remember when Waking in the House of Belonging.* Langley, Wash.: Many Rivers Press, 1996.

Wilhelm, Richard, trans. *The I Ching or Book of Changes.* Princeton, N.J.: Princeton University Press, 1985.

Wisdom Quotes: Quotations to Motivate and Inspire. *www.wisdomquotes.com/001040.html.*

"The Wondrous Path of Difficulties." Buddhadharma: The Practitioner's Quarterly. *www.thebuddhadharma.com/issues/2005/winter/wondrous_path.html.*

Woodward, F. L., and E. M. Hare, trans. *Teachings of the Buddha.* Boston: Shambhala, 1996.

Wyatt, Thomas, trans. *Upanishads.* New York: Penguin Classics, 1965.

Young, Sirinity *Dreaming in the Lotus: Buddhist Dream narrative, Imagery and Practice.* Somerville, Mass.: Wisdom Publications, 1999.

# Index

Abduction Dreams, 125

Abi-l-Khayr, Abu Sa 'id ibn, 163

aboriginal peoples, 13, 39

active imagination, 135

acupuncture, 136

Adam, Eve and, 187

al-Hallaj, 245

amulet, 69, 74

Ananda, 132

Arjuna, 82, 256

Asian

cultures, 64

Philosophy, 11

Attachment, Dreams of, 16, 17, 23, 26, 72, 81, 96, 116, 146, 148-162, 177, 192

Attack Dreams, 136-140

Autumn, 18, 42, 78, 116-117

Awakened Consciousness, 11, 263

Baba, Sai, 101

*Bhagavad Gita*, 82, 256

*Book of Changes* 111, 185 (*See also* I Ching)

Borg, the, 193

Bronte, Emily, 86, 112

Buddha, 9, 23, 56, 84, 86, 132-133, 161-162, 170-172, 178-179, 207, 229-230, 239, 241, 247, 252

Buddhism, 16, 230

Buddhist, 11, 15, 65, 72, 111, 143, 171, 181, 207, 229, 242, 252

Calling, the, 11, 13, 17-19, 23, 28-36, 39-40, 63, 78-80, 102, 106, 16-119, 121, 124, 128, 136, 144, 162-168, 186, 191, 219, 252, 260

Campbell, Joseph, 11, 22, 29-30, 46, 79, 87-88, 99, 117, 141, 174, 242, 251

Chaos Theory, 21

Chase Dreams, 136-137

Chinese

oracle, 88

parable, 110

proverb, 103, 177, 215

text, 179

Christ, 201, 207

cocreation, grammar of, 56-67

codependency, 84-85

Collective Unconscious, 11, 30, 33, 86

Command Dreams, 118-120, 125

Compassion, Mindfulness of, 68, 70, 72, 100, 133, 141, 192, 214

Compassionate
    Healer, the Witness as, 244
    Mentor, 256
    Witness, 73, 226, 256

compassionate
    mirror, 10
    perspective, 85

conflict of opposites, 173

Confucian thought, 111

consciousness
    of contemplation, 93
    of formlessness, 170
    of forms, 170

Control, Dreams of, 16, 17, 23, 26, 66, 72, 81, 92, 96, 103, 108, 109-129, 139, 177, 192, 198, 225

cyclical
    nature of dreams, 37
    nature of the Journey, 37

Dagara tribe, 51-52

Dalai Lama, the, 14-16, 204

dark night of the ego, 176

dark night of the soul, 176

Destroyer, the Witness as, 242-244

Devil, the, 87

Dhammapada, 56

Distraction, Dreams of, 16, 17, 23, 26, 72, 81, 96, 98, 103-108, 116-117, 177, 191

Divine Order, 113

Divine, the, 13, 18, 21, 38, 61, 65, 88, 100, 104, 118, 124-125, 127, 144, 170, 207-208, 213, 220, 244, 264

Dorothy, 27, 30-32, 34, 117

dream
    dictionary, 45
    grammar, 56-67, 103
    images, 45-55
    incubation, 107-108, 111, 129, 246

Dream
    Archaeologists, 44
    Incubation, 24, 64-65

Dreams of
    Abduction, 125
    Anticipating Loss, 148-152
    Apprenticeship, 199, 210-222, 236
    Attachment, 16, 17, 23, 26, 72, 81, 96, 116, 146, 148-162, 177, 192
    Attack, 136-140
    Being, 208, 221, 226, 230-231, 236, 238-246
    Charity, 252, 256-260
    Chase, 136-137
    Chronic Resistance, 190-192
    Command, 118-120, 125
    Defeat, 160-161
    Distraction, 16, 17, 23, 26, 72, 81, 96, 98, 103-108, 116-117, 177, 191
    Embodiment, 208, 213, 221, 229-237
    Embrace and Mastery, 207, 210, 221, 223-228, 252, 253
    Forgotten Love, 150-152
    Formless, the, 221
    Grieving, 149, 157
    Imminent Loss, 153-155
    Immobilization, 125-127
    Impatience, 16, 17, 23, 26, 72
    Judgment, 16, 17, 23, 26, 36, 72, 81, 96, 116, 123, 130-141, 177, 192
    Looping, 127-128
    Opposing the Collective, 190, 193-196
    Paralysis, 124
    Powerlessness, 121-125, 127
    Refusal, 155-160
    Resolve, 252-256
    Return, 250-264
    Suicide and Murder, 155-158
    Willing Sacrifice, 190, 197-199

Dreamtime, the, 13, 39

ego
    inflation, 111
    strategies, 19-20, 33, 66, 70, 81, 90, 116-118, 127, 132-133, 153, 164, 176, 193, 200, 211, 224,
    values, 17, 19, 68, 147

Einstein, Albert, 21, 44, 49, 54, 98, 164, 247
Embrace
    Humility, 69
    of the Present Moment, 68
    self-caring and compassion, 70, 71
    Solitude, 69
embracing
    compassion, 226-227
    humility, 225-226
    non-attachment, 228
    solitude, 224
emotional
    bridging, 91, 95
    mirroring, 204
Eternal One, the Witness as the, 242-243
Eternal Present, 186
Eternal Witness, 263
Eve, Adam and, 187
expanded consciousness, 11, 47
experiential knowing versus logical knowing, 47
fables, 117, 133, 173, 243
fairytales, 57, 83, 117, 133, 173, 243
five
    core ego values (*See* five ego strategies, the)
    ego strategies, the, 16, 17, 23, 26, 72, 81
    favorite habits of the ego (*See* five ego strategies, the)
    lessons in mindfulness, 66, 68, 90
    types of Control nightmares, 117
Force, the, 27, 117
form, formlessness versus, 170, 178, 209, 231
formless consciousness, 170-172, 215
formlessness, form versus, 170, 178, 209, 231
four
    phases of the Journey, the, 11, 35
    stages of the Mythic Journey, 30, 39
Freud, 14, 45, 121, 124
Gandhi, 111, 133-134
Garden of
    Eden, 186-187
    Gethsemane, 179
General Theory of Relativity, 49-50
Gibran, Kahlil, 153, 196

*Glass Menagerie, The*, 28
God, 10, 18, 84, 87-89, 118, 132, 141, 167, 172, 198, 212-213, 232-233, 263-264
    voice of, 118, 120
Goethe, 29, 142
Grail, the, 23-24, 30, 73, 92, 101, 133, 176, 186, 191, 209, 261
grammar of dreams, 56-67
Grief, Mindfulness of, 122, 142-162, 192
growth factor, embrace of the dream experience as, 47
guru, 22, 91, 110, 192, 207, 221, 229
Hanh, Thich Nhat, 20, 84, 175, 219
healing
    dreams, 12
      power of, 11
    energy, 12, 38, 69
    experience, 47
    power, 9
hero, 78-80, 98
Heroic Journey, 11, 70
heroic sacrifice, 79-80
heroism, 79-80
hierarchy of consciousness and intelligence, 51
hologram of living, healing energy, 13
hologram, definition of, 48
holographic image, 48
Holy
    Ark, 92
    Grail, 30
Humility, Mindfulness of, 68, 72, 101, 111, 122, 213
*I Ching*, 69, 88-89, 110-111, 115-116, 179-181, 244
IASD, 164, 265
Illumination, 11, 13, 20, 23, 30, 34, 36-37, 40, 59, 63, 68, 87, 98, 199-209, 211, 221, 223, 248, 261
Imminent Loss, 62, 153-155, 235, 257
Immobilization Dreams, 125-127
Impatience, Dreams of, 16, 17, 23, 26, 72
Implicate Order, 203
incubate dreams, 129, 189
inspirational dreams, 163-168
Integrative Practice, 68-76

International Association for the Study of Dreams, 164, 265

intuitive
     dimension of life, 21
     mind, 21

Jesus, 10, 30, 82, 100, 132, 179, 181, 186, 203, 227

Johnson, President Lyndon, 126-127

Johnson, Robert, 178

Joseph, 10

Judgment, Dreams of, 16, 17, 23, 26, 36, 72, 81, 96, 116, 123, 130-141, 177, 192

Jung, Carl, 10-11, 18, 29, 57, 88, 91, 135, 170, 177, 244

Jungian
     analyst, 202, 241
     jargon, 122
     psychology, 111
     therapist, 48

Kabbala, 202, 263

Kabir, 132, 172

Kiao-chau, 110

kinesthetic memory, 25

King Arthur, 30
     Knights of, 30

Krishna, Lord, 73, 227, 256

Krishnamurti, J., 98, 131, 229

La Queste del Saint Graal, 186

Lao Tsu, 97-98, 107, 142, 155

Letting Go, Mindfulness of, 122, 142-162, 192

Looping Dreams, 127-128

lunar
     attention, 93
     consciousness, 92, 95, 100, 104, 118, 136
     focus, 93

Maharshi, Ramana, 52, 100-101, 263

Matrix, the, 32, 193-194

meditation, 10, 21, 70, 73, 100, 105, 108, 110, 144, 202, 224, 246

Medusa, 92, 94, 227

metaphor, 45-46, 54

Mindfulness of
     Compassion, 68, 70, 72, 100, 133, 141, 192, 214

Formless, the, 215-221

Grief, 122, 142-162, 192

Heart-Centered Values, 91

Humility, 68, 72, 101, 111, 122, 213

Letting Go, 122, 142-162, 192

Solitude, 211-213

Stillness, 211-213

Tension of Opposites, the, 91

Willing Sacrifice, 91

Mother Teresa, 131, 201

Muslim, 9, 230

Mythic Journey, 11-13, 23, 24, 30, 39, 81

nature,
     creative energies of, 22
     natural rhythms of, 22

Neo, 193-194

nightmares, 64-65, 77, 80-81, 88, 90, 101-162

Nin, Anaïs, 35, 90, 190

Non-attachment, 68, 73

Paralysis Dreams, 124

perennial
     cultures, 22
     spiritual traditions, 56

pop psychologists, 84

Positive Psychology, 14

Powerlessness Dreams, 121-125, 127

prayer, 10, 21, 110-111, 202

precognitive dreams, 148

primal energies of nature, 51

problem-solving dreams, 12

psyche, 29, 20, 37, 39, 45, 85, 91, 139, 164, 195

quantum
     physicists, 172
     view of reality, 171

Quest, the, 11, 13, 18-19, 23, 30-31, 33-40, 43, 63, 68-70, 76, 87, 90, 96, 121, 170, 173, 176-177, 186-188, 190-199, 210, 225, 248, 252

Redeemer, the Witness as, 239-242, 244

release
     control, 61, 69
     distraction, 69
     judgment, 70-71

Renunciation, 143

Repairing the Face of God, 263

Return Dreams, 250-264

Return, the, 11, 13, 20, 23, 30-31, 34, 36-37, 40, 59, 63, 68, 183, 208, 216, 247-250, 256, 258-264

Rilke, Maria, 46, 52, 133, 107, 205

Rousseau, Jean-Jacques, 183

Rumi, 38, 63, 101, 200, 217

sage, 52, 99-100, 110, 131, 172, 177, 264

search for bliss, 11 (See also Campbell, Joseph)

seasons, 35-36

Self, the, 23, 91, 100, 103, 138
    compassion, 15
    defeating attitudes, 13
    esteem, 10, 12, 112, 122, 140, 233
    fulfilling prophecy, 67
    hatred, 15
    image, 10, 31, 33, 143, 217
    judgment, 90
    recrimination, 162

shadow work, 132-133

Shaman, 21, 50, 54, 136, 174, 181, 216, 243-244, 258

shamanic healing methods, 136

shock, 88-89

silence, 101, 104, 106

solar
    consciousness, 93-94, 103, 136
    focus, 119
    thinking, 93-94

solitude, 20, 68, 99-109, 126, 233

Somé, Malidoma, 51-2

Sosan, 172, 187

spiritual
    life of the community, 10
    or archetypal dreams, 12

Spring, 18, 36, 42, 248

still face experiments, 203

Sufi
    Mystic, 245
    Path of Love, the, 217
    Teacher, 57, 91, 263

Summer, 36, 42, 248

Supreme Enlightenment, 241

symbol dictionary, 48

Taoist
    Sage, 57
    thought, 111

tension of opposites, the, 10, 75, 170, 195

third perspective, 171-189, 238, 254

thought experiments, 50 (*See also* gedanken)

three
    great fears on the Journey, 59
    greatest fears in nightmares and waking life, 80
    universal fears, 94

Tolle, Eckhart, 99, 179, 202, 211-212, 249, 256

turning-point dreams, 12

Unknown, the, 9, 28

Upanishads, the, 208, 217

Vaughan-Lee, Llewellyn, 57, 90, 263

Voice, the, 118-120, 170

West, the, 15, 243

Western
    culture, 15, 51, 243
    Europe, 99
    perspective, 21
    understanding, 49

wholeheartedness, 98-99, 103, 106

Winter, 18-19, 42, 248

Witness as
    Compassionate Healer, the, 244
    Destroyer, 242-244
    Redeemer, the, 239-242, 244
    the Eternal One, the, 242-243

Witnessing Consciousness, 24, 43, 171-176, 208-209, 212-213, 226, 235, 238-246, 248, 250, 258-262

Zen
    Buddhist, 181
    Master, 57, 172, 201
    monk, 175, 239
    patriarch, 187
    sage, 172

Zen, 22, 52, 81, 208, 264

Zohar, 10, 57

# About the Author

David Gordon, Ph.D., is a clinical psychologist in Norfolk, Virginia, and the founder of The Dreamwork Institute, through which he conducts dreamsharing groups, dream retreats, and workshops throughout the United States and Canada. He is also the founder and director of Studio for the Healing Arts, where he hosts workshops and seminars on indigenous and mainstream spiritual traditions, including Buddhism and Hinduism, shamanism, Kabbalah, Sufism, Christian Gnosticism, and ecstatic dance, as well as Gaian philosophy and Jungian studies.

Currently Membership Chair for the board of the International Association for the Study of Dreams (IASD) and a frequent guest on TV and radio, Gordon has co-hosted the public radio program "DreamWorks" in Norfolk, and written numerous columns on the topic of dreaming. In private practice for the past 30 years, he provides ongoing supervision and training in the area of individual and group dreamwork.

He can be reached at *studioforthehealingarts@cox.net* or *www.studioforthehealingarts.org*.

Made in the USA
Middletown, DE
23 February 2016